"Curiosity can't be taught. Or can it? Good question. The answer is yes, it can—by absorbing the hard-earned but highly accessible wisdom Hal Gregersen offers. This is a book for business leaders but also for artists and anyone else who cares to grow their ability to find answers through sustained, skillful question-asking. I wish I'd had it when I was first heading out into the world."
—SAM ABELL, National Geographic staff photographer
and author of *Stay This Moment* and *The Life of a Photograph*

"I have always been fascinated by the rebels among us—the iconoclasts who see things differently and make things change in positive and constructive ways. *Questions Are the Answer* gives essential insight into how these "deviant" types consistently manage to challenge their own going-in positions—and the most stubborn assumptions of the people around them. A key addition to the literature on creative thinking."
—FRANCESCA GINO, professor, Harvard Business
School, and author of *Rebel Talent*

"People start out in life as fearless questioners, but most learn as time goes by to suppress that impulse. This book has a simple premise—that we can rebuild our questioning capacity by adapting the habits and skills of persistently creative thinkers—and it delivers on that premise powerfully. An invaluable guide for today's leaders."
—AMY C. EDMONDSON, professor, Harvard Business
School, and author *The Fearless Organization*

QUESTIONS ARE THE ANSWER

Also by Hal Gregersen

The Innovator's DNA: Mastering the
Five Skills of Disruptive Innovators
(with Jeff Dyer and Clayton M. Christensen)

Leading Strategic Change:
Breaking through the Brain Barrier (with J. Stewart Black)

Global Explorers: The Next Generation of Leaders
(with J. Stewart Black and Allen J. Morrison)

QUESTIONS

ARE THE

ANSWER

A Breakthrough Approach to
Your Most Vexing Problems at
Work and in Life

HAL GREGERSEN

HARPER
BUSINESS

An Imprint of HarperCollinsPublishers

FIRST EDITION

Designed by Bonni Leon-Berman

Library of Congress Cataloging-in-Publication Data
Names: Gregersen, Hal B., 1958– author.
Title: Questions are the answer : a breakthrough approach to your most vexing problems at work and in life / Hal Gregersen.
Description: New York : HarperBusiness, 2018.
Identifiers: LCCN 2018024871 | ISBN 9780062844767 (hardback)
Subjects: LCSH: Creative ability in business. | Creative thinking. | Brainstorming. | Questions and answers. | Creative thinking. | BISAC:
BUSINESS & ECONOMICS / Leadership. | BUSINESS & ECONOMICS / Management. | BUSINESS & ECONOMICS / Strategic Planning.
Classification: LCC HD53.G7453 2018 | DDC 153.4/3—dc23 LC record available at https://lccn.loc.gov/2018024871

18 19 20 21 22   LSC   10 9 8 7 6 5 4 3 2 1

TO SUZI

CONTENTS

FOREWORD   by Ed Catmull   ix

PROLOGUE   Why Did I Write This Book?   1

1   What's Harder Than Finding New Answers?   11

2   Why Don't We Ask More?   34

3   What If We Brainstormed for Questions?   59

4   Who Revels in Being Wrong?   98

5   Why Would Anyone Seek Discomfort?   124

6   Will You Be Quiet?   151

7   How Do You Channel the Energy?   175

8   Can We Raise a Next Generation of Questioners?   202

9   Why Not Aim for the Biggest Questions?   243

EPILOGUE   What Will You Ask of Yourself?   268

ACKNOWLEDGMENTS   283

NOTES   291

INDEX   305

FOREWORD

by Ed Catmull
Coauthor of the New York Times *bestseller* Creativity, Inc.
and president of Pixar Animation and Disney Animation

When I visited Hal Gregersen recently at MIT, he told me something about Pixar and Disney Animation that I hadn't actually
thought about—despite having spent a lot of time thinking about
how we do things. In fact, Hal had my book describing Pixar's way
of working, *Creativity, Inc.*, in his office. To say it was dog-eared
would be a serious understatement. The spine was so cracked and
it was so scribbled over, highlighted, and stuffed with sticky notes
that it was almost falling apart.

"You are constantly asking questions in that book," Hal told me.
"It's full of questions." More broadly, he said, based on his visits with various colleagues of mine, that our people are great at
asking "catalytic questions" of each other. "It's like you have this
disciplined instinct, or learned habit, that has you constantly operating under the assumption that 'I don't know things that I need
to know.' And then you figure out ways to get them to surface."

I recognized what he was talking about. At Pixar, we have developed several ways, I would even call them institutions, over
the years for pushing ourselves, our stories, and our filmmaking
into new creative territory. For example, our directors all know
that at any point in a project when they are feeling stuck or could
use some fresh eyes on work in progress, they should assemble the

"Brain Trust" of their peers to challenge their thinking. This is not just a random, ad hoc gathering. Brain Trust meetings follow a particular process and have a set of norms around them that we have refined over the years to help the director see new creative possibilities but not rob that director of control. When we merged with Disney, we found we could translate practices that worked in Pixar's environment to the other side of the house—so, for instance, there is now an equivalent to Pixar's Brain Trust, called "story trust," in the Disney Animation world.

To my way of thinking, putting elements like this in place to make creative collaboration more possible is the most important work I can do at Pixar and Disney Animation. (Probably, the same could be said for any manager of an organization that depends on producing a steady stream of innovative work.) Everything depends on the quality of our creative output, and it always improves from candid feedback offered in the spirit of mutual commitment to excellence. A lot of things go into creating the conditions for this, but perhaps the requirement that deserves the most careful thinking is making it safe for people to speak up about problems and offer ideas for how to solve them.

It probably goes without saying that for this sense of safety to exist, the focus has to be kept on the problem and the need to solve it, and not on the person who has failed to solve it so far or the people volunteering suggestions. But even when the focus is wholly on the problem—like, what would make this character more compelling?—any constructive reaction to the work in progress or a comment made about it implies at least some level of dissatisfaction or rejection. And it can really sting. For workers in creative roles, it is very hard to separate their sense of self-worth from how others perceive their capacity for problem-solving.

The challenge is that people work within social dynamics in

which they usually feel they have something to prove. They don't want to expose flawed or incomplete thinking because they fear they will be judged harshly for it. And in fact, that does happen, right? If somebody says something dumb in your presence, you often do take note of that—and if it's you saying the dumb thing, you're probably right in sensing some judgment. To the extent that you are focused on not appearing stupid, or seeming to have something to contribute, or looking as clever as possible, you are not really focusing on the problem to be solved.

So, for the person who is in the position of overseeing a group's work, the best thing to figure out is how to remove that perceived risk that people will be judged for speaking up. How do you create the conditions in which colleagues will rigorously judge an idea that has been put out there, but not judge each other for suggesting the ideas? How do you get to a point where ideas that don't work aren't themselves personalized? Logically, this has to happen for ideas to rise and fall on their merits, but emotionally, it is just profoundly counterintuitive. Again, most of us have a very hard time separating our own sense of worth from how the worth of our ideas is judged.

So this is the context in which I heard Hal make his comment about my colleagues' questioning skills. I think intuitively we probably have gravitated toward the kinds of questions he likes to call catalytic—the kind that knock down barriers by challenging past assumptions and create new energy for pursing solutions along some new pathway. And if we have, it is probably in part because asking a question is a very effective way of introducing a novel way of thinking about something without exposing oneself to judgment. A question, after all, is not a declaration of opinion aggressive enough to draw fire—it is an invitation to think further within a different framing or along a divergent line. If that line of thinking isn't taken up, or fails to lead somewhere valuable, there is no reputational damage to the person who suggested it. And, therefore, a person is more likely to put it out there.

It is interesting when someone holds a mirror up to you and your organization and allows you to recognize something you had not thought about in quite the same terms. I think Hal is right that a certain kind of questioning is present in my colleagues' creative collaboration, and I am now paying more explicit attention to it.

Thinking about the power of questions in collaborative, creative work, I will make one more point. As my colleagues all know, I have never been a fan of organizational mission statements. It isn't that I am against having a collective sense of purpose—any time people are working together in a formally organized way, they should be thinking deeply about why they do what they do. But my exposure to the mission statements that top management teams unveil to their organizations is that they always represent the endpoints of discussions and actually stop people from doing any deeper thinking.

I see better now what bugs me about them: they sound too much like answers. I think it might be better to have mission questions—or at least mission statements that are so ambiguous that they cause people to actively wonder: "What does that really mean?"

When we see the point of our work as all about arriving at smart answers, too often we mistake an answer for the end of an effort. We celebrate arriving at a point from which we need go no further. But that isn't the way life is. Yes, often we are hard at work producing something that needs to be finalized—in Pixar's case, at some point, we release a movie. Boeing ships a jet. A professor finishes a book. And that is an important form of culmination. But for many people, I think, that culmination becomes the goal.

What if, instead, we valued the answers we arrive at mainly because of all the new and better questions they lead us to? Put another way, what if instead of seeing questions as the keys that unlock answers, we saw answers as stepping stones to the next questions? That strikes me as a very different mindset—and one that could take the creative efforts of groups much further.

My hope for you as you read *Questions Are the Answer* is that you will get the same kind of value I have gained: that it will inspire you to think about how a more deliberate use of questions could help you make more progress in whatever problem you are trying to solve. In my case, I have known for a long time that it is my responsibility to create environments where people feel safe enough to give voice to their thoughts and ideas. Perhaps the problem you are trying to solve has nothing to do with managing an organization but relates to a family issue, personal goal, or community concern. Whatever it is, you are probably, like me, receptive to having your thinking productively challenged on the matter—and you might find that questions are the answer.

PROLOGUE

WHY DID I WRITE THIS BOOK?

In the word *question*, there is a beautiful word—*quest*.
I love that word.
—ELIE WIESEL

One compelling reason to write a book is because you discover things so true and important that they deserve tens of thousands of words and hours of a reader's time to explore—and you sense that most people are living unaware of how crucial those truths are. Here's what I've discovered. First, if you want better answers at work and in life, you must ask better questions. Second, if you want better questions to ask, you do not have to resign yourself to chance and hope they will occur to you. You can actively create for yourself the special conditions in which questions thrive. Third, people who ask great questions are not born different. We all start out with the capacity to ask about things we don't know. The ones who choose to keep their questioning skills strong just get better at it.

How do I know all this is true? The most acceptable assurance I can give you is that I have done my homework. I've reviewed the relevant research literatures, formed my hypotheses, and then gone out in the field to test them through hundreds of interviews with creative people. At this point, by my rough estimate, I have pored over transcripts amounting to some three million words, finding the themes and patterns in those fascinating, and at times humbling, conversations. As a scholar, I am committed to that way of knowing. But at the same time I have come to know the truth of what I am sharing more deeply than any standard research process could tell me.

Over the past thirty years I've taught at several universities across three continents. Today I teach in a place with unique conditions—conditions that encourage everyone to challenge old assumptions and invent the impossible. MIT's campus is a place of constant, generative questioning. As my colleague Andrew Lo describes it, MIT "is a safe zone for innovation—and I know that sounds like a contradiction, because innovation is all about taking risk. But this is an incredibly healthy and unusual situation where students feel like they can actually question received wisdom, actually propose things that may be completely out of left field and outside the box." To come to work every day in such an atmosphere is energizing. It is also a constant reminder of what so many people are missing.

Most of us don't live or work in conditions so primed for questioning. We don't even think much about questions and how, by asking more and better ones, we might unlock entirely different answers. We started out life with great creative curiosity, but we lost it along the way. For a long time, this was true of me as well. I grew up in a home that wasn't much of a safe zone for questioning. To ask what seemed like obvious questions about why things were as they were was seen as outright defiance. At the same time I found early on that certain kinds of questions could shield me, if only by redirecting people's attention to topics that felt safer to focus on. I vaguely grasped that some questions held more power than others.

Later, as a graduate student, I studied under Bonner Ritchie, who was unbelievably skilled at asking tough questions that caused others to do their best thinking. I sought him out as a mentor because of how eye-opening the effects could be. I learned more from time spent with him than I did with other teachers. He systematically pried open my mind and heart to new possibilities with questions. Many of us have had mentors and friends who do the same, if we stop to notice and value that special trait in them.

For the past decade my focus as a scholar, consultant, and coach has been on corporate innovation, studying the effects of asking new questions in start-ups and large organizations in established industries. Twenty-five years ago, my first conversation with Clay Christensen—the Harvard Business School professor who first gained fame for his theory of disruptive innovation—focused on what causes people to ask the right questions. Our collaborations ever since have sharpened my appreciation of the role of questions in breakthroughs. We have both found inspiration in writings by Peter Drucker, who grasped more than fifty years ago the power of changing what you ask. "The important and difficult job is never to find the right answers," he wrote. "It is to find the right question. For there are few things as useless—if not dangerous—as the right answer to the wrong question." When Clay and I worked with Jeff Dyer to identify five behaviors that make up the "innovator's DNA," the first of those five was the habit of asking more questions.

Many of the innovative entrepreneurs we interviewed could remember the specific questions they were asking at the time they had the inspiration for a new venture. Michael Dell, for instance, told us that his idea for founding Dell Computer sprang from his asking why a computer cost five times as much as the sum of its parts. "I would take computers apart . . . and would observe that $600 worth of parts were sold for $3,000." With that "Why should it cost so much?" question in mind, he hit upon the business model that made Dell such a force in the industry. From others we heard about long-standing predispositions to challenge assumptions and conventions. "My learning process has always been about disagreeing with what I'm being told and taking the opposite position, and pushing others to really justify themselves," Pierre Omidyar, founder of eBay, told us. "I remember it was very frustrating for the other kids when I would do this." Innovative entrepreneurs love to imagine how things could be different. Asking themselves, or others, what is being taken as a given today that should not be assumed or accepted can be the best way to catalyze original thinking.

Over the years I came to appreciate that perspective-changing inquiry wasn't just about business innovation and organizational change. Questions have a curious power to unlock new insights and positive behavior change in every part of our lives. They can get people unstuck and open new directions for progress no matter what they are struggling with. Reframed questions, in whatever setting, turn out to have some fundamental things in common. For one thing, they have a paradoxical quality of being utterly surprising in the moment they are asked but in retrospect seeming obvious. In other words they carry with them a quality of inevitability without having been inevitable at all. For another thing, they are generative. They open up space for people to do their best thinking. They don't put anyone on the spot, demanding correct, often predetermined answers under threat of public humiliation. They invite people down an intriguing new line of thought that offers some promise of solving a problem they care about. I often use the word "catalytic" for these kinds of questions, because they act like catalysts in chemical processes: they knock down barriers to thinking and channel energy down more productive pathways.

On a personal level, too, I keep discovering how crucial it is to raise the right questions—sometimes by being caught out by not asking them. In January 2014, for example, I suffered a heart attack while giving a speech. Later, I had to come to terms with the fact that, for a few deep reasons, I had chosen to make some convenient assumptions about the state of my health, and it had almost cost me my life. A year later, in the spring of 2015, I had the chance to join my friend David Breashears, a renowned mountaineer, expedition leader, and cinematographer—he co-directed and filmed the IMAX film *Everest*—at Everest Base Camp and to climb up into the Khumbu Icefall. We embarked on the adventure after having formulated what we thought was a great research question about leadership. The many expeditions that attempt to summit the mountain every year amount to a fairly controlled experiment: every team uses similar equipment and follows known paths. Yet some make it and some don't. Are there key differences to be found in the leaders of the successful ones—and the systems they cultivate around themselves? Meanwhile, though, in my planning of the trip, I hadn't been so focused on a quite fundamental question: Did I, who live these days literally at sea level, have any hope of being productive in a short jaunt above 18,000 feet?

Adding insult to injury, even my research approach turned out to have embedded assumptions I hadn't thought to question. David Breashears has seen many attempts on Everest fail in the many years he has been climbing on the mountain, some tragically. He was there in 1996 when the terrible events resulting in the loss of eight lives that were later described in Jon Krakauer's 1997 book *Into Thin Air* unfolded. Whenever I listened to his stories, I processed them in the mode of a leadership scholar, dispassionately forming hypotheses about, for example, cognitive

Sunrise below Mt. Everest (second peak on the right) taken during an exhausting ascent of Kala Patthar (18,519 ft.).

Ang Phula Sherpa (on the right) and I pause in the Khumbu Icefall, with majestic Pumori (23,494 ft.) behind us. David Breashears

Step by step, I (second from right) ascend the Khumbu Icefall with Ang Phula Sherpa (far right) always nearby. David Breashears

Turnaround time in the Khumbu Icefall, with Everest Base Camp (17,598 ft.) spread out below our shoulders (Ang Phula Sherpa right). David Breashears

biases in decision-making. On my trek from Lukla to Base Camp, I realized that it's one thing to be in an MBA classroom talking about bad calls like Rob Hall's fatal choice to try to get a straggling client to the summit even though it was far past the "safe time." It's another thing to actually be at an altitude where even breathing or thinking clearly is a challenge. I realized how wrong I had been to believe I was in possession of sufficient information to judge.

If you picked this up as a business book reader, expect to encounter a somewhat different style of narrative. Maybe that is already clear. I am fascinated by issues of leadership and innovation in organizations, and many of the interviews this book draws on are with CEOs and other high-level executives in the most innovative companies and social enterprises I know. But I have talked with these leaders as whole people whose lives are bigger than their very big jobs. The truth I have stumbled across—that the way to find better answers is to ask new questions—is not a truth that applies only to one part of life.

Think for a moment of your own life and those occasions when the right questions have unlocked a new solution to an issue that you had just been wrestling with. My central question is: What kinds of conditions (or forces) were in place when that happened, both inside of you as well as around you? Are there certain circumstances that help you frame your best questions—or others that you can sense shutting them down? This book pulls together the collective response of several hundred creatives to these questions. My hope with it is to get you, too, to better appreciate the importance of questions as catalysts for change in general, and to enable you to be more reflective about how you can generate those questions.

Finally, I am writing this book in the first person. If you have read Henry David Thoreau's *Walden*, you may remember his apology on the first page for doing the same. "In most books, the I, or first person, is omitted; in this it will be retained . . . ," he informs the reader. "We commonly do not remember that it is, after all, always the first person that is speaking. I should not talk so much about myself if there were anybody else whom I knew as well. . . ." Then he turns this mild defense of his own voice into a demand of others: "Moreover, I, on my side, require of every writer, first or last, a simple and sincere account of his own life, and not merely what he has heard of other men's lives . . ." His hope is that any author would give him "some such account as he would send to his kindred from a distant land . . ."

I have valued that kind of authentic voice in many books I cherish—among them, great books about questions like Parker Palmer's *Let Your Life Speak* and *A Hidden Wholeness*; Twyla Tharp's *Creative Habit*; Victor Frankl's *Man's Search for Meaning*; Mary Catherine Bateson's *Peripheral Visions*; John Steinbeck's *East of Eden*; and Donald Miller's *A Million Miles in a Thousand Years*. (In the last, the fact that a film is being made about the author's life causes him to question the story of his life and then change it for the better.) Picasso once said, "There is only one way to see things, until someone shows us how to look at them with different eyes." All these authors have given me new ways to see things—and eyes that remained different as a result.

I don't want to adopt some disembodied "expert voice" as we get into the chapters. I want to be that kindred person who has struggled with serious impasses in various areas of life and worked to overcome them—by asking tough questions that took my head, heart, and hands down entirely new paths.

1

What's Harder
Than Finding
New Answers?

The important and difficult job is never to find the right answers,
it is to find the right question.
—PETER DRUCKER

When the first group of visitors arrived at a newly opened event
space in Shanghai in June 2017, they were promptly immersed in
a situation unlike any they had encountered before. First, they sat
through a concert combining music and poetry. Then they made
their way through a full-scale mockup of some typical features of
a town: a park with a pond offering boat rides, an outdoor market
with a playground for the kids among them, a café full of chat-
tering patrons. Not so remarkable, you think? Here's the catch:
they experienced all this in utter pitch-blackness. They stumbled around. They bumped into things. They laughed but at the
same time were deeply bewildered. None could have managed it
at all except for the help of their expert and agile guides—who, of
course, were blind.

This is "Dialogue in the Dark," the brainchild of Andreas Heinecke, who created the first such installation in Frankfurt, Germany, in 1989. Today, the social enterprise he built operates in dozens of countries, simultaneously creating jobs for blind people and helping sighted people understand how they go through life. Millions of visitors have experienced it, and for many it sparks a life-changing moment.

And it all started with a question—actually, with a reframed question. Some thirty years ago Heinecke was working for a radio station, when he learned from a manager that a former employee would be rejoining the staff there soon. The man had been in a terrible car accident and left blind by his injuries, but he wanted to work again. Heinecke was asked to help that colleague accomplish his reentry into the workplace. It was a challenging assignment, since Heinecke had no experience in any assistance of this nature, but immediately he started trying to solve the problem of what a person with such a disability could still do at a passable level. It was only as he got to know his colleague well that he realized he had been asking a terribly reductive question. He switched it around to something more positive: In what kind of job setting could a blind man capitalize on his relative strengths? The idea for "Dialogue in the Dark" sprang to mind and showed the way to what would be his life's work.

My contention in this book is that this is how a great deal of progress happens. Questions are reframed in ways that prove catalytic. They dissolve barriers to thinking, like limiting prior assumptions, and they channel creative energy down more productive pathways. People who have been feeling stuck suddenly see new possibilities and are motivated to pursue them.

The chapters that follow will deal with how this insight might let you operate differently in work and life. What if the key to finding better answers is to start by asking better questions? How would you go about doing that? As we'll see from many creative people's efforts in all kinds of settings, it is possible to create conditions in which new angles of attack on problems will more likely be voiced and paid attention to. It is possible to build habits of pausing to revisit questions before rushing to formulate new answers. But before we move on to exploring these methods, there is the work of this chapter to accomplish: convincing you that this is a line of effort worth pursuing. You need to appreciate first the power of a certain kind of questioning, and avoid the traps of only working to solve problems presented in the same old ways.

BEHIND EVERY BREAKTHROUGH IS A BETTER QUESTION

Trace the origin story of any creative breakthrough, and it is possible to find the point where someone changed the question. I have seen this as a longtime student of innovation; the stories in that realm abound. For example, consider the origins of the snapshot. Photography had been invented well before Kodak founder George Eastman was born in 1854, and he took an interest in it as a young man. But as he prepared to take an international trip at age twenty-four, he found it was too much of an undertaking to pack along the elaborate and expensive equipment. The technology for capturing photographic images had steadily improved over the years in terms of speed and quality, but the assumption remained that this was a process for professionals, or at least for serious and well-heeled enthusiasts. Eastman wondered: Could photography be made less cumbersome and easier for the average person to enjoy?

It was a promising enough question to motivate Eastman to dive into research mode, and exciting enough that he could recruit others to help. By age twenty-six he had launched a company, and eight years later, in 1888, the first Kodak camera came to market. Not only did it replace wet emulsion plates with new dry film technology, it featured what managers today call a "business model innovation." There was no longer an expectation that the customer would acquire the skills and the setup for developing the film. Instead, after shooting a whole roll of a hundred pictures, he or she sent the compact camera back to the company for developing. The Kodak was a smash hit, but the question lived on. By 1900, Eastman and his colleagues launched the Brownie, a one-dollar camera simple enough for a child to operate and durable enough for soldiers to take into the field.

Today, as I sit in the midst of MIT's buzzing hive of innovators, I see plenty of people arriving at and articulating questions with the same power to excite the imagination and engage other clever people's efforts. For the moment I'll name one: Jeff Karp. He's a bioengineer in charge of a lab devoted to biomimicry. If that's an unfamiliar term to you, let me suggest that the best way to understand it is with a question: *How does nature solve this problem?* Say the problem in question is the need for a bandage that will stay stuck to a wet spot, such as a heart, bladder, or lung that has just been operated on. In that case, what could be learned from slugs, snails, and sandcastle worms? Perhaps it is not surprising that this particular question had never been posed—but once it was, scientists in Karp's lab made rapid progress toward a product used widely today. As Karp puts it, nature offers an "encyclopedia of solutions" for those who think to consult it. "By exploring nature for new ideas," he explained, "you uncover insights you would have otherwise missed by simply staying in the lab."

Sometimes the outcome of asking a different question is an immediate insight—a novel solution that has people slapping their foreheads at how obvious it should have been.[1] (I can imagine someone in the early days of magazines asking, "Why don't we charge the subscribers next to nothing, and take on advertising?" Or someone in a more recent decade asking, "Would we accomplish more if we stopped condemning alcoholism as a moral failing and instead treated it like a disease?") It's as though the new answer is so embedded in a question that you effectively unlock the answer as soon as you ask the question. More often, discovering an answer takes time, but framing the question makes the pursuit possible. As with Eastman's or Karp's question, catalytic inquiry opens up space for new lines of thinking; it recruits help, often from people trained in other disciplines; and it generates new appetite for the work.

It's also important to note that while I tend to accentuate the positive as I talk about the power of questions—their ability to reveal opportunities and yield breakthrough ideas—they are just as powerful in helping people tackle negative threats. One way to think about what a great question can do is to acknowledge the inherent danger in what "you don't know you don't know." Imagine a simple diagram: a two-by-two matrix describing the state of your knowledge of a situation. One axis presents two possibilities: there are things that are important to your success that you know all about, and other things unknown to you. The other axis reflects how cognizant you are of those knowledge assets and gaps; that is, you may or may not be aware that there is a piece of information out there that you need to solve your problem. Thus, there are things you *know* you don't know. For example, if you are an army general, you might know that the enemy has a weapons cache but be unsure about where it is. You know that you don't know that. Far more troubling, though, are the things you *don't* know you don't know. These are things that have not even crossed your mind to ask.

Donald Rumsfeld invoked this framework in a famous discussion of the Bush administration's suspicion of weapons development in Iraq, and pointed out that the "unknown unknowns" often turn out to be one's downfall. Business strategists, too, recognize this as the realm from which business-destroying disruptions usually emerge. We can return to Kodak for a classic example. After a century of success, it was decimated by something it didn't know it didn't know: how fast it would need to retool and reorganize in response to a sudden, large-scale consumer shift to digital photography. Or, more recently, think of the taxicab industry, whose "unknown unknown" was the impact of thousands of ordinary car owners turning into ride providers through services like Uber and Lyft. Was this question even raised in a Yellow Cab management meeting as recently as five years ago? If so, it was not taken to heart. (The company, San Francisco's largest traditional taxi firm, filed for bankruptcy protection in January 2016.)

You might say that such developments should have been foreseeable—and who could argue with that? After all, they were foreseen by the disruptive innovators who triggered the radical change. But for the people who were busy going about their business in the old mode, gaining the same insights would have required venturing into uncomfortable territory—beyond the usual realms of work where they knew they didn't have all the answers, to realms where they weren't even asking the right questions.

In the face of positive opportunities, then, and also negative threats, my claim is that, by revisiting the questions they are asking, and asking better ones, people arrive at dramatically better answers. In fact, I would push this to a bolder declaration that no dramatically better solution is possible *without* a better question. Without changing your questions, you cannot get beyond incremental progress along the same path you've been pursuing.

IT PAYS TO FOCUS ON QUESTIONING SKILLS

There's a corollary to the thesis that breakthrough solutions spring from better questions: by getting better at questioning, you raise your chances of unlocking better answers. Talk about things you didn't know you didn't know: Has it ever occurred to you before now that some people are better questioners than others, and that this is a learnable skill? If you agree that this is a capacity you should deliberately expand in yourself and perhaps others around you, do you have any idea how to go about it?

Now that the idea has entered your head, I suspect you will start to notice that highly creative people mention this capability a lot—and always have. Reading an interview with Tesla and SpaceX founder Elon Musk, for example, you might now pause over the point where he says, "A lot of times the question is harder than the answer. And if you can properly phrase the question, then the answer is the easy part."[2] Reading the blog of Ellen Langer, the Harvard psychologist who pioneered the concept of "mindfulness," you might engage with the post that begins: "Outside of *Jeopardy* and the game '20 Questions,' we typically worry about answers more than questions. Yet, questions direct our information search and all but determine the answer."[3] Scrolling through your Twitter feed, you might retweet the observation by disruption theorist Clay Christensen: "Questions are places in your mind where answers fit. If you haven't asked the question, the answer has nowhere to go." You might suddenly glimpse the respect for questions behind

Picasso's great pronouncement: "Computers are useless. They can only give you answers." You might start to see calls for better questions everywhere.

Fast Company magazine recently profiled how a particularly creative engineer, Chris Gentile, goes about his work. Gentile, who is now president and CEO of iBoard, figured out, for example, how to integrate holograms into mass-produced toys. He is the force behind other innovations in virtual reality as well, such as 3-D Web graphics and gaming devices. The journalist behind the story said he felt like "a young monk climbing the mountain" as he approached such awesomeness. And he did not come away empty-handed: Gentile gave away his top four pieces of advice for anyone trying to generate a breakthrough idea. Number one? "Change the question." The simple example he gives is described by the reporter:

> Gentile was once asked by some researchers to help them figure out how they might commercialize robots they had been working on. When Gentile stepped into their lab, they eagerly walked him over to their robots that were swinging their arms in their best effort to mimic human movement. But Gentile got distracted by some computer screens across the room where he saw stick-figure depictions of the robots moving seamlessly. He asked, "What are those?" and learned that the researchers had developed software to read and depict their movement. Gentile's eyes gleamed and he said, "Forget the robots!" He changed the question from "How can we commercialize robots?" to "How can we commercialize the software?" The idea led to a new form of more realistic animation for video games and movies.[4]

The urgings of all these people to get others to pay more attention to questions is, in itself, a challenge to a deep-seated assumption many of us make. We tend to believe that creative ideas are just lightning bolts of insight—*eureka* moments—that can't be summoned on demand. Even more helplessly we tell ourselves that it must take a special kind of brain—on the order of Einstein's—to serve as the lightning rod to such epiphanies. The truth is we can do much more than passively wait and hope. We must do much more.

It would surely be malpractice on my part to suggest that no one else has already been researching the notion of building questioning capacity. That work has been going on for decades, beginning, not surprisingly, in the field of education. You may, for example, have heard of "Bloom's taxonomy," which outlines six distinct levels at which a student's cognitive capabilities can be challenged by a question or problem. They range from the very basic application of knowledge one performs by recognizing or recalling a piece of information, to the much more complex processes used in analysis, synthesis, and evaluation. Benjamin Bloom, an educational psychologist, published that taxonomy over six decades ago, in 1956—and legions of education theorists since have explored how better questions can activate the higher levels of cognition. In more recent decades, experts in other disciplines have turned their attention to settings beyond classrooms. In the context of workplaces, for example, my MIT colleague Edgar Schein has urged leaders to engage in "humble inquiry," which he defines as "the fine art of drawing someone out, of asking questions to which you do not already know the answer, of building a relationship based on curiosity and interest in the other person."[5]

The result of this ongoing work is that, even if no definitive recipe book for arriving at great questions exists, we have gained many ideas and practices that have proven effective in various settings. More broadly, this work raises awareness of the fundamental idea that questioning is a skill and capacity that a person, with deliberate practice, can strengthen. Understanding the power of questions and emphasizing that you should get better at asking them offers a critical choice. You can begin to ask: What am I doing today and tomorrow and the next day so that better questions come into my work and my world?

NOT ALL QUESTIONS ARE GOOD ONES

One theme that runs through the work of every researcher focused on questioning is that not all questions are created equal. Building a questioning capacity isn't simply a matter of asking more questions—of yourself or others. There are different *kinds* of questions, and while some are inspiring, and some instructive, others are downright toxic.

Bloom's taxonomy is one way of thinking about the qualitative differences in questions: they vary according to the mental processes demanded of the person attempting to answer them. More complex cognition is required for problem-solving, for example, than for simple retrieval of memorized facts. Along similar lines, Robert Pate and Neville Bremer proposed another way to divide up the world of questions: some are convergent, while others are divergent. Convergent ones seek a single right answer, which in a teaching setting is already known to the teacher. These "closed" questions—like "What is the average temperature in Hawaii?"— test someone's knowledge or ability to arrive at a logical answer. Divergent ones invite more than one answer, like "How should societies respond to climate change?" "Open" questions like this invite more creative thinking.[6]

While "open" sounds better than "closed," and "complex cognition" sounds smarter than "simple cognition," there is no inherent value judgment going on in these systems of classification. The theorists behind them stress that they all have appropriate places, depending on the purpose at hand. But let's say we do have a purpose in mind—and it's to arrive at novel insights by exposing "unknown unknowns." Let's even say we are convinced that, as a general rule, the world needs a lot more people devoted to that purpose. In that case, we are making a value judgment. The best questions, then, are the ones that excite the imagination and spur positive change.

Meanwhile, the goodness or badness of a question is also determined by the spirit in which it's asked. Take the question that Apple design chief Jony Ive says his old boss, Steve Jobs, used to ask him "nearly every day." Ive had always noticed Jobs's ability to maintain a laser focus on the task where his attention would make the most difference. One day Ive told Jobs he admired that, and admitted it was something he himself struggled with. Evidently, this became one of the people-development problems Jobs then decided to prioritize. In their daily encounters, Ive said, Jobs "would try to help me improve my focus by asking me, 'How many times did you say *no* today?'"[7]

That in itself is a great question, because it forces a perspective shift: it recasts the challenge of staying focused from sustaining engagement in a task to rejecting distractions from it. But it is easy to imagine that having Steve Jobs repeat the same question to you day after day could start to feel like a form of abuse. The reason it didn't for Ive is that Jobs genuinely wanted to help. The same question in different hands can be an expression of caring or a cudgel.

For me, the best questions—the ones this book focuses on—are catalytic; that is, they dissolve barriers—which, in idea generation, usually come in the form of false assumptions—and channel energy down new, more productive pathways. Let's take a look at each of these powerful qualities in turn.

GREAT QUESTIONS BREAK DOWN ASSUMPTIONS

Some questions knock down the walls that have been constraining a problem-solver's thinking. They remove one or more of the "givens" in a line of thinking and open up space for inquiry that had been closed off. We commonly call this reframing.

Tina Seelig, a Stanford professor who writes about creativity and innovation, is a big advocate of reframing. In her words, "All questions are the frame into which the answers fall. And . . . by changing the frame, you dramatically change the range of possible solutions." Seelig quotes the often-told story about Einstein, in which he says: "If I had an hour to solve a problem and my life depended on the solution, I would spend the first fifty-five minutes determining the proper question to ask, for once I know the proper question, I could solve the problem in less than five minutes." Seelig suggests that one way to reframe things is to think of someone quite different from yourself and try to adopt the perspective they would take on the situation. Would a child interpret something differently than you do as an adult, or would someone from a different place, versus a local, start with a fundamentally different set of assumptions?[8]

At Alphabet, the parent company of Google, an entire unit of the company exists to operate as a "moonshot factory," trying to devise very ambitious solutions to big problems. Called simply X, it likes to take on "age-old, world-hurting problems," as one of its managers, Phil Watson, puts it, that could be solved in a dramatically better way given new technological capabilities. Since transportation is that kind of problem, for example, Alphabet's driverless car initiative started within X before turning into Waymo, a standalone Alphabet company. The same goes for Loon, which started in the X unit as the "Project Loon" effort to provide Internet connectivity to Earth's most remote areas using stratospheric balloons to suspend networks nodes in the sky. Always, the effort starts with an attempt to map the problem space correctly before jumping into building a solution. The leader of the group, Astro Teller, constantly reminds teams to "start with the hardest part of the problem," Watson tells me—which of course begs the question, since at the outset of any effort to imagine a solution that doesn't exist, it can be hard to predict exactly where the going will get tough.

What people at X have learned to recognize, however, is that the human tendency is to start digging in and making progress on whatever part of the effort is easiest. So, just calling out that tendency and advising against it can help. The comical example Xers use is that, if the vision was to get a monkey to sit on top of a pole reciting Shakespeare, the typical team would go straight to work building that pole with its nicely balanced platform at the top. It's the part of the problem they already know how to approach, and solving it feels and looks like momentum-building progress. But everyone knows the hard part is going to be teaching the monkey—and if that proves impossible, any time spent on other parts of the solution will turn out to have been wasted. To keep themselves focused on where their energies should be directed, people at X sometimes toss a hashtag into their team communications: #monkeyfirst.

Cognitive psychologists know there are deep reasons that humans readily settle into comfortable frames of thinking and generally resist breaking them until the feeling of being thwarted by them becomes unbearable. In social groups, moreover, this tendency is compounded. Sociologist Amitai Etzioni, who finds strong evidence that people's social identities and personalities are shaped mainly by their community relationships, observes that we cling to "stable knowledge" rather than allowing "transforming knowledge" to challenge the basic assumptions of our systems. When we engage in producing stable knowledge we only play with secondary assumptions within a larger framework which is taken for granted. To question the frame of our knowledge system is, for most of us at most times, to upset the applecart too much. As Etzioni puts it, "Once consensus has been reached on a basic worldview, a self-view, a view of others, or strategic doctrine, it is politically, economically, and psychologically expensive for the [decision-makers] to transform these assumptions . . . Therefore, they tend to become tabooed assumptions, limiting the production of knowledge to specifics within the confines of these assumptions."[9] The status quo marches on.

Questions turn out to be the most effective way of breaking through this wall of resistance to reframing. In a tentative, nonaggressive way, questions crack open taboo territory and encourage us—individually and collectively—to reexamine fundamental assumptions we are making. Elon Musk's favorite term for this is "first-principles thinking." When his electric car company, Tesla, landed at the top of the *Forbes* Most Innovative Companies list a few years ago, the team of us who compiled that annual ranking talked to him about his knack for coming at enormous problems from new angles.

First-principles thinking, Musk explained, hacks away all the things that have been treated as givens but shouldn't be, until it gets down to the base layer of incontrovertible truth. Then it works back up from there. Musk's easy example for us was one from the automotive world in which Tesla competes. Why simply accept that in putting lightweight aluminum wheels on its cars Tesla must incur the going rate of $500 apiece? Instead he would likely say: "Well, that seems odd, because the cost of cast aluminum is maybe two dollars a pound. And the wheel is twenty-five pounds, so that's fifty bucks. Okay, there's some processing costs involved, so let's double that and now we're at a hundred. This wheel should not cost five hundred." Musk is very aware that people don't normally push back so hard on what is presented to them as reality. They are "more likely to say: 'Well, we looked at what other people pay for wheels and they seem to pay somewhere between $300 and $600. So, we think our $500 number is not that bad.' But that just means everybody else is getting ripped off, too!" Analysis of a problem by first principles, as he summed it up, "is where you try to boil things down to the most fundamental truths in a particular area by asking 'What are we *sure* is true?' The things you're highly sure of are base truths, your axiomatic elements, and then you apply your reasoning using those."

Reframing, this example suggests, is almost always a case of "larger framing"—opening up a space of inquiry that has been closed down to some extent. Similarly, this is what my colleague Clay Christensen does when he advises innovators within firms to stay focused on "the jobs to be done" by the goods and services they produce.[10] If, for example, a company produces cars, it should not fall into the trap of saying "What would make our cars better?" It should take the larger perspective of remembering that a car is just a solution the customer "hires" to get a job done, which is to transport her to where she needs to go. Think in terms of "How can we transport the customer better?" and the frame for innovation in the company's offerings suddenly becomes vastly larger.

GREAT QUESTIONS ENGAGE AND ENERGIZE

Malcolm Gladwell is the modern-day master of persuasive rhetoric, or what is called in the twenty-first century "narrative nonfiction." At the outset of his bestselling book *Outliers: The Story of Success*, he invites us to come along with him on his journey of discovery:

> *What is the question we always ask about the successful? We want to know what they're like—what kind of personalities they have, or how intelligent they are, or what kind of lifestyles they have, or what special talents they might have been born with. And we assume that it is those personal qualities that explain how that individual reached the top.*
>
> *. . . In* Outliers, *I want to convince you that these kinds of personal explanations of success don't work. . . . It's not enough to ask what successful people are like, in other words. It is only by asking where they are* from *that we can unravel the logic behind who succeeds and who doesn't.*[11]

Please note here that Gladwell is starting his book by saying, essentially, "Let's reframe the question." He does that because it immediately engages his audience's attention. He is telling them that, while they have always looked at a topic they care about in one way, they really should be looking at it in another way. He knows their reaction will be "Ooh, cool, this should be interesting. I will enjoy poking around in that space for a while." This is the second quality of a certain kind of questions, the kind I am trying to encourage more of. They excite and engage others' creative thinking. They unleash energy and channel it down a new pathway that presents the potential for new solutions.

Great insights, on their own, are next to useless. They take on their world-changing power only when someone turns them into practical reality. And turning insight into impact almost always entails hard work. Usually it requires more work than one person can do, both in terms of their time and personal skill sets. To do big things—even to change big things about one's own life—means recruiting and motivating others to take up the cause.

Recruiting others to a cause is something a group of parents in New Jersey had to do, for example, when they were feeling stuck for solutions. Their kids, whose autism spectrum disorders made it difficult for them to function independently, were about to age out of the programs provided through the local school system. In 2000 they began by forming an informal club of parents who were in the same boat, who all contributed some funds to provide a range of recreation activities for their kids. As these parents got to know each other better, conversations among them kept landing on their biggest worry: "What will happen to our child when we are not around?" That changed one day in a very productive way. "As our kids aged up," they report now, "we saw we had to take action. And the first thing we did is reframe the question." The group started asking itself: "What can we do to make sure our child has a purposeful life today, and in the future?"[12]

On one level, that is a simple shift in language—yet, isn't it obvious how the first question trapped people in helpless dread, while the second motivated productive action? The new question not only energized the parents; it gave them a focal point for sharing ideas and a basis for inviting others—like clinical psychologists and nonprofit agency advisors—whose help they would need. Today, the Quest Autism Foundation they created together provides a range of services as a state-approved "Real Life Choices provider" of adult day programs and, thanks to a capital campaign, is about to combine its two sites into a home of its own.

Was it really instrumental in the beginnings of the Quest Foundation that a *question* was posed instead of a declarative statement sharing an idea or setting forth an inspiring vision? I think so, for a few reasons. Questions, when they are seen as sincere requests for help, invite creative contributions from others rather than merely campaigning for their support. In most cases that additional thinking makes for better solutions, but if nothing else it generates more active support.[13] People who cognitively engage with an issue become more invested in getting it resolved. Since so much of what we struggle with in life and work is bigger than we are, it is essential that we use the tools we have to recruit help from others, and good questions are among the best of those tools.

TIME TO GO BEYOND ANSWERING

A few years ago I gave a speech to a group of CEOs and senior leaders in Singapore at a *Wall Street Journal* conference, presenting findings from *The Innovator's DNA*, for which Jeff Dyer, Clay Christensen, and I had researched behavioral differences between businesspeople who were and were not highly innovative. One of five key skills that distinguished innovators from non-innovators was their questioning behavior. (For example, we found that innovators often demonstrate a high Q/A ratio, referring to the number of questions versus answers we found in their transcribed conversations.) In Singapore, someone from the crowd came up to me afterward. "Here's my concern," he said. "All the way up from the bottom to the top of my company, I've been promoted primarily for having all the right answers. Now I'm in the CEO role I realize, uh-oh, it's not about answers up here. It's probably more about asking the right questions. And I'm not quite sure I know how to do that."[4]

I wasn't surprised to hear that he had made it so far in his career without becoming a more deliberate questioner. When people spend a lot of time in hierarchical organizations, they are rarely encouraged to ask questions of any kind. Instead, abundant signals clue them in to the grim reality that asking convergent questions—seeking simply factual information—makes them look dumb. And even harsher signals discourage them from asking divergent questions, which often challenge matters that are supposed to be settled at pay grades higher than theirs. And, by the way, when I refer to hierarchical organizations, I am hardly limiting that term to corporations. It describes the vast majority of nonprofit organizations, educational institutions, government agencies, and the military. (There's a reason Alfred, Lord Tennyson, wrote of the Light Brigade, "Theirs not to make reply, / Theirs not to reason why, / Theirs but to do and die.")

In such environments, the keys to surviving and thriving are smart answers. People get ahead by standing and delivering solutions to problems just as they are presented to them. Time goes by, the solutions incrementally improve, and no one has paused to revisit the questions. And who ends up in charge of the whole operation? Someone who is the product of that process. Like the CEO I met in Singapore, these are managers who have had questioning beaten out of them so long ago that they don't even know how to go about it when they get their turn at the top. Yet the future of the enterprise, and the livelihood of everyone who works in it, depends on senior leaders spotting when assumptions need to be called out and raising basic questions about how to serve customers better. Most often when I learn of leaders who are the exceptions, they are entrepreneurial founders as opposed to classic risers through the ranks. At Salesforce, for example, chief marketing officer Simon Mulcahy tells me that Marc Benioff (cofounder, chairman, and CEO) is constantly asking what the future will look like and how the company should adapt. Importantly, though, he always stresses the need to approach these questions with a "beginner's mind"—constantly seeing the world with fresh eyes. "You need to have a beginner's mind to create bold innovation," Benioff says. In older enterprises more focused on execution than invention, the potential "movers and shakers" who challenge conventions are too easily dismissed as "dreamers of dreams."[15]

Focusing on answers to settled questions is fine in many situations. In fact, it's essential that good questions should lead to periods of good answering.[16] The point is not to remain in constant questioning mode, always stepping back to rethink things instead of stepping up to make a decision and get on with life. But answering yesterday's questions is not good enough at times when we are feeling stuck, or when innovation is imperative, or when change must happen more continuously.

And so I was also not surprised that the CEO who approached me in Singapore was, in his new leadership role, now realizing that the most important personal development task he faced was improving his ability to frame and reframe questions. I've heard the same from many others. For example, Mark Weinberger, who leads the professional services firm EY, told me: "CEOs are expected to have the answers—and obviously you do need to have some answers. But sometimes it's not easy for other people to realize that one of your biggest jobs, in the CEO role, is to ask the questions." He was quick to add that those questions also have to be asked in the right spirit. "You can't make people feel like you think they're wrong if they can't answer what you're asking about. That can't be the purpose of the question. The real purpose is to help them think differently."

For Narayana Murthy, founder of Infosys, this is the only way to keep growing as a firm. "At the end of the day, for us to succeed in the marketplace, we have to create sustainable differentiation—and sustainable differentiation comes from the power of the human mind," he told me. "And that power is expressed in terms of the right questions—and then the right answers to those questions." He summed up his line of thinking by stressing that the job of the leader is to ensure the organization is "creating differentiation through the power of innovation," and that implies certain priorities for how leaders think and behave: "I believe that asking the right questions is the first step."

THE MORE WAYS WE'RE STUCK, THE MORE QUESTIONS WE NEED

As it happens, we are collectively—and in many cases individually—in need of the power of innovation in numerous realms. There are scientific mysteries to unravel, social issues to resolve, personal difficulties to overcome. In many of these areas, progress has stalled as old ideas have run their repetitive course. Only new questions can show the ways forward.

For example, one problem that many people have noticed is the lack of gender diversity in certain fields, especially science, technology, and engineering. One entrepreneur I know, Debbie Sterling, was especially bothered by it when she came out of college. She herself had majored in engineering at Stanford, but she and the other women in her program were vastly outnumbered. They knew this wasn't a case of discrimination by the admissions staff: across the board, there just weren't enough women applying to engineering programs.

Sterling told me about the day she discovered something she

could do about it. "The idea first started at a club that I started with my friends called 'Idea Brunch,' where we would get together every couple of months and make breakfast, and each person would get up and pitch an idea—like for an art project, or a business, or an app— and we'd brainstorm for a few minutes and then go on to the next." At one brunch her friend Christy used her turn to recall the experience of being a little girl playing with her older brother's Lincoln Logs and Erector Set. Those toys got her interested in building at an age when "she didn't know any better—that this wasn't something for a girl to do." Sterling recalled her friend asking why those had been the brother's toys and not hers. "Christy's question was: What would make those toys appropriate for girls, too? . . . And I remember sitting there so mesmerized by that. It was just an epiphany moment, like: Oh—this is what I was put on this earth to do."

Sterling took that sense of purpose and ran with it, coming up with a product idea and using Kickstarter crowdfunding to get it prototyped. Today the company she founded, GoldieBlox, makes a range of toys—and is proud to proclaim why. "GoldieBlox is on a mission to inspire the next generation of female engineers," its website says. "Our goal is to get girls building." I like even better how Sterling put it to me: "Our question is: How can we disrupt the pink aisle?"

It's just one example of someone seeing a problem that has others throwing up their hands, and then finding an unexpected new angle to approach it from. In chapters to come, this is a continuing theme, with people challenging how cybercrime gets thwarted, how traffic problems get solved, how gun violence is combated, and more. Their work suggests not only that new answers are always out there but also that we should always be working to turn more people into catalytic questioners.

TIME TO GET BETTER AT QUESTIONING

In case it is not already evident, I need to make something clear: this is not a book that "gives you the questions" any more than it is a book that gives you the answers. Other books often hand over question sets, and their formulaic approach can be effective in the specific use cases they target.[17] However, this book aims higher, to equip people to generate unique, unlocking questions relevant to their own situations.

In that quest, the focus here is on a special class of questions, a small subset of the whole universe of questions. This is why, perhaps, those other books extolling questions and questioning have not been as useful or satisfying as they could have been. It isn't simply a matter of asking more questions; indeed, the questions raised in many settings are time-wasting diversions if not downright toxic. Instead, it's a certain kind of question that inspires creative problem-solving because it energizes collective thinking, inspiring collaborative work to make serious progress. By keeping a focus on these questions, we can learn how to bring more of them to the surface of our lives and work.

Breakthrough solutions start with reframed questions, and we are in need of breakthrough solutions in many, many realms. We can all benefit by grasping in a more disciplined way something we have tended to see as pure serendipity: the flash of inquiry that leads to insight. This last point is really the rationale for the book: the belief that something that seems like a once-in-a-lifetime stroke of luck—the insight, seemingly out of nowhere, that shows the way forward—is actually not something we should leave to chance or assume must be rare. We can make such moments happen by putting more emphasis on the questions that precipitate them.

2

Why Don't
We Ask More?

And you, Scarecrow, have the effrontery to ask for a brain?
You billowing bale of bovine fodder!
—THE GREAT AND POWERFUL OZ

When you look at a provocative political piece of art, you often suspect that an outsize personality lies behind it. That seems to have been the case with the late Tim Rollins. He was a New York artist known for his longtime collaboration with high school kids, many of them with learning challenges, from the toughest neighborhoods in the Bronx. Tim Rollins and K.O.S. (for "Kids of Survival") was a darling of the art world in the late eighties, and the "Kids'" output continues to this day—but a *New York* magazine article at the high point of the collaboration's sales attempted to show a less attractive side of the story. It used quotes from disaffected students to paint an unflattering portrait of the studio's dynamics.[1] For example, one student complained that if Rollins didn't go for one student's suggestion for a painting, the rest would pile on: "He'd be like 'Well, nope.' And everybody would say, 'Nope, nope, nope.'"

But if it was Rollins's own idea, everybody would go overboard to support it: "He'd say, 'How about this?' 'Oooh, yeah, we like that, Tim.'"

I don't presume to know the truth of the situation—and probably multiple truths were in play—but it would make sense that the kids were struggling to sort out just how this unusual arrangement worked. One young woman told the *New York* reporter, "The kids would never say anything because they didn't want to hurt Tim's feelings." They were conscious of being beneficiaries of the program and were afraid he would think they were using him. But at the same time, she noted, some knew the kids' involvement was exactly why the work held so much appeal to buyers. So, she said, "the kids felt like, 'Wait a minute—who's getting used here, anyway?'"

Take sides if you want on the answer to that question, but the crucial point here is that the question was a legitimate one to ask. Raising it within the studio itself, in a spirit of perspective-taking rather than accusation, might have headed off some resentments. It could even have proved catalytic, strengthening the partnership so that it would become even more creatively productive than it was. So why didn't the students who had that question express it? Why don't big, path-affecting, fair questions like this get raised? In this chapter we will explore that puzzle. The answer I propose is complex, since various elements conspire to kill off questions, but in the end it will boil down to something simple and solvable. Most of the spaces where social discourse happens in our world are not conducive to questioning or to developing people into more creative, constructive questioners—but if we recognize that deficit and resolve to change it, we can build the spaces that are.

LEARNING NOT TO ASK

The first reason that questions don't spring naturally to many people's lips is that, early in life, the natural desire to ask them was checked many, many times—so much so that questioning impulses weakened and the desire withered away. The process takes place at school and at home, and continues as young people head off to work. By the time they are in positions where they feel at liberty to ask challenging questions, and are even required to do so for their own good and that of others, they don't know how to do it.

Anyone who has spent much time around kids knows that humans start out full of questions and are uninhibited about asking them. Most of this questioning is simple knowledge seeking and sense making, but mixed in with the factual questions are inevitably some discomfiting ones, and now and again there's one that touches a third rail, however inadvertently. As their questions provoke responses, kids learn on two levels. They get answers (when they're lucky) to what they are curious about, and at the same time they get signals about whether they should keep asking.

Often, questions are very much alive in young people as they head off to school, but on first contact with most formal education systems the questions start getting rebuffed. Tony Wagner and Ted Dintersmith capture this dynamic well in their recent book *Most Likely to Succeed*. Teachers beholden to administrators to improve their districts' showings in standardized examinations spend their days "teaching to the test," trying to cram as much codified knowledge into students' heads as possible. Questions from students create unwelcome delays in the march through the curriculum, and in the typical classroom of twenty to thirty students the teachers' own questions are hardly models of generative inquiry. Plenty get asked, but they are designed to test recall and keep students paying attention, if only from fear of being called on next.

Education researchers have long been aware of this imbalance. Edwin Susskind, for example, went into elementary classrooms in the 1960s and rigorously recorded every spoken interaction. He found that, on average, an hour of class time featured eighty-four questions by the teacher, and just two questions asked by the pupils—that is, by *all of the pupils combined*. He counted one question per pupil per month.[2] Even earlier, in 1942, psychologist George Fahey observed 169 pupils in six high school classes across an academic year and found the same: one question per student per month.[3] William D. Floyd found among primary teachers a ratio of teacher questions to pupil questions as high as 95 to 5.[4] Summing up the body of research that existed by the late 1980s, the education scholar James T. Dillon said, "Students do not ask questions in classrooms. Whereas teachers have consistently been observed to ask a great many questions, students are heard to ask remarkably few if any at all."[5]

We might expect that this "stand-and-deliver" mode of questioning in classrooms would fade as students advanced in their studies, to the point that the use of questions would not be so one-sided, and students would have sufficient knowledge to start probing for new discovery. In his landmark book *Productive Thinking*, Max Wertheimer examines how Einstein, for example, came to develop his theory of relativity. At age sixteen, he reports, Einstein "was not an especially good student, unless he did productive work on his own account. This he did in physics and mathematics, and consequently he knew more about these subjects than his classmates. It was then that the great problem really started to trouble him. He was intensely concerned with it for seven years." Einstein is an extreme case, but the point is that he couldn't seriously engage with questions about a field until he had spent years with existing literature—and, at the turn of the twentieth century, it was possible at age twenty-three to be on top of it. (While we are on the subject of Einstein and questions, I can't resist including the next few lines of Wertheimer's account: "From the moment, however, that he came to *question the customary concept of time* . . . it took him only five weeks to write his paper on relativity—although at that time he was doing a full day's work at the Patent Office" [emphasis mine].[6] What an astonishing testimony to how catalytic the right question can prove to be.)

In any field, students generally need a grounding in fundamental facts and theory—that is, foundational knowledge of what has already been established beyond question—to be able to make insightful, productive inquiries of their own. Science education researcher Philip Scott explains that in a classroom the discourse among students and their teacher comes in two flavors. In the "authoritative" mode, the teacher is just transmitting, aiming to convey information to students. Yes, students ask questions, but only to obtain factual answers or explanations. The questions coming from teachers are frequent but only designed to test comprehension. When teachers shift to a "dialogic" mode, they encourage students to venture ideas of their own and consider different points of view. They draw out students' tentative responses with intriguing questions, and, equally important, they welcome such questions in return. Scott's point is that both modes are necessary and that effective classrooms feature a mix, but that the proportion of dialogic discourse rises as students advance.[7]

You can likely see a built-in problem implied here that logically gets worse with every passing decade. In any given discipline, the foundational set of knowledge keeps growing. Thus, for each generation, it takes more years of formal schooling for students to clamber up onto the shoulders of the giants that came before them and begin to look farther. For most people, that is more years than they can commit to expensive formal schooling. Instead, they spend their entire educational careers in classrooms designed for transmission of information, not questioning or learning to question the foundational concepts.

From there they move into workplaces. Some join the military—again, not a sector historically known for cultivating questioning behaviors. Others go into public and private sector jobs highly regimented by standard processes and rules. If anything is perfectly designed to head off questions, it is a detailed procedural manual, handed to an employee with a heavy workload to put through its explicit steps. So workers whose habits were formed in question-hostile educational settings usually find themselves in execution-focused workplaces where learning goals to encourage creativity are conspicuously absent (though the world's most innovative companies are exactly the opposite).

From classrooms to offices, then, people spend their days in question deserts where creative inquiry is ignored and silenced in the interests of efficiency. Stopping to consider how a problem might be solved differently, or how a different problem might get solved, is a regrettable cause for delay and, if the question is really challenging, can bring activity to a halt. This love of productivity is a reason why questioners are discouraged, but usually it is not the whole reason. The bigger, darker reason for shutting down questioning is that these settings are also rife with power struggles.

POWER CORRUPTS THE QUESTIONING PROCESS

In every realm of human interaction, people jockey for power—even in my own world of academia, where, as Wallace Sayre famously observed, the politics are especially intense "because the stakes are so low." But if you want to see how world-class power players do battle, there is no place like Hollywood. We could choose to zoom in on just about any major studio in any month to find a struggle playing out, but here's a well-documented one from the 1940s that I especially like because it pits people with different powers against each other—the rich producer Samuel Goldwyn and the respected writer Lillian Hellman—and more than hints at why most people lose their taste for questions.

As Goldwyn's biographer A. Scott Berg tells the story, Hellman was ordered by Goldwyn to show up at his Hollywood home one day in 1943 after she had dramatically declared a film he had made from one of her scripts "a piece of junk":

> As she entered the house, Goldwyn shouted, "I hear you tell people that Teresa Wright was your discovery!"
>
> "What does this have to do with anything," she asked.
>
> "Answer my question," he demanded.
>
> "No," she said. "I will not answer any questions. I told you this afternoon, I take no more orders from you. Ever."
>
> Goldwyn commanded her to leave. "I will not get out of this house," she said, "until you have left this room." All the color draining from his face, he reissued his order. She restated hers. They stared each other down, and he blinked first, crying out for [his wife,] Frances. She ran into the room, trying to make peace, and he stormed up the stairs. Upon his exit, Hellman walked out the front door.[8]

It's a ridiculous, petty encounter, but at the same time hard to read without feeling one's blood pressure rise. What we're witnessing is a contest of who's calling the shots—and we instinctively get that the winner will be the one who gets to pose the questions, and the loser will be the one who is forced to answer. In this case, the result is a standoff. An unstoppable questioner has met an unquestionable object.

This encounter does not, of course, feature the kind of catalytic questions that open up new space for creative breakthroughs. These are a more common kind of question—a kind that is easily deployed as a weapon. We see this all the time in political affairs. As Douglas Walton writes, the "questioning and reply characteristic of much political debate . . . is an overly aggressive question, an overly evasive reply, and then a complaint by the questioner" that their target has ducked the question.[9] Those attempting to gain or maintain power don't use questions to ask permission, gain others' perspectives, get to know others better, or seek their counsel. They use questions to put others in their places, to catch them out and make them look stupid, or to remind them that they are obliged to stop whatever they're doing to respond. The power hungry aren't seekers of truth; they are seekers of advantage.

This explains further why ordinary people don't venture to ask many questions: seeing them used in these ways by power seekers creates the lasting impression that questions are acts of aggression. Noting this, those who do not wish to challenge others or be seen as trying to take charge opt quietly to keep their questions to themselves. Thus, many people who should be asking more questions—in the nonaggressive ways that would yield knowledge, resolve ambiguity, and inspire fresh thinking—engage in constant self-editing to avoid giving offense. They

In Hamburg, this street scene forced me to stop and reflect on how power-hungry people close off windows of crucial inquiry in our lives.

internalize the power dynamics around them and hold their tongues.

The most alarming example that comes to mind for me is the classic study of nurses conducted by psychiatrist Charles Hofling in the 1960s. To test the actual "situational" behavior of workers in power hierarchies and how it differed from their own predictions of how they would behave under certain conditions, he had a researcher posing as a doctor phone in orders to nursing staff on actual hospital wards. The order was for a drug named Astroten—actually nonexistent, but a bottle of placebo pills labeled as such had been planted in the supply cabinet—to be administered to a particular patient without delay. This request not only violated the hospitals' protocols for how prescriptions must be communicated, it called for twice the dosage level marked clearly on the bottle as the "daily maximum." Yet twenty-one of the twenty-two nurses who picked up the phone did not question the order and had to be intercepted to keep it from being carried out.

For someone who lives to control others, such unquestioning obedience is nirvana. The single best measure of power, in fact, may be the extent to which one's edicts and actions can go unquestioned. Thinking again of Hollywood and the source of this chapter's epigraph, recall the scene in the classic film *The Wizard of Oz* when the misfit heroes arrive in the Emerald City and are granted an audience with the Wizard. The audience is meant to perceive that this eminence, who the protagonists hope will be beneficent, is actually an imperious bully. How does the film make that immediately clear? By having him shoot down questions. When Dorothy speaks up with a tentative "We've come to ask you . . ." she is promptly cut off. "Silence! The Great and Powerful Oz *knows* why you have come." It is too much to expect, however, that because he *knows* their request he will respond to it. Instead, she and her friends are issued an order—"Step forward"—then subjected to the wizard's barrage of insults and given an assignment that serves his own needs. It's just a movie, but the point is, we all get it. This is just how imperious bullies act.

Power-seeking people are tuned in to the fact that questions steer the course of conversations and that the ones doing the asking are therefore in the driver's seat. They use questions to maintain control and, when others pose questions, ignore them or try to turn them to their advantage. In a career advice column on *Forbes* magazine's website, plenty of letters come from office workers frustrated with domineering bosses. One named Josh writes:

> *I got halfway through the presentation and one of the VPs asked a simple, logical question.*
>
> *Bart jumped in before I could speak. . . .*
>
> *The VP said "My question is for Josh" and then I answered the question.*
>
> *Bart said "Josh, you should really let me answer a question like that! This is not your area of expertise. The VPs and I know better than you do."*
>
> *The presentation is about a topic that is exactly in my area of expertise.*[10]

This pattern of behavior shows up in many workplaces, evidently. When a website called the Muse asked contributors for tales of their worst bosses, one office worker recalled this: "I once had a boss who, while I was replying to a question addressed to me by their boss in a meeting (with whom I had worked before and had developed rapport), actually put their hand less than an inch in front of my face to silence me so that they could answer instead."[11] Lest you wonder if this experience is unique, Bob Sutton, professor at Stanford and author of *The No Asshole Rule* and *The Asshole Survival Guide*, provides ample research evidence to suggest the opposite. He tells me it's far more prevalent than most would imagine or admit.

To sum all this up, there are good questioners and bad questioners, and the worst questioners make use of questions to dominate others. But most people never pause to think that questions come in different shades of good and bad, and therefore the stinging effects of toxic questioning taint all questioning activity for them. On a deep level they come to believe that to ask a question—especially one that challenges any edge of the status quo—is to behave obnoxiously. The higher that people rise in hierarchies—based on position, expertise, ownership, charisma, or, heaven forbid, all four—the more their questions tend to pack a wallop and fail to encourage the challenging inquiry that could lead them and others to better ways of thinking and doing.

More than a century ago Lord Acton made a wise observation based on his study of senior government and church officials. "Power tends to corrupt," he concluded, "and absolute power corrupts absolutely." He built further on that thought: "Great men are almost always bad men, even when they exercise influence and not authority: still more when you superadd the tendency or the certainty of corruption by authority. There is no worse heresy than that the office sanctifies the holder of it. That is the point at which . . . the end learns to justify the means." I would extend Lord Acton's observation into the territory of this book by saying: Power tends to corrupt the questioning process and absolute power corrupts the questioning process absolutely.

LACKING THE GROWTH MINDSET

Why do people put up with this kind of thing? Barbara Kellerman ventured an explanation in her book *Bad Leadership*: "Our need for safety plays itself out at many levels other than the original, familial one, and this is why we follow the leader in everyday life. To be a well-behaved child is generally not to question the teacher, even when the teacher is somehow bad. When we are adults on the job it's the same: By and large we toe the line. We do what we're told and play by the rules, even when the rules are unfair, and those who set them badly equipped or disposed. We follow because the cost of not following is, more often than not, high."[12]

So we yield too easily to the power games others play on us. But the self-editing doesn't end there. We also have our own self-serving reasons for not asking more questions. We may, as Bill McDermott, CEO of SAP, told me, "not want to learn what uncomfortable answers our inquiries might yield, or to take responsibility for doing something with our newfound knowledge." The example of Kevin T. Hunsaker comes to mind. He was the "director of ethics" at Hewlett-Packard in 2006 when the company reacted to a boardroom leak of sensitive information with an aggressive effort to uncover which director had shared the secret with a reporter. When a member of the security team complained to Hunsaker that HP's investigation tactics had crossed a line in obtaining private phone records and were "very unethical at the least and probably illegal," Hunsaker felt compelled to ask the company's top investigator if all was aboveboard. Informed that it was "on the edge," he didn't push for details. Instead, he emailed back: "I shouldn't have asked."[13] What a terrible irony, given that the entire rationale for having an ethics officer position was to give someone the power to ask. Instead, an overzealous investigation went unchecked, and everyone involved was tainted by it, if not indicted.

People often hesitate to ask questions because they would rather not gain information that would make them confront a need for change. Even when, rationally, it is evident that things are not going as well as they could, there is something within individuals that is ferociously protective of the status quo.[14] Recall the matrix discussed in Chapter 1 with its one quadrant full of things "you don't know you don't know." For most people, that territory is blocked off by various barriers, including emotional ones that keep them from wanting to venture into it.

Carol Dweck's work on people's beliefs about intelligence is relevant here. The groundbreaking research behind her book *Mindset: The New Psychology of Success* shows that people differ according to whether they believe a person's level of intelligence is fixed or subject to development. People who believe the latter have what Dweck calls a growth mindset, and it gives them the motivation to work harder and achieve more than their fixed-mindset counterparts. But Dweck is quick to point out that the growth-mindset advantage "isn't just about effort": while a willingness to work hard matters, people who want to keep learning "also need to try new strategies and seek input from others when they're stuck."[15]

Dweck specifically addresses how learners from each mindset react differently to having questions posed to them. Imagine, she proposes, that you sign up for a course in an unfamiliar subject and, a few sessions into it, the teacher brings you to the front of the class and asks you a series of questions about the material. "Put yourself in a fixed mindset," Dweck instructs. "Your ability is on the line. Can you feel everyone's eyes on you? Can you see the instructor's face evaluating you? Feel the tension, feel your ego bristle and waver." Now switch, she invites, to putting yourself into the same situation with a growth mindset. "You're a novice—that's why you're here. You're here to learn. The teacher is a resource for learning. Feel the tension leave you; feel your mind open up."

While I've just devoted a fair bit of space to the questioning behaviors of powerful people, Dweck's comments here are an important reminder that there is another side of the coin to consider. Beyond how others in your presence are deploying their questions, there is the matter of how you are receiving them. Are you responding with a growth mindset or a fixed mindset? My hunch, too, is that the kinds of questions people *ask* are very different depending on whether they have a growth mindset or a fixed mindset. Those who lack the mindset that invites change and growth are less comfortable raising the kinds of questions that challenge assumptions and invite creative thinking about what could change. For them, even the seemingly benign questioning that would not disrupt things doesn't happen. The questions with potentially bigger implications—the ones with transformative potential—are truly off the table.

I mentioned Kodak's founding in Chapter 1, spurred by a catalytic question. But consider again how, many decades later, that company's story turned out. In 2012, Kodak found itself in bankruptcy. The destruction took place because someone else had asked and answered all the right questions—about how digital technology could transform amateur photography—before Kodak did. This happened despite the fact that in 1974 Kodak engineers had invented the first electronic camera: it may have delivered only a 0.01 megapixel image, but it was a start that could have been pursued far more seriously. Instead, Kodak management saw no compelling reason to commit significant resources to pursu-

On a recent Disneyland Park trip with our grandchildren, we noticed a changing of the guard where decades-old "Kodak Picture Spot" signs had been replaced by "Nikon Picture Spot" ones.

ing the invention. With images so low in resolution, and no PCs or high-speed Internet at home or work to share or print images, Kodak's digital camera sat on the shelf.

Fast-forward twenty years, and while Kodak had seen the light and was running a successful consumer digital business, it had squandered a huge opportunity in a rapidly moving new market. The mystery is: Why had the company become incapable of the kind of imaginative, catalytic questioning it had been founded on? And why do so many others? My theory is that, as organizations grow and gain market power, power-seeking people are attracted to them and gravitate to upper managerial roles. The ranks, in turn, fill up with the kind of people who can stand working for such bosses—people who lack the growth mindset that would make it impossible to go through life without questioning. Thus, even places that once changed the world can lose their abilities to generate and pursue exciting new questions.

QUESTIONS NEED PLACES TO FLOURISH

Among the many problems in our world crying out for better solutions is the difficulty of protecting endangered species. Especially galling to any conservationist is the plight of the white rhino, constantly poached for the alleged but completely bogus medicinal value of its horn. A few years ago a nonprofit organization in South Africa won an innovation award for an idea that sprang from changing the question. All previous efforts had focused on how to dissuade or intercept the poachers who found it so easy to trespass on the animals' habitat. This new effort asked: Why don't we *move the animals* instead? The result was Rhinos Without Borders, which has already transported dozens of rhinos to an area of Botswana where poachers have no operations and networks and are easier to keep out.

It's a great story about a question, but I tell it here because it also serves as an apt analogy to what questioners themselves need. It just won't work to attempt on some large scale to convince question killers to back off so that question-hostile environments will transform into places where creative inquiry thrives. The forces against this are too entrenched and too great. Those who want to cultivate more questioning should instead create new spaces designed and protected as areas where the rules are different and different conditions prevail.

Consider a comment by Vijay Anand, an executive at Intuit, a software company that is very attuned to the need to keep innovating. "As a leader, it's your job to set the big goal, envision the big dream," he says, "but as a good leader, it's also your job to step aside, let people run with the idea and build it. Stay out of the nitty-gritty, and give people the freedom to do their own thing. A lot of times, that's all you need to do. My one question is always, 'What is your billion-dollar product idea for India?' And it is remarkable how inspired everyone is to answer that question and bring that dream alive."[16] This is a philosophy that Brad Smith, Intuit's chairman and CEO, has worked to spread in the company throughout his fifteen years in the job. He is a big fan of the "grand challenge" style of questioning that gets lots of people thinking about what it would take to realize an inspiring vision. He cherishes any question "that gets our heart beating really fast and causes us to step back and say: 'Wow, to achieve that, I'm going to have to think and act completely differently.'"

For that matter, listen to Lionel Mohri, Intuit's vice president of design and innovation, for whom the task of creating good spaces for questioning is a full-time job. A strong advocate of the "design thinking" approach to product and service innovation, and more generally of engaging people in systems thinking, he provides the frameworks and resources to help others in the organization develop ideas for fresh solutions. But fundamentally, he told me, "I don't think innovation is actually about solutions—it's actually about the right questions. . . . If you don't ask the right questions, you're not going to get the right solutions." Especially if people are interested in "breaking paradigms and doing disruptive innovation," he says, they have to go to this higher level of reframing the question. This is what he considers "the biggest takeaway from design thinking and systems thinking": it solves the problem he faces of "How do you make it so that people can go there?"

All these comments are evidence of a much broader Intuit effort to create a "culture of innovation"—in other words, a kind of "conservation land" for questions to survive and multiply over months and years. In the chapters to come, I will introduce many other people who care about doing the same: creating an oasis here and there with hopes that creativity-friendly conditions will spread.

WHERE IN THE WORLD DO QUESTIONS THRIVE?

The notion that we can do more to create spaces conducive to questioning isn't just about organizational cultures inside companies. Whole societies' cultures also vary in terms of how encouraging they are of questioning. Nitin Nohria, the dean of Harvard Business School, recalls the exhilaration he felt on leaving Bombay for the first time in his life and arriving in Cambridge, Massachusetts, to do his PhD at MIT:

I had this simultaneous sense of, on the one hand, being in a small place, but on the other hand, being in a limitless place intellectually. What was striking is that nobody said that just because you're a graduate student, you're supposed to think small thoughts and you have to wait until you get tenure to think big thoughts. In India, you almost always felt that you had to find your place. It was a very hierarchical society, and when you were young, you were never supposed to challenge a professor.

Here, to suddenly be liberated to imagine whatever you wanted to imagine for yourself, to be encouraged to sit in seminars—your right to ask a question, if you asked an intelligent question, was the same as anybody else's right to ask an intelligent question.[17]

To be sure, India is a different place than it was decades ago—so is the United States—and at any time, it is possible to overstate this cultural angle. "TK" is a Korean law professor in Washington, DC, who complains about "culturalism"—a term he coined in his popular blog called "Ask a Korean!" By way of definition, he writes that culturalism is the "unwarranted impulse to explain people's behavior with a 'cultural difference,' whether real or imagined."[18] The post where this critique appears was prompted by his close examination of a theory, endorsed by Malcolm Gladwell, purporting to explain why an infamous disaster happened to Korean Air Lines. No one will ever know for sure why the crew of Korean Air Flight 801 so misjudged its approach to a Guam runway that it crashed into neighboring high terrain. But this theory posits that, because the plane's first officer and engineer were too respectful of the hierarchy of the cockpit, they failed to question the decisions of their tired captain even as they saw him making mistakes. The idea that an overly deferential Korean culture is the blame for the crash is, however, a theory TK doesn't buy. "Because the culturalist impulse always attempts to explain more with culture than warranted, the 'cultural difference' used in a cultural explanation is more often imagined than real," he writes. "To paraphrase Abraham Maslow, to a man with a culturalist impulse, every problem looks like a cultural problem."

While culturalism can certainly be taken too far, a large body of research does confirm that real differences exist between country cultures, and some of these differences must influence whether people ask and encourage challenging questions. For example, a renowned researcher in the field, Geert Hofstede, and his colleagues have studied six dimensions of cross-cultural differences for several decades. Among them is "power distance," defined as "the extent to which the less powerful members of organizations and institutions (like the family) accept and expect that power is distributed unequally."[9] In a culture with small power distance, many aspects of life are observably different from those in large power distance societies. For example, where inequality is not as great, "subordinates expect to be consulted," whereas they expect, in places with high inequality, "to be told what to do." The implications for raising questions that challenge the status quo are obvious.

A second cultural dimension that makes a difference when it comes to questions is "uncertainty avoidance," or the degree to which members of a society feel stressed by ambiguity, unstructured situations, and the prospect of an unknown future. In cultures where uncertainty avoidance is high, people are comfortable with strict behavioral codes, laws, and rules. There is "disapproval of deviant opinions, and a belief [that] 'there can only be one Truth and we have it.'" Among the observable differences on this dimension, Hofstede points to schools in which teachers can say "I don't know" versus schools where teachers are "supposed to have all the answers." Again, it is easy to see how these cultural differences would translate to very different propensities to ask thought-provoking questions.

Hofstede's third dimension of cultural difference relevant to questioning is the extent to which a society's people tend toward individualism versus collectivism. In individualist cultures, ties among individuals tend to be looser, as people look after themselves. In collectivist cultures, people are more likely to be found living in strong, cohesive groups at home and work. Individualist cultures value speaking one's mind while collectivist cultures focus on maintaining harmony. If the latter is the goal, questions tend to suffer, as people value the stable knowledge that is foundational to their mutual understanding and cooperation over transformative knowledge that might disrupt many existing arrangements.

Hofstede's work is a constant reminder to those who deal with people from other cultures that the attitudes and behaviors they may think are universal are not at all. For those of us particularly interested in questioning behaviors, it also reinforces the notion that the natural curiosity humans are born with can be encouraged or discouraged to very different degrees depending on the circumstances in which they find themselves. If we acknowledge that whole societies, and certainly whole organizations, can trend toward keeping questions from surfacing, that should reinforce our resolve to carve out the special places in which we know they can flourish.

CLEARING A SPACE FOR INQUIRY

The Quakers have an institutional practice that sounds like a wonderful example of a space specifically carved out for productive questioning. I discovered it from Parker Palmer, an educator and activist who has touched millions of people through his books, including my favorite, *Let Your Life Speak*. He recalled a time when he was offered a plum job as a college president. Certain that he would accept, he nonetheless followed his faith's practice: "As is the custom in the Quaker community, I called on half a dozen trusted friends to help me discern my vocation by means of a 'clearness committee,' a process in which the group refrains from giving you advice but spends three hours asking you honest open questions to help you discover your own inner truth. (Looking back, of course, it is clear that my real intent in convening this group was not to discern anything but to brag about being offered a job I had already decided to accept!)"

Palmer's memory of the meeting is that the questions at the beginning were easy to field. They weren't too much different from the ones he had prepared for and answered well in his interviews for the new post. But at some point a question came at him that "sounded easy yet turned out to be very hard." It was: "What would you like most about being a president?" Some hemming and hawing followed, with Palmer making evasive answers that were seen as such by the committee. After cycling through the question a number of times, he finally gave the honest reply, "an answer that appalled even me as I spoke it":

> *"Well," said I, in the smallest voice I possess, "I guess what I'd like most is getting my picture in the paper with the word president under it."*
>
> *I was sitting with seasoned Quakers who knew that though my answer was laughable, my mortal soul was clearly at stake! They did not laugh at all but went into a long and serious silence—a silence in which I could only sweat and inwardly groan.*
>
> *Finally my questioner broke the silence with a question that cracked all of us up—and cracked me open: "Parker," he said, "can you think of an easier way to get your picture in the paper?"*

The committee had done its job. Its questions had caused Palmer to look within himself and discover that his desire for the prestigious position "had much more to do with my ego than with the ecology of my life." When he made the call shortly after to withdraw his candidacy, he knew he was avoiding a step that "would have been very bad for me and a disaster for the school."[20]

I bet that an experience like that would turn anyone into a lifelong fan of questions, and it also drives home the truth that crucial questions don't and won't arise naturally in the normal course of life.

To borrow Hemingway's phrase, questions need a clean, well-lighted place to unfold in. I see many people trying to create such spaces as deliberate responses to the many forces arrayed against curiosity and questioning. People are deliberately designing places and times to operate by different norms than the ones we traditionally follow. In the business context, for example, Mark Zuckerberg has institutionalized a weekly "question time" with his Facebook employees during which they are encouraged not only to seek information but to bring up tough issues they think the company's leadership might be missing or might not be addressing actively enough. Others invest in expertly facilitated offsite sessions devoted to forward-thinking questions.

In the family context, parents such as Tiffany Shlain (an Emmy-nominated filmmaker who founded the Webby Awards in the early days of website design) and her husband, Ken Goldberg (an artist, writer, and researcher at UC Berkeley), specify "device-free" hours in the day or week when everyone engages a different mode of communication. My friend Bea Perez, chief public affairs, communications, and sustainability officer at Coca-Cola, has a "table talk" routine in her own family that provides this kind of break for conversation and crucial questions.

Among friends, something like Debbie Sterling's brunch club (which we heard about in Chapter 1) can pull people out of their routine and create a space for floating crazy ideas. Any type of therapy or coaching session, for that matter, is ideally a space reserved and designed for asking and answering transformational questions.

In a sense, this chapter has been one long response to an objection you might have had after reading Chapter 1: If questions are key to progress (large or small), why have we reached the twenty-first century without people knowing and embracing that? Why are we not celebrating, encouraging, and inviting questions more often?

Our answer began with the startling (and ample) evidence that questions get actively discouraged in the very places where people are expected to learn the most—and should be asking the most. As Neil Postman famously put it, "students enter school as question marks and leave as periods"; they are turned into masters at answering and novices at asking. Rigorous studies conducted across decades show that very little inquiry takes place in most classrooms and workplaces—not because of an innate lack of curiosity, but due to social conditioning. Humans begin life as active, enthusiastic questioners, but as childhood progresses and the years pass, that quality fades.

I shared my belief that this innate behavior vital to survival and happiness is effectively suppressed by social dynamics, as powerful people in hierarchies resent and therefore restrict the asking of questions, and too many people, often lacking a growth mindset themselves, conclude that life is easier without asking. To question anything fundamental is by definition to challenge, as leadership scholar John Gardner put it, "the crusty rigidity and stubborn complacency of the status quo."[21] (Think: Why are we doing this in the way we are? Are we really focusing on the most important goal?)

No wonder, then, that the combination of personal reticence and powerful resistance to questioning sets up, in groups, a terrible lack of innovative thinking. We have a society with a seriously stunted capability to question, and it will take active, deliberate work to break our "mind-forged manacles" (William Blake's metaphor) and reactivate questioning in our teams, classrooms, and families. We may not be able to change the whole world into a questioning place, but we can carve out spaces in which we establish question-friendly conditions. The chapters to come will show us how.

3

What If We Brainstormed for Questions?

You can tell whether a man is clever by his answers.
You can tell whether a man is wise by his questions.
—NAGUIB MAHFOUZ

About twenty years ago I was leading a brainstorming session in an MBA class on creative strategic thinking, co-taught with colleague Jeff Dyer, and it was like wading through oatmeal. We'd been discussing something that many organizations struggle with: how to build a culture of equality in a male-dominated environment. Although it was an issue that the students cared about, they clearly felt uninspired by the ideas they were generating. With just a few minutes left till everyone had to leave, we had done a lot of talking, but the energy level in the room was essentially nil.

Glancing at the clock, I closed my eyes briefly and resolved at least to give us a starting point for the next session. "Everyone," I improvised, "let's forget about finding better answers for today. Let's just write down some better questions we could be asking about this problem. Let's see how many we can generate in the time we have left." They dutifully started to throw out questions— and I kept to my word, redirecting anyone who started responding with an answer. To my astonishment, the room quickly reenergized. It was as though I had flipped a switch. Instead of trudging out at the end of the session, people left talking excitedly. And with good reason: among the questions scribbled on those chalkboards were a few that deeply challenged assumptions we had been making and opened up unexpected spaces for potential solutions.

Brainstorming for questions, not answers, wasn't something I'd tried before. It just occurred to me in that moment, probably because I had been reading and reflecting on sociologist Parker Palmer's early work about creative discovery through open, honest inquiry. But it was a gambit I soon tried again and have since used in many, many sessions, with constant refinement of the exercise. Virtually every time, I see this lift in positive energy and creative insight. What is going on in these rooms?

Over the years I have come to realize that it is a simple matter of creating a different kind of space for people, in which the usual rules and norms are suspended and different behaviors are encouraged. More broadly, this small-scale exercise has convinced me that breakthrough thinking isn't just a product of superior gray matter. It's not all about the cognitive processes going on inside people's heads. To a great degree it's a matter of the conditions in which they find themselves—which usually discourage questioning but can be altered to invite it.

CONDITIONS APPLY

This emphasis on conditions deserves some explanation, because it is not always assumed. If you ask yourself why people behave the way they do, your answer might put you into one of various philosophical camps. Whether or not you've ever engaged with the arguments of, say, Hegel versus Marx versus Popper, you might be more inclined to believe that people's thinking is determined by their environments or that it transcends those. This has been a question I have discussed repeatedly with a man I count as a great mentor and friend, Clay Christensen.

I've mentioned Christensen in passing already, and many readers will recognize him as the author of *The Innovator's Dilemma*, which describes how large businesses are often disrupted by scrappy start-ups. He is a big believer that behaviors—the actions and decisions, that is, that people default to habitually—cannot be legislated in isolation; they always emerge in context. As an example, he points to the often unsuccessful attempts by capitalist democracies to export their practices to nations of the world that have not grown up with them. Christensen observes that where these have failed to take hold, it is because a general climate was not already established in which people voluntarily obey the law, honor their contracts, and respect the rights and property of others. Shifting the focus to these underlying preconditions changes the understanding of what needs to be done. The question becomes: What institutions could be established or strengthened to cultivate these instincts?

Christensen is also a longtime believer in the power of asking the right question. He tells a story about the precise moment when this struck him, back in his student days at Harvard Business School. One day, when a classmate made a brilliant comment about a case study, he realized it came from a very different angle than his own analysis. He made a note to himself: What *question* did they ask of the case that led to such a great insight? And after that, as he prepared for discussions, he forced himself to pause before diving in to figure out a solution. He says: "The rare and valuable skill, I came to realize, was to ask the right question. That done, getting the right answer was usually quite straightforward."

It wasn't until recently that he and I put these two beliefs together. When reflecting on the research behind our book *The Innovator's DNA* (coauthored with Jeff Dyer), we recalled that our interview data showed that innovative leaders had a much greater propensity to ask questions, especially ones that challenged the status quo. While it looked like an inborn trait—"part of their DNA," so to speak—Christensen wasn't so sure. Maybe this is one of those behaviors that only emerges or proves successful in certain places. Maybe, if you want more productive questioning to be done, you have to create the conditions that favor it—instead of, for example, trying to hire more "questioning types."[1]

To say that someone is a product of their environment is not to say they have no agency, that they are simply acted upon by forces greater than themselves. In fact, sensing the environment and adjusting to it can be a very rational process. Incentive systems in large organizations, for example, are one of the conditions in which employees find themselves, as are the stories people tell about past victories and defeats. Such drivers of culture and conditions are built by people and can be consciously designed and altered to change the likelihoods of different outcomes.

Understanding this has made me recognize the importance of what some leaders in large organizations are trying to do as they grasp that the key to their enterprises' thriving is constant change, not stasis. Tony Hsieh, CEO of the online shoe retailer

Zappos, comes immediately to mind. He is nothing if not a space maker, as I experienced personally in a few days spent at "Llamapolis," the funky trailer park he established in an abandoned parking lot in downtown Las Vegas. The very entrance to the park, a tunnel strewn with holiday lights, signifies that the visitor is entering a place different from the world around it. This is Hsieh's home, but also the place where he often does his best thinking, so he has tried to create a setting where different conditions prevail. The point is to maximize the "creative collisions" that happen among the interesting and diverse residents and guests staying in the thirty trailers and tiny houses—moments of connection that are random but also intensified by a lot of careful thinking about how the layout will enable them.

Hsieh thinks on many levels about how to hit the reset button on the prevailing conditions in which people interact. In management circles, he is probably best known for his experiment in what he calls "Holacracy," a dramatic alternative to bureaucracy that imagines an organization's structure not as a pyramid or some other classic engineering construct but rather as an ecosystem in which success is a holistic phenomenon that emerges from constant, dynamic interactions among interdependent contributors. That is what Hsieh designed Zappos to be, and anyone who has worked at Zappos after working elsewhere can attest to the different behaviors it gives rise to. On the level of urban renewal, too, Hsieh came to Las Vegas with an ambitious intent to change the city's entrepreneurial vibe, hoping to make it a hotbed of innovative start-up businesses and a magnet for what Richard Florida calls the "creative class." After Amazon acquired Zappos, he was able to put serious money to the task, funding local ventures and nonprofit interventions. It's been a controversial experiment, to be sure, and Hsieh has trimmed his vision over the years, but no

Life *can* be beautiful when question marks become this big.

Miguel Hernandez, a full-time artist-in-residence at Zappos and creator of uncommon questioning spaces.

An equal rights resident explores "Llamapolis"—Tony Hsieh's trailer park in a revived and vibrantly alive downtown Las Vegas.

"When you eliminate the impossible, whatever remains, however improbable, must be the truth." —S'chn T'gai Spock (quoting Sherlock Holmes)

To think outside the box at Zappos you might find yourself inside an unusual one.

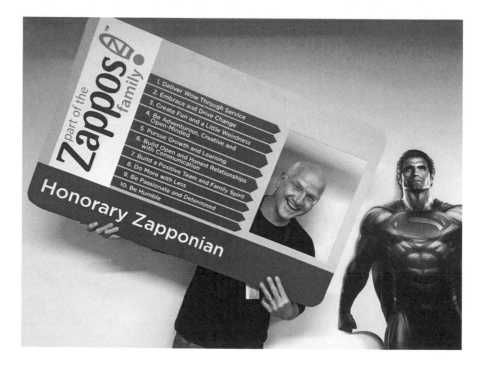

one can doubt his commitment to the idea that, if you want different behaviors to take hold, you must start by changing the settings
in which people find themselves. As in his trailer village, his idea
for downtown Las Vegas is that its public and commercial spaces
should maximize serendipitous conversations that will spark
ideas and therefore yield what he calls a "return on collisions."

A SMALL-SCALE RESET

By comparison, my "Let's brainstorm for questions" exercise was
decidedly small-scale and spontaneous. Still, as an easy, effective
intervention—especially in the form it has taken after more de-
liberative design since—it is worth unpacking a bit in terms of the
conditions it creates. At a minimum, what I now call a "Question
Burst" may be an exercise that you will want to try if you are, individually or as part of a group, looking for new insights to solve
a problem you care about. With that in mind, let me describe it in
detail. It consists of three steps.

Step 1: Set the Stage. To begin, select a challenge you care deeply
about. Perhaps you've suffered a setback or you have an indistinct
sense of an intriguing opportunity. How do you know it's a problem ripe for a breakthrough, given the right unlocking question?
It's probably a good candidate if it "makes your heart beat fast," as
Intuit CEO Brad Smith put it. You'll give it your full attention and
want to engage others in thinking about it.

BOTTOM LEFT I asked Kristen, my Zappos tour guide, "Where is a good place
to get my picture taken?" Her answer, with a smile, "You're empowered,
Hal. Where would you like to take it?" Ouch. I felt a tinge of wrongness and
discomfort as she had unknowingly poked at my "disease-to-please" default
approach to such a simple task. Kristen Anderson

Next, invite a small group to help you consider that challenge from fresh angles. You can do this exercise on your own, but bringing others into the process provides a wider knowledge base and helps maintain a constructive mindset. When you ask others to participate in a Question Burst, you're also summoning empathy and energy, which directly support idea generation and, ultimately, idea implementation. It's best to include two or three people who are starkly different from you in terms of their "insider" understanding of the problem and their general cognitive style or worldview. They will come up with questions that you would not—questions that might prove surprising and compelling—because they have no established ways of thinking about the problem and no investment in the status quo. They're more likely to ask third-rail questions and point to elephants in the room—because they don't know not to.

With your partners in the exercise assembled, give yourself just two minutes to lay out the problem for them. Once you've gone to the trouble of engaging willing helpers, it would be a pity to pollute their minds with your preconceptions before you've gained any benefit from their thinking. People often believe that their problems require detailed explanations, but that is because they have explored them in depth themselves. Quickly sharing the challenge forces a high-level framing that doesn't constrain or direct the questioning. So just hit the highlights: Try to convey how things would change for the better if the problem were solved. And briefly say why you are stuck—why it hasn't already been solved.

Before launching into question generation, it's important to clearly spell out two critical rules of engagement. First, ask people to contribute only questions. Explain that those who try to suggest solutions will be redirected by you, the leader of the brainstorming session. Second, announce that no preambles are allowed. Explanations and details, short or long, mainly guide people to see the problem in a certain way—the very thing you're trying to avoid.

You'll also want to do a quick emotion check up front. Reflect on the challenge right now: Are your feelings about it positive, neutral, or negative? Jot down your baseline mood. No need to spend more than ten seconds on this. You'll do it again after the session is over. These checks are important, because emotions have an impact on creative energy. Remember that this exercise not only sparks valuable new questions but also provides a positive emotion boost, making it more likely that you will follow up.

Step 2: Generate the Questions. With the problem now presented in broad-brush fashion, and everyone apprised of the rules, set a timer and spend the next four minutes collectively brainstorming surprising and provocative questions about the challenge. As in all brainstorming, no pushback is allowed on others' contributions. Your goal is to jot down on paper at least fifteen to twenty questions (best for verbatim capture and for consulting later).

Is there some precise magic about four minutes and twenty questions? No, but it works, for several reasons. The time pressure forces participants to stick to the "only questions" rule. I often see that people find it excruciatingly difficult to resist responding with answers—even for four minutes—when people start venturing questions. For example, one time when I was at a manufacturing organization and a small group started throwing out questions related to supply chain issues, one manager in the group kept launching into answers—whether out of defensiveness or to display his knowledge, I don't know. This impulse is understandable. But in this exercise the emphasis is on quantity. Any time spent answering someone else's question means less chance of hitting the twenty-question goal. Also, if people are focused on generating as many questions as possible, they'll more likely generate short, expansive questions that are unburdened by qualifications and assumptions, and will not feel obliged to explain questions that come from left field or carefully couch their language around charged topics.

Throughout the four minutes, you'll write everyone's questions down. Capture everything verbatim and ask your partners to keep you honest on this; otherwise, you might unconsciously censor something you don't immediately "get" or want to hear. As you're writing, add your own questions to the mix. Doing so may reveal patterns in how you've habitually framed the problem (and unknowingly perpetuated it). Karl Weick, the renowned organizational theorist, likes to say: "How can I know what I think until I see what I say?" That applies here.

Once the timer goes off, do the second quick emotional check. How do you feel about the challenge now? Are you more positive than four minutes ago? If not, and you're doing this in a setting that allows it, try rerunning the exercise. Or get some rest and try again tomorrow. Or try it with some different people. Research has established that creative problem-solving flourishes when people work in positive emotional states. I am convinced that much of the initial power of the Question Burst lies in its ability to alter a person's affect toward the challenge by dislodging that negative feeling of being stuck.

Step 3: Unpack the Questions. Your partners have now done their job, and you should be feeling more energized by the possibility of making progress. On your own, study the questions you jotted down. Be on the lookout for ones that suggest new pathways. About 80 percent of the time, this exercise produces at least one question that usefully reframes the problem and provides a new angle for solving it. Select a few questions that intrigue you and strike you as different from how you've been going about things. A few criteria can help as you consider each question: Is it one you have not asked or been asked before? Is it one for which you honestly don't have a good answer? Is it one that evokes an emotional response, positive or negative? In other words, subject the questions to a surprise test, an honesty test, and a gut-check test.

Now try expanding those few into their own sets of related or follow-on questions. A classic way of doing this is the "five whys" sequence developed by Toyota founder Sakichi Toyoda—and the variation on it suggested by Stanford's Michael Ray in *The Highest Goal*. Ask yourself why the question you chose seemed important. Then ask why the reason you just gave is important. And so on. The point is to keep opening up the space the problem occupies, which also broadens the territory of possible solutions and deepens your resolve to do something about it.

Finally, commit to the quest—the pursuit of at least one new pathway you've glimpsed—and do so as a truth seeker. (I steal that term from NASA engineer Adam Steltzner's account of working at the Jet Propulsion Laboratory, where the "right kind of crazy" people manage to accomplish things like landing a robotic rover on Mars.) Set aside considerations of what might be more comfortable to conclude or easier to implement, and instead focus on what it will take to get the problem solved. Devise a near-term action plan: What concrete actions will you personally take in the next three weeks to find potential solutions suggested by your new questions?

Recently an executive from a company with four major units participated in a Question Burst and went away with a resolve to track down some facts. He had been wrestling with concerns about behaviors he observed in his business unit, which was set up along different lines than the other three. In that session it dawned on him that he had been making a big assumption: that the founders who had set up his division had given it a different financial compensation scheme and so on because they had *intended* to create a different culture within it. But was it true? His to-do list started with getting on the founders' calendars to ask. Guess what: not only was this not a culture they had aimed for, but they were dismayed to learn it even existed. Those meetings turned out to generate a series of interventions to check the toxic behaviors.

So, that's it—the Question Burst exercise I invented all those years ago and have kept refining since. But is precipitating a fresh insight as simple as this? Can anyone willing to engage in this brief exercise summon up a valuable reframing of a problem big enough to have life-improving impact?

On the one hand, I am tempted to say yes. The simple implication of what is described here is that we would all be more likely to come up with innovative solutions if we made it a regular practice to engage in Question Bursts. Think of it as a sheer numbers game. Most questions aren't earth-shattering, but given enough repetitions—and I always advise doing at least three rounds on a given issue—the technique will reliably yield its share of great ones. For example, recently I heard from someone at a global software company who had decided to try a series of Question Bursts to make progress on a chronic management problem. "I feel extremely positive after the third round," she wrote, as "the questions became much deeper." The exercise actually exposed that the original conception of the problem she faced was "superficial"— and, by persisting with questioning, she "arrived at a much more meaningful challenge to conquer."

Meanwhile, the investment required is almost nil. Jonathan Craig is chief marketing officer at the brokerage firm Charles

Schwab, which has made "the power of questions" central to its brand ever since it realized its best customers were the ones asking the best questions. As Craig puts it, "It's hard to imagine hugely striking out by virtue of simply asking a question." He explains: "I often use it with my leadership teams, where if we're struggling with a big issue, a big challenge, rather than just trying to answer it, we'll just, for fifteen minutes, write up on the board all the questions we would love to have the answers to, to help answer the final question. . . . As a leader, using that approach of catalytic questioning, or other approaches to just pull out people's questions, will get you the better outcomes. We see it all the time."

Essentially, this is a road-tested process for increasing your chances of recasting problems in valuable, new ways. I've used it with countless other corporate teams (including at Adidas, Chanel, Coca-Cola, Danone, Discover, Ernst & Young, Fidelity, Genentech, and General Motors), with nonprofit organizations (for example, UNICEF and the World Economic Forum), and with individual leaders I've coached. Whether at work or in life, this is a quick way to rapidly bring different perspectives to bear on a problem you are wrestling with—and if you can make it a regular practice in a larger organization (using it at least three or more times with different groups of people about the same problem), it can help create a broader culture of collective problem-solving and truth seeking.

On the other hand, I also want to acknowledge that exercises don't always travel well. James T. Dillon made this point in his book *Questioning and Teaching*: "As a souvenir of our visit, we may be tempted to take home some exotic technique of questioning. But all techniques are better left just where we have found them. That is their rightful place, the one place where they can do any good. Back home we would only look foolish using some outlandish technique," he writes. "The smart thing to bring home is some understanding—theoretical notions that enliven practical actions [and] come home with a new understanding of how to turn the elements of questioning to our purposes in our circumstances."[2]

I agree with that advice, and in this case the larger takeaway is the one of creating spaces for questions to be asked. The important objective is to find ways to create the right conditions for questioning on a much broader scale so they are more pervasive in your organization and life. The Question Burst achieves its goals by imposing conditions that are nothing like participants' usual ones, causing them to suspend their usual behaviors. It is a one-off session, not intended as a whole solution. But if, by creating artificial conditions that work, this exercise causes people to value questions more—and to think more broadly about the conditions that favor them—then it can have lasting influence. Less forcing will be necessary to get more questions to come to the surface naturally.

EMOTIONS BEFORE AND AFTER A QUESTION BURST

During the past few years I've used Argomento polling software to collect data from more than 1,500 leaders about their experience with the Question Burst methodology. It has confirmed what I've sensed over the past twenty years as I used simple hand-raising techniques with more than 10,000 participants in classes, executive off-sites, and conference sessions. First, I ask people to quickly type into the app a few words that best reflect how they feel about their challenge, before and after the four-minute Question Burst segment. Here are the word clouds that were generated from that data:

Before doing a Question Burst how do you feel about your challenge?

questioning · discouraged · inspired · neutral · open · vulnerable · pressured · energized · marketing · know · eager · hopeful · **conflicted** · **scared** · alone · worry · pessimistic · hopeless · energised · **optimistic** · **confused** · afraid · tough · **nervous** · start · sad · sick · global · **annoyed** · zone · help · happy · opportunity · right · defeated · daunting · **helpless** · irritated · motivated · challenge · constrained · disappointed · **anxious** · **worried** · unsure · thinking · **overwhelmed** · perplexed · unclear · **stressed** · empty · bad · exited · impatient · don · fear · uncertainty · preoccupied · **curious** · **uncomfortable** · insecure · **lost** · exhausted · now · **concerned** · stupid · **excited** · **challenged** · puzzled · positive · blocked · passionate · upset · difficult · **stuck** · committed · frustrating · tired · drained · unknown · **uncertain** · resigned · time · urgent · lack · challenging · **interested** · **angry** · frustration · negative · agitated · stress · daunted · exposed · apprehensive · enough · control · bewildered

frustrated

© argomento.fr

After doing a Question Burst how do you feel about your challenge?

concerned · enthused · feeling · neutral · stressed · progress · clear · intrigued · ready · relaxed · different · powerful · engaged · refreshed · opportunity · **supported** · hope · **enlightened** · depressed · **energized** · **motivated** · stuck · enriched · focused · good · want · **encouraged** · eager · options · action · many · helped · **confident** · **excited** · less · **relieved** · can · invigorated · ease · zen · go · feel · full · interesting · **optimistic** · new · still · **hopeful** · curious · clarity · frustrated · get · relief · alone · confused · way · **inspired** · **better** · determined · comfortable · bit · anxious · committed · helpful · **ideas** · **open** · scared · **positive** · happy · little · perspective · dd · **empowered** · informed · validated · hard · exited · creative · work · thoughtful · understood · overwhelmed · nervous · need · challenge · exciting · surprised · daunted · slightly · amused · mejor · idea · minded · contemplative · annoyed · solutions · right · approach

© argomento.fr

We usually project both word clouds at the end of the session, and groups are always stunned at the difference. The same dramatic emotional shift is evident when people are asked directly if their feelings have changed after doing the Question Burst. Overwhelmingly, they report feeling at least a little better about the challenge they are trying to tackle.

After doing a Question Burst how do you feel about your challenge?

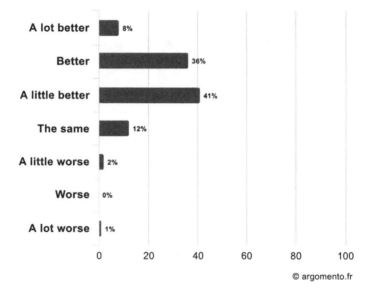

© argomento.fr

A NEW PERSPECTIVE

Spending just four minutes intensely generating questions gives most leaders a way to reframe their challenges. Here's a typical breakdown of how people report their shift in perspective after doing the exercise, and, below, their yes/no responses to whether they came away with at least one new idea to potentially solve the challenge:

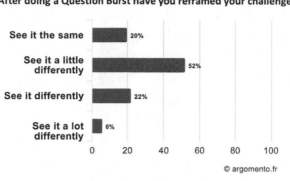

After doing a Question Burst have you reframed your challenge?

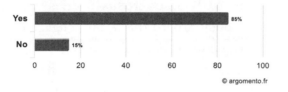

After doing a question Burst did you discover at least one new idea?

OTHER FORCING FUNCTIONS

I closed the previous chapter with the observation that many of us—maybe all of us—do seek out and create spaces in our lives and work that operate by different rules, with the express hope that this will open up our mental processes. Not only do questions occur to us in these settings, but we take the time in them to notice and engage with the questions that arise. That essentially describes many vacation getaways, religious retreats, corporate off-sites, and sessions with mentors, coaches, and therapists. It explains minutes carved out of busy days for meditation, walks, and probably no small share of hot baths.

A friend of mine, Mark Widmer, provides a unique service for families that is based on the idea that, if people are plunked into different places, they become more capable of creatively re-framing the problems they are fighting. He and his colleagues at Ampelis find scenic settings—ranging from the red-rock terrain of Moab, Utah, to the Dolomites of Italy—and stage retreats with careful thought to the conditions they are creating for dialogue. He tells me about one couple who came from humble means but grew rich, as one of them invented a valuable product, built a successful business on it, and ultimately sold that business. Along the way, the couple raised a family, but, not having been raised in wealth, they sensed there were many things they "didn't know they didn't know" about how to avoid the negative dynamics that can come with money. Widmer credits a series of gatherings in places away from home where the family engaged in activities they didn't usually pursue, creating a climate in which they could ask the right questions. The couple was in the habit of worrying: *Will leaving this money to our children end up tearing them apart? Will inheritance make it harder for them to be good people?* Together the family shifted to: *What is it that great parents do leave their children that helps them lead great lives?* As great questions often do, this one had a catalytic quality. It pointed to a very different pathway, because the immediate answer was "Their values"—and it energized the whole family to think together about those and find ways to pass them along.

In the corporate world, I would say a close cousin to this kind of family activity is the team off-site—assuming it is designed for the purpose of getting away from the daily grind to think about strategy for the long term. Sometimes it can feel like a needless expense to have managers decamp from their usual headquarters buildings and convene in another place, but a change of venue really can trigger a change in modes of thinking—as well as shake up the usual patterns of interaction among colleagues. In the past decade, as companies have become more focused on the need to innovate, off-sites have become much more thoughtfully designed and facilitated to focus people on the questions that really matter.

One interesting format is an innovation consulting service that enterprise software maker Salesforce has created for its biggest clients, which it calls "Ignite." It is designed not only to provide a process but also to create the conditions in which a management team can arrive at a shared vision of a company's future. At the outset of this six-part method, participants engage in a "question and reframe" exercise that is built around the Question Burst method. For example, at a recent session, a Salesforce team worked with leaders of the newly formed business Berkshire Hathaway HomeServices to frame the right questions as it embarked on building its brand as one of the few residential brokerage franchisors that is also an operator of properties. How could it ensure that its approach to selling was reliably of a relational (versus transactional) nature? How could its frontline people go beyond working as real estate agents to succeeding as trusted advisors? The benefit of the session to Berkshire Hathaway managers was that it gave them the chance to step back from the constant busywork of running the business and assess whether key activities were aligned with the biggest priorities. In other words: Was it responding to the right questions? CEO Gino Blefari and business development SVP Chris Stuart later wrote to Marc Benioff that the session exceeded their expectations in terms of the strategic clarity they were able to take away from it.

Not incidentally, some of these Ignite sessions are now hosted in very special locales within Salesforce campuses around the world. For example, the sixty-first floor of the Salesforce Tower in San Francisco, which is the tallest building in the city and has amazing 360-degree views, is one of what Benioff calls the

"Ohana" floors—named for the Hawaiian word for family. "The Ohana floors are also a place to give back to others," Benioff says. "Religious groups, nonprofits, NGOs, and schools are able to use those spaces when we're not using them."

Why the Hawaiian motif as an integral part of Salesforce's offices and culture? There's a story behind that, and it is also about the value of questioning. Marc Benioff came up with the idea for Salesforce itself when he was in a setting where the conditions were good for questioning. This was in 1999, when no one was in the business yet of what is now called enterprise cloud software as a service. Back then, every large enterprise had a massive IT organization tasked with purchasing the hardware and software required to run various parts of the business and then installing it on their premises. It was also a time when everyone in tech was marveling at the growth of two consumer-oriented Web-based businesses: Amazon and eBay. Benioff had been working himself to a state of exhaustion as an executive at Oracle and was ready for a break. So he took an extended sabbatical and went to Hawaii, where he spent his days connecting with locals, swimming with dolphins, and giving his mind free rein to go where it would. One day the question struck him: *Why are we still loading and upgrading software and running our own hardware in the way that we have been doing all this time, when we now have the Internet?* Given the connectivity and simplicity it afforded, why shouldn't software be provided like a service instead of a product? That time in Hawaii, and that one query, proved transformative for him, and was the genesis of a business whose fiscal 2018 revenues topped $10 billion.

Since that time, Benioff has been a huge advocate of cycling back into questioning mode before moving on to answers. In fact, he has come up with a set of five big questions that he brings his teams back to whenever a set of decisions has to be made about what Salesforce will sell or how it will operate going forward. They are: *What is it that we really want? What's really important to us? How are we going to get it? What is preventing us from having it? And how will we know that we have it?* This five-question sequence keeps everyone going back to reconsider vision, values, methods, obstacles, and measures—so much that everyone knows it by its acronym, V2MOM. Benioff told me in an interview:

> There's a lot of asking, and then listening, involved in the innovation process. Salesforce was founded on a simple question: Why isn't all enterprise software as easy to buy as a book on Amazon .com? Then we evolved that question. We saw how people were communicating and collaborating on social media and how mobile devices were becoming pervasive and we asked: Why isn't all enterprise software like a Facebook app? A few years ago, we looked at how consumer apps were getting smarter, and we asked: How can we make enterprise software more intelligent? We observe what's happening in the world, and we ask: How can we apply it in new ways?

The Ohana floor, with its wide-open spaces and breathtaking views of land and ocean, is Benioff's attempt at creating a space where this expansive questioning can happen more readily. "If you want people to think differently," Noah Flower from the Salesforce Ignite team explained when I visited an Ohana floor, "you need to put them in a different space." Meanwhile, it is also a highly visible reminder of the origin story of this company that was founded on innovation and must keep innovating. The floor is not reserved for executive use; it is there to be a resource for all. And as people use it, Benioff hopes they will soak up the message: it all started with questions. Keep asking.

Salesforce is an interesting organization for me, and Benioff is an interesting leader, because there seems to be a multilevel attempt going on there to establish the conditions that will give rise to catalytic questions. I will mention one more approach that comes with a good story. It is a chat group on the company's own enterprise collaboration platform, Chatter, called "Airing of Grievances." If that doesn't sound like a name a company would normally apply to an internal social media forum, that's because it was created at the grassroots level. The "grievances" being aired range from complaints about various aspects of life at the company to tricky problems engineers would like to get others' input about. The story goes that when a couple of people in the top management ranks of Salesforce first caught wind of it, they mentioned it to Benioff and suggested some kind of intervention might be called for, possibly to take it down. Benioff's response was to ask them to pull it up on the big screen and give him a look. What he saw there instantly made up his mind: "Are you kidding? I need this." Salesforce's senior VP of corporate messaging, Al Falcione, told me that Benioff even makes a habit of pulling up the Airing of Grievances page when he does product demonstrations for the CEOs of Salesforce customers. That can be a little scary for Falcione, who says he has more than once said, "Marc, you're really going to just put that up on a screen? You don't know what people might be complaining about at the moment. You're going to show that to other CEOs?" But Benioff's attitude, he says, is "This is how I stay in touch with my company now. I can go through this, and I can read what everybody's having problems with." And since it gives him that valuable sense of connectedness, he wants other CEOs to see that they could get it, too, by installing Chatter themselves. (If this sounds like people at Salesforce are airing grievances without being aware that the boss is watching, nothing could be further from the truth. Benioff occasionally throws his own comment into the mix to make that transparent, and to remove any doubt, he posted to his Twitter account—now closing in on a million followers—"My favorite internal Salesforce group is Airing of Grievances!")

Salesforce relies on several forcing functions to keep questions flowing. In most companies, it is a challenge just to get people to engage in the unnatural act of posing more questions, using a few exercises like the Question Burst. Salesforce is using such techniques left and right. But Benioff is on a larger mission to get people questioning as the rule and not just the exception. He is trying to establish conditions across the board by which it comes naturally to his colleagues and himself, and isn't something they must be placed in special circumstances to do.

I would say the same is true for the folks I have met at Pixar, at Amazon, at EY, and at Charles Schwab. Probably none of them are under any illusions about how hard it is to establish widespread conditions in a company that are different from what people experience in other parts of their lives or have known in other workplaces. But these leaders are in a position to have that breadth of influence and know that their organizations' futures depend on innovation, and this is what they are working to do.

TO QUESTIONING AND BEYOND

Pixar, the filmmaking company that brought you such masterpieces as *Finding Nemo*, *Coco*, and *The Incredibles*, is another great questioning environment, under the leadership of Ed Catmull, who has been at the company since its founding and is now president of Pixar and Disney Animation Studios. I have had the chance to spend a fair bit of time in Emeryville, California, talking to

When cruising Pixar's parking lot, it's hard not to wonder what new movie character will appear on this car's spare wheel cover.

Dan Scanlon, director of *Monsters University*, shared a bit of insider wisdom, "In early development, movies are just tiny little candles that you need to shield from the wind because they're not a raging fire yet."

The world's largest Luxo invites all to stop and ask, "Wait, what?" before strolling into The Steve Jobs Building.

As a visitor, it's jaw-dropping to see this case full of Oscars shimmering in the sun. Each one reflects how countless catalytic questions create compelling storylines here.

An end-of-day moment at Pixar's bridge brought Buzz Lightyear's "To infinity and beyond" battle-cry to mind.

Pixar's people and observing some of their processes and practices. My conclusion is that this is a place where the mean quotient of catalytic questions is substantially higher than in other organizations. Catmull has worked very hard and has in turn inspired other leaders to create a culture of candor from the start. Yet, in spite of these broad-based foundation-laying efforts, Catmull is acutely aware of how hard it is to get catalytic questions out on the table. So he and others have been very deliberate about adding specific, structured, purposeful settings where creative questioning flourishes.

The Pixar "Brain Trust" is a perfect example. In the process of making a film, directors voluntarily enter a room where the whole point is to get the raw, unadulterated feedback of their peers. This is a potentially devastating experience, because at Pixar they hold a strong, shared belief that directors should work on projects in which they have, or acquire, a deep emotional stake in the storyline. Historically, this makes for the best films, but it also means that directors display deep vulnerabilities. One producer told me that, after his directors go through a Brain Trust session, "we have a brief debrief for a half hour or so and then I send the director home for the rest of the day. They need it, because it is hard to take. Even though they know it is coming, it is still highly personalized and difficult."

A feedback session that leaves someone needing to go home from work might sound cruel, but it turns out not to be, because of everyone's awareness that Brain Trusts are a special setting where different rules apply. Everyone in the room knows that the questions raised must be in the spirit of making the creative product as good as it can possibly be. A lot of careful design thinking has gone into making the Brain Trust process one that respects and leverages the director's emotional investment in the project.

Beyond the Brain Trust, Pixar has designed other purposeful spaces and places to open up possibilities for creative inquiry, insight, and ultimately impact. One important event that has taken place a couple of times already is "Notes Day." The inspiration is the longtime tradition in filmmaking for people high up in a studio hierarchy to periodically ask for a screening of a film in progress so that they can provide feedback in the form of "notes." Notes Day took that familiar practice and extended it to the task of assessing whether the studio itself, rather than one of its products, could use some serious tweaks or rewrites. Notes Day, it may not surprise you to hear, began with a question. Katherine Sarafian, the producer behind *Brave*, gave me her account of the day Pixar's senior leadership went for a management off-site at Cavallo Point, a conference center in Sausalito, to discuss how the company could do a better job of reining in costs and staying on top of other operational issues. "It was January 19, 2013, that we hatched this idea of 'Why don't we Brain Trust the company?'" she recalls. "'What if we shut down for a whole day? Get everyone in the company thinking? What if—ah, wait, let's do it!'"[3]

The idea was first proposed in the room that day by Guido Quaroni, Pixar's head of software R & D, but it soon became Sarafian's task to turn it into reality—and ever since the March 2013 event took place, she says, she has practically "built a career trying to deliver on the promise of Notes Day." In many ways, when she looks back over what has been accomplished, she feels much more could be done. For all the literally hundreds of positive changes that have been implemented based on employees' thinking, some of the big questions that were on the agenda of that original off-site in 2013 remain unresolved. Still, she is proud to "put a marker on that day. That was a day that we put questions and questioning on the front door of the company," she says. "Where we shut down and we said, 'We only want to know, with all curiosity, how could we work better? How can we operate better? How can we be more efficient?'" Not incidentally, along the way, Sarafian says she herself has become more aware of the power of questions and more likely to use them with the teams she leads. She has, she says, seen "the positive outcomes and results based not on having the answers but on the very Ed Catmull–ish process of peeling the layers and asking questions and inquiry."

That comment speaks to the last factor I will mention about Pixar for the moment: the undeniable influence that leaders have as they model the behaviors that the rest of the organization will interpret as the keys to success. More than any specific practice, like the Brain Trust or Notes Day, it is the constant positive pressure exerted by leaders who truly believe it is important to ask the right questions that manages to build a culture of questioning over time. This is what leads to multiple experiments being tried in the name of boosting creativity and challenging assumptions; only some of these experiments produce results and take hold, but collectively they raise the organization's questioning quotient. What strikes me most about Pixar is that, thirty years after its founding, the point has not arrived when Ed Catmull has determined that his job is done and a perpetual-inquiry machine has been built. Even in an enterprise steeped in the fundamental value of creative thinking and utterly dependent on the originality of its output, Catmull knows that specially carved-out spaces and places are still necessary, and Pixarians must consciously and collectively keep fueling the constructive effort of questioning.

SAFELY UNSAFE SPACES

The reason that questions bubble up in the kinds of settings I've been describing is that, in large and small ways, the prevailing conditions have been altered to do a few key things: to signal that asking questions is a valuable activity worth focusing on; to compel people to linger in a questioning frame of mind longer before diving into their search for answers; and to grant people more distance from their close-in work so they can broaden their perspective on a problem and view it from different angles. In a world that is largely hostile to potentially disruptive thinking and thinkers, these are spaces deliberately constructed to be safe for questioning.

This notion of providing safe spaces is a big topic, and not without controversy. Many people react against the phrase because it is associated with the desire, often seen on college campuses, to be sheltered from challenging views from other parts of the political spectrum. Perhaps even more troubling, the term sometimes refers to requests to be isolated from people of other racial, ethnic, or religious backgrounds. As a *Los Angeles Times* columnist notes, "Students' frequent demand for protection from uncomfortable ideas on campus—such as so-called trigger warnings—is now paralleled by calls to be physically separated too. Groups contend that their well-being depends on living with their own kind."[4] Any such group desire to huddle within a bubble or be exposed to nothing but an echo chamber is 180 degrees away from the kind of safe space I am talking about. What I am advocating are spaces where people can dare to take in disconfirming information and where the questions occurring to them as a result—questions that might well be perceived as contrarian, or annoying, or flaky—can be voiced and heard. These are spaces for exploration beyond safe comfort zones.

Among the masters of creating safe spaces for questioning are group psychotherapists. Sally Barlow, author of *Specialty Competencies in Group Psychology*, is an expert practitioner of the trade who thinks about how to create the conditions in which clients can see their challenges with fresh eyes and find better, more productive paths. Of course, much of this depends on her own well-crafted questions, but the breakthrough often happens when a person who seeks counseling recognizes the question they came in with is not framed productively. She told me about one woman who joined a group hoping to understand "Why don't people like me?" That must be a hard question to give voice to in a group setting, and it's a testament to the space Barlow created that the woman could do so. Moreover, once it was asked out loud, other questions followed from the rest of the group. One was cued by something the woman did in that very session that others found somewhat intrusive and irritating. Had she noticed the cues that her behavior had crossed a line? Barlow says the woman left that session with a different question than the one she arrived with: it was "How can I become more aware of some things I do unconsciously that really put people off?" Framing the problem that way gave her a handle on it, and as result, Barlow says, "she really changed, and started caring about her impact on other people."

If the term "safe space" is less loaded in management circles, it has everything to do with the research Amy Edmondson, author of *The Fearless Organization*, has done on effective team dynamics. In a widely cited research study, she surveyed and tracked the performance of fifty-one work teams within one large manufacturing company and found behavioral patterns in the ones that learned and performed at the highest level. Her findings led her to develop the concept of team psychological safety—"a shared belief held by members of a team that the team is safe for interpersonal risk taking." Edmondson made clear that team psychological safety was "not the same as group cohesiveness, as research has shown that cohesiveness can reduce willingness to disagree and challenge others' views, such as in the phenomenon of groupthink." And neither was safety a simple matter of a team's permissiveness or "unrelentingly positive affect." Rather, the key to feeling safe was having "a sense of confidence that the team will not embarrass, reject, or punish someone for speaking up."[5]

The question of what makes some workers more productive or innovative than others is a perennial one in management research, and often the findings point to interpersonal dynamics. Back in the 1950s, for example, Bell Labs was in its glory days as the R & D arm of AT&T, responsible for many breakthrough innovations. One of the scientists there, C. Chapin Cutler, later recalled a talk by a member of AT&T's patent department, Bill Kefover, in which he told this anecdote:

> The patent people one time made a study to find out what is responsible for innovation? What do people who have been so inventive have that characterizes them? We studied them to find what made them different. We couldn't find anything common in religion, we couldn't find anything unique in schools or education—although they generally came from better schools, they came from all over the place—and, oh, color of hair, background, all these things. The only thing we found that seemed to be common amongst Bell Labs innovators was: most of them had had breakfast or ate lunch sometime with Harry Nyquist.

Cutler always remembered that story because, as someone who had himself lunched with Nyquist, it made sense to him. "Nyquist was full of ideas, full of questions," he said. "He drew people out, got them thinking."[6]

Much more recently, another study of workers in an innovative firm generated a lot of attention. It was Google's "Project Aristotle," a multiyear effort involving the study of hundreds of internal teams to pinpoint just what made the difference between the ones that excelled and the ones that didn't. As reported in the *New York Times Magazine*, the findings were surprising to the researchers because they didn't make the case for either the highest IQs or the hardest workers. The strongest predictor of team success was a high level of psychological safety.[7]

CREATING CONDITIONS FOR YOURSELF AND OTHERS

In the first two chapters of this book, I argued that questions are the keys that unlock insights . . . and, unfortunately, also established that we don't pay enough attention to questions. Indeed, questions are discouraged in us and we discourage them in ourselves. I also suggested that, where questions flourish, it is because someone has created the space for them to do so. This chapter pushed that point further by explaining that the spaces in which questions thrive are spaces where *different conditions prevail*. My final observation here is that individuals can get themselves into such productive circumstances in three ways.

First, they can consciously seek out more settings where questioning conditions prevail. On a personal level, a coaching or therapy session, a sabbatical, or even a camping trip, can be a forcing function—a carved-out safe space for questioning that does not resemble the normal conditions in which one operates. For example, my friend Maureen Chiquet, who was president of Gap and Banana Republic before becoming CEO of the luxury goods company Chanel, tells the story of setting aside her silk-lined tweed jackets for a weekend at a horse ranch, where a horse whisperer introduced her to "equine life coaching." Quite to her surprise, the experience was deeply affecting. It caused her to question her work as a leader in important ways—which led to her engaging other senior leaders in a multiyear leadership journey that included, among other exercises, taking them to visit the same ranch.

Second, you can *create* those conditions in pockets around you—and not only for yourself but perhaps for others as well. This is what I did on that day decades ago when I shifted my class of MBA students into questioning mode, and I have since learned to do better with other groups. Rod Drury, who founded one of the world's fastest-growing software-as-a-service companies, New Zealand–based Xero, creates that kind of space virtually for his colleagues with enterprise social media tools. He doesn't limit himself to reviewing what others post; he also shares his strategic thinking and snippets of market intelligence and encourages anyone in the organization—"even someone who's just joined the business ten minutes ago"—to ask questions, offer perspectives, or call out assumptions that no longer track with reality.

Mike Inserra of EY is a big believer in reverse mentoring, which takes the same idea to a richer, face-to-face level. He says that the habit he has made in recent years to carve out time and space to learn from younger people in his organization has changed his thinking on many levels. In fact, he says, it is "reprogramming my thought process." The reason this is so is that he truly works to understand the perspective the younger person is sharing, even when "some of the concepts they bring forward, candidly, just don't naturally flow to me." Rather than pass over what others might dismiss as immature thinking, Inserra says, "after the conversation, you've got to take it, digest it, and then come back— because I may get it intellectually, I hear them. But not having had their experiences, it will take me more time to process and then really think about the next set of questions or steps forward" implied by it. Inserra referred in our conversation to the habit many managers have of telling their people: "Don't come to me with a problem unless you have a solution." Instead, he says to people, "Anytime you have a problem, bring me your problem, but bring me a *thought process* on a solution." This is important, first, because it develops the person's problem-solving, which is after all "a learned behavior, and you get better at it." Second, when someone brings their problem-solving approach to him, it might also change how he himself thinks about their problem. "At its core," he says, "it goes to creating environments where people can express dissenting points of view and then iterate on those points to try to reach an outcome."

Third, in your daily comings and goings in circumstances you cannot easily change, you can pack along the condition of assuming greater wrongness as a purely personal perspective. This is akin to the idea of mindfulness, a state of active awareness of and attention to what is happening in the moment. If you can, by sheer dint of will, refuse to capitulate to the conditions that are suppressing your imagination and voice, you can make a questioning space for yourself. In places where others are at best tentatively raising a hand in a hunched-shoulder posture, barely daring to ask what is on their minds, you can stand straight and give voice to the query. And you can grant an audience to the tentative, contrarian questions trying to assert themselves around you, and inside your own head. You can focus on changing your own attitudes, activities, and behaviors. More specifically, as an attitude change, you can stop assuming your first instincts and default answers are right and instead assume that you are probably wrong. As an activity change, you can spring yourself from your usual haunts and start venturing into places that challenge you—out of your comfort zone. As a behavior change, you can quiet your impulse to assert a position and spend more time in receiving mode as opposed to transmitting.

These are not just three pieces of advice I thought up; they are what I found people doing who I consider to be especially productive thinkers. You'll meet many of them in the next three chapters as we take each of these changes in turn.

Putting the Question Burst to Work in Life

Recently I did some executive coaching work with the CEO of a global nonprofit organization. We started out with typical work-related issues, but at one point the discussion took a turn toward home. The CEO expressed concerns about his eldest daughter, who was just turning thirteen. For all those years, he had cherished his relationship with his daughter, but as the transition to teenhood became real, he felt her pulling away—and he was worried about losing that close connection. We decided to take a few minutes to do a Question Burst about his concern. Here are the questions that we generated together in four minutes:

1. Am I a good father?
2. Do I listen enough or do I tend to want to solve/act too much?
3. Do I push too hard?
4. Do I hover or "helicopter" too much?
5. What hurts the most? Why?
6. What is she the best at?
7. Do I recognize (and praise) that enough?
8. How is she better than you?
9. What talents complement yours?
10. When was the last time you just watched her for more than thirty minutes?
11. What do her eyes say when she expresses concern?
12. How can you slow down to see what you're missing?
13. What does your schedule say matters most to you?
14. What are her greatest worries?
15. How well do you know who she is?
16. Who would she be if her last name wasn't yours?
17. What is uniquely independent about her?

18. What country would change her life the most?
19. When do her eyes sparkle?
20. What will you do when she gets married? Why?
21. What are her greatest areas of independence from me?
22. What has she learned lately from her own experience?

This executive's review of the questions immediately afterward turned into a deep conversation about the role parents play in the lives of daughters. I recall talking about how some parents can do too much handholding as their children grow—and even with adult children—and rob those young people of their own journeys. By the end of our conversation he had arrived at an approach he felt good about: "I had been focused on how not to lose her, but I now realize the real question is how to support her growing and flourishing on her own. I need to let her find her." His insight, painfully brought to the surface, brought tears to my eyes then, and does now as well.

4

Who Revels in Being Wrong?

If you're not prepared to be wrong,
you'll never come up with anything original.
—SIR KEN ROBINSON

Lior Div, cofounder and CEO of Cybereason, spends a lot of time assuming there's something he is missing—even something he is fundamentally wrong about. It's what makes him good at what he does, which is coming up with effective countermeasures against cybercriminals. Cybercrime is an underworld full of "unknown unknowns," with its legions of shadowy hackers relentlessly devising new ways of breaching allegedly secure systems. If there's any problem realm crying out for fresh thinking, this would be it.

The numbers are all going in the wrong direction. According to those who study the phenomenon, just in the twelve-month span from fall 2016 to fall 2017 there was a 2,200 percent rise in phishing—sending people deceptive messages that infect their devices with malware if they click a link. Almost two-thirds of those malicious URLs were set up to install ransomware, which renders all files on a computer inaccessible unless its owner pays a named price. Another 24 percent were Trojans designed to steal online banking credentials. One expert analysis predicts total annual cybercrime costs of $6 trillion for the next few years. Since that will make cybercrime more profitable for its perpetrators than the global trade in all major illegal drugs combined, Steve Morgan of Cybersecurity Ventures says we're in for "the greatest transfer of economic wealth in history" and "one of the biggest challenges that humanity will face in the next two decades."[1]

Div's innovative breakthrough came when he recognized that most of his profession was fixating on a flawed question. Everyone, he says, was working on the problem of how to keep the bad guys out. But notice the assumption embedded in that question: that the bad guys are outside. "The thing is," Div tells me, "they're *already in*. In most organizations, when we are deploying a solution, we find an adversary active in the environment." Recognizing that raises a really good question: What do you do if you assume they're already in? That reframing opens up a world of different solutions, because here's what you do: you monitor what they're doing, you find earmarks of different actors, and you piece together their intent. This takes you beyond treating cybercrime as an IT problem and past the hopelessly reactive strategy of building higher walls and slapping on more patches. "The problem we're dealing with," Div says, "is not fundamentally a bits-and-bytes problem; it's *people*. There is an adversary behind the scene with an agenda." Focus on the reality that there are people out to get you, and your solutions become much more oriented to the fact that "they are very, very, very creative and they will keep trying different ways."

The solution Cybereason created as a result of this line of thinking uses machine learning and artificial intelligence to respond to threats in real time, all the while gathering intelligence and connecting the dots about the attackers and how they work. It is acclaimed as a breakthrough innovation. But if you think about it, its approach only made sense—once Div asked the right question.

I'll say more later about Lior Div's habit of assuming that he might be wrong and the history behind it. The point for the moment is that he has acquired the habit, and it keeps him looking at problems from different angles. This is why a different question could penetrate his thoughts in the first place, and it's also why he stopped to engage with it. And it's a habit he loves to see in others. His model colleagues are "challengers"—since they challenge the status quo—who "wake up in the morning asking questions, because they understand that the world is bigger than what they can see." They accomplish great things because they always suspect there is some other, better way to get something done, or another thing they can do, and they "put a question mark on everything we are doing, all the time."

WRONGNESS AS A CONDITION

Nothing shuts down questioning activity more than the determination to be—and be seen to be—unquestionably *right*. When we are sure we are right, or convinced that a decision must be made without delay, we leap to ready answers and shut down further inquiry. We resist opening up the discovery process and pressure others to close it down.

By contrast, when we know we are wrong about something, we stay in a questioning mode because we must. If something we are trying is unequivocally not working, we can't kid ourselves that we are right about it, so the questions keep flowing.

Here's the implication: if in more areas of life and work we can slow down our rush to rightness and instead cast about longer in wrongness, we are far more likely to stumble over catalytic questions we and others have not yet thought to ask—leading to answers that are unprecedented in their rightness. The rest of this chapter will bring more examples of people who have consciously developed habits that have worked for them and could work for others. Several common themes emerge in what they are doing. First, they try to make themselves more conscious in general of their probable wrongness. Second, they cause themselves to be more receptive to disconfirming evidence and other challenging information they have avoided noticing or taking seriously. Third, they spend more time with people who deliver different views and data and who actively confront them with the truth they are missing.

Questions don't arise whenever we are wrong. It's only on those rarer occasions when we *think* we're wrong. And for most of us it's only when we are practically hit in the face with how wrong we have been that questions start to get our attention. Sometimes new information makes it obvious. This tends to be the way with scientific discovery. Take for example, the 423-million-year-old armored fish fossil that turned up in China in 2016, greatly surprising evolutionary biologists. Because the implication of the fossil is that the jaws of all modern land vertebrates and bony fish originated in a bizarre group of animals called placoderms, *Science News* reports that "the new find . . . is helping rewrite the story of early vertebrate evolution." Paleontologist John Maisey of the American Museum of Natural History put it more bluntly to the reporter: "We've suddenly realized we had it all wrong."[2]

Most of us do not work in enterprises where exposures of ignorance are met with such delight or where the evidence that should overturn some prior assumption is so cut-and-dried. In our work and daily lives we don't always get the signal that we should be admitting we're wrong. And if we do, all kinds of pressures, on top of our personal egos, keep us from acting on it.

This key takeaway, for example, comes from a study of organizational learning by Anita Tucker and Amy Edmondson. They investigated how it was that many basic flaws and failures persist in a mission-driven organization full of highly educated workers. Organizational learning refers to the process by which enterprises overall get better at achieving objectives because the people within them notice what's not working, try new ways to do better, and keep tweaking standard procedures accordingly. But in the hospital setting Tucker and Edmondson studied, frontline workers weren't calling out the flaws in processes, and in the absence of that feedback, performance wasn't rising over time. Why not?

The researchers found their answer in a powerful set of prevailing notions about how "ideal employees" behave—which unfortunately celebrated conduct that actually undermined organizational learning. Worse, they realized that these ideal-employee norms were not some odd quirk of the hospital they were studying; they are common to most enterprises. "For example," they write, "most managers would identify an ideal employee as one who can handle with ease any problem that comes along, without bothering managers or others." But if the problem is a recurring one, because of a flawed process design, that quiet competence only guarantees it will come up again. From an organizational learning perspective, then, "the ideal employee is instead a noisy complainer, who speaks up to managers and others about the situation, thereby running the risk of being seen as someone who lacks self-sufficiency."[3]

"Noisy complainer" doesn't sound like something you would want to put in boldface type on your résumé or like anything ever listed in a job description's relevant qualifications. But Tucker and Edmondson want you to go further than that. Instead of going along to get along, covering for colleagues' mistakes, they say ideal employees are *nosy troublemakers*, quick to call out lapses. To the point of this chapter, they are *self-aware error makers* who don't strive to present an image of flawless performance but openly acknowledge their slip-ups. And, at the core, they are *disruptive questioners* who won't leave well enough alone. They are "constantly questioning, rather than accepting and remaining committed to, current practices."

I mention the study because it puts such a strong emphasis on the cultures that groups create—cultures in which, paradoxically, it's often so important for people not to be wrong that they won't engage in the behaviors that would lead them to be more right. It underscores that the best way to encourage more of the behavior you want is to create the conditions in which that behavior will arise naturally. This is absolutely true of the questioning required for process improvements in a workplace—and, I would add, for any kind of positive transformation at work or in life.

If you want to find a new angle on a problem and ultimately find a breakthrough solution, you must rid yourself of the impulse always to display deep competence. For the right questions to surface, you must spend more time feeling mistaken.

STALE MENTAL MODELS

One of the more thoughtful people I have talked with about embracing wrongness is Jeff Wilke, a top executive at Amazon. At some point during his college years he became interested in how creative thinkers manage to update their mental models—or, as some prefer to call them, heuristics. Essentially, we carry around sets of assumptions in our heads about how things work, allowing us to operate on autopilot in many respects so we can allocate our rational attention to things that really do require new thinking. The thing is, mental models themselves have shelf lives, so we need to find mechanisms for revising and updating them.

Wilke believes in two main ways to challenge and reset our mental models. One way is through "crucible" experiences. Here he is recalling work by leadership scholars Warren Bennis and Bob Thomas, who studied how people are transformed by intense episodes of adversity that push them into periods of self-reflection. In crucible moments, people are forced to question assumptions they have made and get more clarity about what they value. This crystallizing effect gives them better judgment going forward. The other way—less traumatic and less dependent on outside events—is through the deliberate practice of raising questions to challenge our models. Wilke sums it up: "If you never ask questions and you never experience anything new and you never enter any crucibles, your model becomes stale. You don't really build any new awareness of the world. But if you seek out things that you don't know, and you have the courage to be wrong, to be ignorant—to have to ask more questions and maybe be embarrassed socially—then you build a more complete model, which serves you better in the course of your life."

By focusing on mental models, Wilke goes straight to the deepest level of potential wrongness, the level that is hardest and most valuable for us to question in ourselves. It's hardest for a few reasons: it requires not just learning but unlearning; it's the kind of questioning that we get the least practice doing; and it exposes a layer of knowledge most people give no thought to at all.

All of these reasons are called out in research by Michelene Chi, whose focus as a scholar is on conceptual change, or mental model

Our grandson checking in with dad for Day 1 work.[4]

Hunter Freyer's mind-warping question in the hallway: "If you stripped away all the rules of car racing and had a contest which was simply to get a human being around a track 200 times as fast as possible, what strategy would win? Let's say the racer has to survive."[5]

Gazing down with Nana on the Spheres, a creative rainforest space for sparking bigger questions.

Checking out from Day 1 work with dad.

transformation. She notes a big difference in learners' responses to new information depending on what kind of learning they are doing. Most learning involves just *adding new knowledge* where none existed before, or *filling in gaps* where some did. No one balks at these kinds of learning, because they only enrich one's knowledge. But sometimes new information serves to correct "prior misconceived knowledge," so the effect is not enriching but "concept changing."[6] In other words, you were wrong, and you need to be set straight. This is much harder to enjoy, even at a trivial level; none of us likes getting dinged by a fact-check. But when the wrongness being exposed is at a more fundamental level of understanding—what Chi calls a "category mistake"—it hurts all the more.

Chi further notes that category mistakes—flawed mental models—are hard to acknowledge because most of the time this layer of our thinking serves us so well. Having to readjust the assumptions we've learned to make is, as she puts it, "a low frequency occurrence in everyday life . . . because, in our everyday environment, our initial categorizations are mostly correct . . ." No one gets much practice in second-guessing commitments already made to their mental models. But even though it's rare in everyday life to have a fundamentally flawed mental model, Chi says wrongness at this level is the "fundamental source of robust misconceptions" in fields like science, where people miss the importance of anomalies by staying stuck on flawed models. Most people, meanwhile, are not even aware of the fact that underlying assumptions do so much of the heavy lifting in their minute-by-minute decision-making. Like oxygen in the atmosphere, mental models provide their essential service whether we think about them or not.

The bottom line here is that flawed mental models do not naturally present themselves to people. If you want others—or if you want yourself—to confront the possibility of wrongness, the only hope is explicit instruction. Chi sums up: "The lack of awareness of the need to shift categories laterally is due to the low frequency of such shifts in the real world," and therefore instruction aimed at promoting such shifts "must begin by making students aware that they have committed category mistakes" whenever such mistakes occur.[7]

Back to Lior Div, since now we can appreciate how hard it is to do what he—like Jeff Wilke, Mike Inserra, and some others I have met—does in his daily life. He is a smart guy, and intellectually curious, like a lot of people. But he routinely takes it beyond gathering data within his broadly established understanding of some realm. Rather than just filling in his mental models, he throws challenges at the models themselves. He and his colleagues, he says, "come to every environment not trying to say that we know in advance what we will see there. . . . We know that there is a blind spot out there and we need to kind of sense and find out where."

When I asked how he developed this habit, I was surprised by how definitively he could pinpoint its genesis. It was when he reached the third grade and suddenly realized he could not read. It turns out Div was dyslexic, but no one had noticed this because of his strong memorization powers. So this was a double realization: "What I discovered was not just that I can't read; it was that everybody else thinks that I *can* read." And, to make that a triple, he also saw that, up to that moment, he himself had thought he could read. "Nobody tells you as a child what 'reading' is," he explains. "I would ask somebody to read something, and then I would look at the ceiling and start 'reading' it." It was only when the assignments reached a certain level of difficulty that he had to confront the possibility that there was something about this reading thing that was escaping him. Once he had that aha moment, he attacked the problem and closed his substantial reading deficit within a year.

That shock-to-the-intellect experience left him with an enduring conviction. He routinely suspects now that there is probably some big principle important to his progress that he isn't grasping, just as there was then. His unconventional road to reading also taught him that just because there is a usual path to reach an objective, it doesn't have to be the only path. "Just the realization that another path exists and that the boundaries of a problem are bigger than you thought," he says, "enables you to think different—and not to be afraid of being different." Looking back, Div says he feels very lucky to have been dyslexic, because "in the world that I was living in . . . nobody encouraged you to ask questions. There was a system and you needed to work according to it." He thinks he would not have formed the habit of questioning his basic assumptions about problems if he hadn't had this early, dramatic need to do so. And, having formed that habit, he is determined not to break it.

TRY BEING WRONG MORE

The people I know who excel at questioning are equally deliberate at creating conditions for themselves in which they feel less certain. It might sound like an odd goal, but it isn't that hard to pursue. One way is simply engaging in activities and being in places where you find it hard to get your bearings; this will give you practice in being unashamedly ignorant. It will start to normalize the activity of constantly gathering and processing information to assess your situation. Take a class in pottery or needlework and be shocked by your fumbling fingers (or, in my case, a dancing class to highlight clumsy feet). Land—or better yet, live—in a foreign city and work your way through the subway. Go to a festival and confront art that mystifies you.

Creative people know they need to prod themselves in such ways to retain their creative curiosity. I asked Stewart Brand, founder of *The Whole Earth Catalog* and subsequently the WELL, the Global Business Network, and the Long Now Foundation, how he managed to keep his spark alive. He responded immediately with a favorite quote from a novel by Jim Harrison: "Every day I wonder how many things I am dead wrong about." Brand says he tries to live by that, greeting each day with a hope to debunk some misconception. A couple of years ago, I shared this with Hasso Plattner, cofounder of SAP, and he almost shouted out, "That's exactly how I wake up in the morning!"

People who set out to discover where they're wrong make special efforts to surround themselves with people who will tell them so. As Pixar and Disney Animation Studios president Ed Catmull advises, "Seek out people who are willing to level with you, and when you find them, hold them close." This is easier said than done, of course. Rationally you might agree you need people around you with the brains and guts to tell you your thinking is flawed. But when it happens, you pretty much hate them. As the popular economics author Tim Harford writes, "The irony is that disconfirmatory feedback is the most useful kind of feedback imaginable. If I'm making serious mistakes while cruising along in a complacent bubble of self-satisfaction, I badly need someone to explain exactly what I'm doing wrong. But what I need and what I might enjoy are, of course, quite different."[8]

Catmull has been very thoughtful about how to overcome this natural resistance. He is always pushing himself to move further into the territory of what he doesn't know he doesn't know, always listening for the weak signals he might be missing. His real impact as a leader, however, has been his success in engendering the same habits across Pixar's organization. More than most corporations, Pixar is in the business of creativity. Its market demands creative entertainment, and across the twenty feature films it has released as of this writing, it has consistently delivered. Catmull is convinced that the key to sustaining that performance is candor. It's one of his favorite words, something he brings up again and again—as in "Lack of candor leads to dysfunctional environments" and "Candor could not be more crucial to our creative process." He is under no illusions about all the dynamics that get in the way of it.

I've already mentioned the "Brain Trust" that Pixar assembles to help people see what they are getting wrong. In these intense sessions, debates are encouraged and feedback demanded. Catmull expects everyone to give "brutal" feedback to the director of a film in progress. Why? Here's his own answer: "Because early on, all of our movies suck. That's a blunt assessment, I know, but I choose that phrasing because saying it in a softer way fails to convey how bad the first versions really are. I'm not trying to be modest or self-effacing. Pixar films are not good at first, and our job is to make them so—to go, as I say, 'from suck to not-suck.'" What we are seeing here is a habit of declaring at the outset of a creative process, "We are probably getting this all wrong." Maybe it's true and maybe it's not for any particular project, but Catmull knows his people have to assume it is true if they are to be receptive to constructive criticism.

I have heard from many people that the Brain Trust experience is tough yet cherished as essential to great filmmaking. When Pixar became part of the same corporate structure as Walt Disney Animation, and Pixar's leadership team gained responsibility for leading the Disney studio as well, the Brain Trust practice was the first thing they decided to port over to the new environment. President Jim Morris explained to me why this kind of collaborative feedback session, which would seem to have obvious value (especially in light of Pixar's success), is actually very rare. The usual dynamic among directors of films is that they are intensely competitive, vying for scarce resources and hoping to see their projects moved to the best possible slots in a release schedule. In most settings, filmmakers stand to benefit if other projects flounder, because that allows their efforts to take more prominence and their projects to advance. Pixar, by contrast, is "much more like an old-fashioned studio of the '30s or '40s, where everybody is an employee essentially" and they care about the performance of the whole enterprise. "There's an interesting social contract that goes with it," Morris says, because "everybody in that room is going to be in the hot seat in that room at some point and going to need the help of those other directors when it's their film." Therefore, "nobody ever goes in and tries to shoot down the project. They only go in to try to say, 'Here's what I don't think is working and here is a possible way to fix it.' That is deeply refreshing, because you almost could not do it in Hollywood."

At Disney Animation, the essentially equivalent practice is called the "story trust." I spoke with Byron Howard and Jared Bush there, the directors who brought us *Zootopia*, and was amazed to hear how thoroughly its story had been transformed over the several years the film spent in development. Both were quite honest about how painful the process can be. In all of these movies, Bush said, "as a filmmaker, you're putting yourself out there. It's not just a product. These stories are incredibly emotional. . . . So when you say, 'Here's a deep piece of my psychology,' and then you have

Jared Bush (left) and Byron Howard were as animated as their movies when talking about the crucial role of questions in their work. I left them inspired to acquire a far more fun-loving style of inquiry.

Walt Disney once said, "It's kind of fun to do the impossible"—which captures how Disney and Pixar Animation continue their cutting-edge work.

people say, 'Here's why that sucks,' it's hard not to feel that like a personal attack." Those few hours of feedback make for a very uncomfortable experience. "At the end of it, though, you know you are going to learn something," Bush says. "Someone's going to say something that I never even thought of . . . so, weirdly, you dread it, but you also look forward to it." He says that his own approach is to try to anticipate what will be said, because he is acutely aware of some parts of the execution that are weaker than others. "Usually when I go into these meetings, I think, 'Here's the five things I think people are going to say about this movie.' Then it's the *sixth* one, that you had no idea about, that turns out to be even more important or a bigger concept or more fundamental."

From the outside, it's easy to imagine Pixar and Disney Animation as a place full of play, with constantly happy people collaborating to create content that makes them, and everyone else in the world, laugh. But these are people working hard to be creative, and who are successful enough that they could be forgiven for believing they have the right instincts. It's at least as hard for them as for anyone to have someone question the path they are going down.

Another effective way to develop a more prevailing suspicion that you might be wrong—and not just at the top layer of facts but at the deeper layer of assumptions and mental models—is to educate yourself about cognitive biases. This has been a major theme in the current culture of ideas, with bestsellers like *Thinking, Fast and Slow* (by Daniel Kahneman) and *Nudge: Improving Decisions About Health, Wealth, and Happiness* (by Richard H. Thaler and Cass R. Sunstein) helping large swaths of the public gain a greater awareness of cognitive quirks and limitations. A big one, for example, is confirmation bias. This is the very human habit of seeing what we want to see. Having formed a hypothesis that something is true about the world, we are more apt to note and file away evidence that helps to confirm that while passing over the evidence around us that would suggest otherwise. This isn't a deliberate refusal to acknowledge the challenging data; missing it is an unconscious phenomenon. That's just one form of cognitive bias; some attempts to list all the others run to over a hundred entries.

Spend enough time with this literature and you realize what folly it can be to go with your instincts. One entrepreneur I interviewed, Rod Drury, who founded the New Zealand–based software company Xero, has a funny way of describing how this affects his decision making. "I love the George Costanza theory of management," he told me, referring to a famous episode of the *Seinfeld* comedy show: "If every instinct you have is wrong, doing the exact opposite must be right." Drury uses prods like this to push for more creative thinking—which he knows is especially crucial for a start-up trying to compete head-to-head with bigger and more established businesses. It not only leads to novel solutions; it means "We do the exact opposite of what an incumbent would expect us to do."

Part of the value of waking up to the general failings of the human mind is that it also causes you to become more reflective about your own tendencies as a thinker. Whether or not the old left-brain/right-brain theory is valid, the past decade in neuroscience has revealed how idiosyncratic humans' mental processes are. The term "neurotypical" has become nearly meaningless. Once you recognize that people have a great range of different tendencies in how they process information and translate learning to action, you realize that dynamics deeper than you know may be blocking your perception of the truth.

CHECK YOUR CERTITUDE

Despite the popularity of books about our limiting cognitive habits, and despite the fact that we live in an era where it is easy to access information that could reveal so much of our wrongness to us, some observers of modern society worry that people are actually becoming *less* willing to entertain doubts about their rightness. They note that our increasingly digitally intermediated lives also grant us a greater ability to surround ourselves with inputs that only reinforce our going-in assumptions and exclude ones that challenge us.[9]

Chuck Klosterman, for example, makes this point. Klosterman himself is an iconoclast, and the essays that make up his bestselling books suggest no hesitation about offering strong points of view. In his latest book he declares: "My perception of reality is so inflexibly personal that it has almost no correlation to what's happening in the world outside of my own skull."[10] But I really like the way he started his last book. The first sentence reads: "I've spent most of my life being wrong."[11] He soon makes it clear that he doesn't think he's alone in this. The whole story of civilization's progress, he notes, is the repeated discovery that some belief, assumption, or conventional wisdom that guided people in the past was deeply, deeply wrong. Yet we go through life without doubting that these days we have it right. One might think that, as time goes on and the historical record grows, people would be increasingly willing to admit the likelihood that something they believe wholeheartedly will turn out to be hogwash. To the contrary, Klosterman's book, *But What If We're Wrong?*, points to a "modern culture of certitude." He worries about "our escalating progression toward . . . ideology that assures people they're right about what they believe." Fighting that culture of certitude is essential because it "hijacks conversation and aborts ideas. It engenders a delusion of simplicity that benefits people with inflexible minds."

Roger Martin makes a related point. Martin is former dean of the University of Toronto's Rotman School of Management and founder of the Martin Prosperity Institute, and earlier in his career was a strategy consultant to Fortune 500 companies. He has seen the rise of digital networks change business decision-making and economic policymaking. Commenting on the widespread perception that people have become more polarized in their views, he offers a different twist on the problem. "I think any thoughtful analysis of differences of opinions would suggest that the positions staked out today are not more sharply contrasting or farther apart than 25, 50 or 75 years ago," he says. "However, it is arguable that views are held with more certitude. And the more certain one is of one's view, the more difficult it is to find superior solutions when confronting views that are only a small distance away." So it isn't that people form more extreme opinions in the age of social media; it's that they lose the ability to question those views and improve upon them. "If you are certain that you are looking in the eyes of 'the truth,'" he notes, "you won't even attempt to find a better solution, and you will be trapped into either/or decisions."

This is especially important to Martin because it relates to his high regard for "integrative thinkers." In his book *The Opposable Mind*, he writes that the most innovative thinkers have "the capacity to hold two diametrically opposing ideas in their heads." Somehow, he explains, "without panicking or simply settling for one alternative or the other, they're able to produce a synthesis that is superior to either opposing idea." It's easy to see how synthesis gets short-circuited by too much certitude on one side or the other.

Now that I have brought Roger Martin into the narrative, it's a good moment to share a great story he tells about a breakthrough he himself experienced because he was willing to admit he'd been wrong. This happened in the early years of his consulting career, when he was a smart engagement manager providing data, analysis, and advice to some of the world's best-known brands. He was confident in his project teams' solid work and proud of the beautifully packaged and intellectually bulletproof recommendations he handed over as deliverables. The problem was that, time after time, he would notice—months later—that the original issue or indecision persisted. The client's management team wasn't acting on the advice.

At some point, rather than dismissing yet another client as hopelessly unable to change, Martin thought to question his own assumptions about what a good consultant does. Perhaps there was something he was doing wrong? That chink in the armor of his certitude let entirely new questions find a voice inside his head. He had been approaching every engagement with what seemed like the obvious one: *What is the answer to the client's problem?* Now he wondered if a better question might be: *How can I help the client's management arrive at the answer?* His whole approach began to shift with the reconception of his role as a facilitator of problem-solving rather than a bearer of better solutions. Building on that insight, he crafted new questions to use in that process—questions that could open up space for teams' creative thinking and help them test ideas in collegial, productive ways. His favorite (and now one of mine) became "What would have to be true for the option under consideration to work out fantastically?" Martin credits this question alone with creating a dramatic change in the success of clients, because it allowed ideas to be refined in group discussions without their originators feeling directly challenged.[12]

The side benefit of achieving this kind of epiphany is that a person can learn to love that scales-falling-from-the-eyes moment. They can enjoy it so much that they start to probe other areas where they suspect they could be wrong or missing something big. This brings us to another habit that many creative questioners have acquired. When wrongness gets revealed, perhaps because something they tried did not work out, they do not rush to sweep it under the rug and distance themselves from it. Instead, they hold it up to the light to get a good look at it. This is the "embrace failure" school of thought, and there is no need to explain it here; it is already well-plowed territory in the innovation literature. But I do want to emphasize that creative people don't just use phrases like that; they live by them. For example, Sara Blakely, the founder of Spanx, reports that she frequently brings up her own failures in conversations with her team because she wants to create a climate in which people will fearlessly test their new ideas. She even devoted a chunk of her time on the stage at a companywide meeting to describing mistakes she had made. It was an upbeat talk—every mistake got a snippet of music, such as Britney Spears's "Oops! . . . I Did It Again," as its soundtrack—but the message got through. Lior Div tells me he is so serious about raising the comfort level with failure that he is measuring each of Cybereason's departments on it. How many new things did they try, and how many of those didn't pan out? "If they are not failing enough, they're not good," he says, because they must be playing it too safe.

One of the many things that makes it hard to spend more time being wrong is that you run the risk of looking dumb. By the same token, a good sign that someone will entertain the possibility of their wrongness is that they ask very basic questions—sometimes even embarrassingly dumb-sounding ones. Adrian Wooldridge, a veteran journalist for the *Economist*, told me about a time in his life when he was a young reporter and resolved to learn from the best. He got to know Bob Woodward, half of the legendary team that exposed the 1972 Watergate break-in, and started paying attention to how he worked. Woodward, he quickly noticed, asked questions of his sources that sounded as if he didn't have the first clue about the matter he was investigating. Wooldridge was a little mortified on Woodward's behalf, but soon realized he shouldn't be. Because the reporter hadn't signaled any established line of inquiry, his interviewees often told him things that were genuinely surprising.

I thought of Wooldridge's comment while I talked with Jeff Karp, the scientist whose lab focuses on biomimicry. He told me: "A lot of the questions that I ask in lab meetings are fairly simple questions, or questions where I'm trying to understand what's been done and what the data really means." He does this because he really does need to understand, but he also appreciates that these group presentations are an opportunity to "show the people in the lab that often I don't know and I'm trying to figure things out." He suspects that a lot of the people around the table, whether they get the current presentation or not, have their moments of struggling to figure things out, "but they're not necessarily saying it." By showing some vulnerability, he is trying to create an environment where everyone agrees: "We should be striving to understand and not just sitting back and not asking questions."

GETTING SYSTEMATIC ABOUT IT

If you really want to hear about someone fully aware of the power of wrongness, then let me tell you my Schwab story. Walt Bettinger, CEO of Charles Schwab, is one of the most deliberate CEOs I have met when it comes to entertaining doubt and inviting fresh questions. His adamant belief is that "the difference between successful executives and unsuccessful ones is not the quality of their decision-making. Each one probably makes 60 percent or 55 percent good decisions, or something like that. The difference is the successful executive is faster to recognize which were the 40 or 45 percent that were wrong and adjust, whereas the failing executive often digs in and tries to convince people, even when they're wrong, that they were right." Think about that for a moment. If it were truly your conviction that the winners in any group of executives were the ones fastest to discover where they were wrong, it would give you real incentive to try to find that out. In my interactions with Bettinger, I learned at least five ways he does this systematically and with real discipline.

He requires "brutally honest reports" from the people who work directly for him. This is not just a glib phrase; it's a real thing: an institutionalized, twice-a-month set of observations under five headings (one of which is "What's Broken?"). Everyone knows they need to get their "BHRs" done, and everyone knows that, if someone loses their job working for Walt, it's probably because a problem exploded that had been brewing but never flagged in a BHR. Not surprisingly, the practice of requiring BHRs has cascaded down through the ranks.

He checks in with different vantage points. There are various constituencies with different perspectives on problems—employees, owners, analysts, clients—and Bettinger is disciplined about hearing voices from each camp regularly. For example, he makes frequent visits to work sites away from headquarters and consciously works to improve his approachability.

He explains to people why he depends on them to educate him. Knowing that many people will hesitate to give him "the honest information, questions, challenges" he wants, he lets them in on his dilemma. "I actually say to people: 'The number one challenge I deal with every day is isolation,' and then I walk through the forms it takes and I'll personally ask them to help me in this regard."

He finds ways for people to tactfully say, "You don't get it." Beyond employees, even Schwab's independent owners and the analysts who follow the company may not be inclined to volunteer to the CEO what he is missing or wrong about. To pry observations out of them, Bettinger frames the inquiry as an act of imagination. He consistently asks: "If you were in my shoes, what would you be doing differently than what you see us doing today?"

He visibly encourages the issue raisers in the ranks. Hoping to deepen the search for "where we are wrong" as a cultural norm, he constantly invites employees to reach out to him by email or phone with issues they notice. "I probably get twenty-five emails a day from random employees," he says, "because of this investment made over the years." Three or four times a year, he flies a batch of them to San Francisco to spend a day at headquarters—"not as reward system but as an encouragement system for those people."

Anyone wanting to set—or reset—the conditions in which they find themselves should take note of the conscious, deliberate way in which Bettinger is trying to "formalize the accountability to minimize isolation." His tactics might or might not be "best practice" for others, but certainly any of us can start with the questions that gave rise to them: Whose different perspective do I need? How do I keep surprising information flowing to me? How can I get people to tell me I'm wrong? What am I failing to ask about? And how do I encourage imaginative probing of our assumptions in every corner of the organization? Bettinger sums it up by saying, "I guess I've always felt that fear of 'what you don't know you don't know,'" he says. "And to informally hope that you will figure out ways to get that information, I think, has always been dangerous." His words remind me of something Jeff Bezos, founder of Amazon, told me years ago: "When you're in a box, you've got to invent a way out of that box."

THE ORIGINS OF QUESTIONS

Lawrence Krauss is a physicist at Arizona State University and the inaugural director of its Origins Project, which got its name because it studies the origins of the universe, although it also engages with other "fundamental questions that are at the heart of the twenty-first century's greatest challenges" relating to life, disease, and complex social systems. Not long after the discovery of the Higgs boson in 2013, he predicted that there would also be other new things at the Large Hadron Collider that would help a field that had been "like people locked in a room with sensory deprivation for forty years."

Krauss noted that, under such conditions, we are usually reduced to hallucinating, and that "most of the hallucinations we've had, namely theoretical physics, will be wrong." But Krauss didn't seem to be in too much of a hurry for the field to declare what was right. When he was asked what direction the next era of discoveries would take, he said he didn't know: "I mean, I have speculations. I have ideas and so do other theorists. But I always hope I'm wrong. I've often said the two greatest states to be in if you're a scientist is either wrong or confused, and I'm often both."

The line got a laugh from his audience, but Krauss followed up with his point in all seriousness. "Mysteries are what drive us as human beings," he said. Not knowing is more exciting than knowing, because it means there is much more to learn. To be in that great state of feeling wrong and confused is to be more open to new possibilities and more apt to challenge old understandings. "We are fortunate enough, for whatever reason, to have an intellect and . . . to have evolved a consciousness that allows us to ask those questions," Krauss said, "and to stop asking them is just a tragedy."[3]

5

Why Would Anyone
Seek Discomfort?

What makes us human, I think, is an ability to ask questions,
a consequence of our sophisticated spoken language.
—JANE GOODALL

Climate change is a polarizing issue that can divide people into
warring camps. Some want a momentous reaction to a tipping-
point situation before it's too late to save the earth. Others want
measured responses, if any, to a situation that they believe may
not even be within humans' power to reverse. The fact that these
positions align with views on other social issues transforms a
mainly scientific topic into a wholly politicized one. Us-versus-
them emotions run so high that it's hard to imagine arriving at
any mutually agreeable decision. Yet the dividing lines can be deceptive, as a group of climate activists found recently when they
ventured into the enemy territory of West Virginia coal-mining
country.

This was a set of highly educated and well-heeled urbanites involved in different companies and nonprofits who had recently decided to join forces on an initiative. But making this trip together

wasn't entirely their plan. It was Lindsay Levin's bright idea to take them on what she calls a "leaders' quest"—a trip that combines fact-finding, perspective-taking, deep dialogue, and reflection by a group collaborating on a significant challenge. Levin's aim in designing one of these experiences is always to take participants out of their comfort zones. In this case, "uncomfortable" was an understatement. The group must have known going in that they would come face-to-face with people who were serious climate-change skeptics. But, in the end, what really made them squirm was discovering their foes were just as human as they were.

As Levin told me the story, one day of the trip involved a tour of a working coal mine. It was dirty, it was claustrophobic, it was disorienting for a group accustomed to pristine, knowledge-worker-filled offices. Afterward the group gathered in a "shack-y kind of building outside the mine" for a more personal conversation with the foreman and a few of the miners. As Levin began asking questions, the miners first talked about their faith. The foreman brought up the topic of evolution, joking that "maybe you all think your grandmothers came swinging through the trees, but my people date back to the Bible." They talked with affection about the natural world around them and the region's wildlife—but made clear how little they thought of the US government's Environmental Protection Agency. And of course they celebrated the prospects for their industry's revival, given recent political victories. "So we had this conversation that jarred on so many levels," Levin recalls, "and the group with me—I knew this would happen—was at a loss for words."

Then the conversation took an entirely unexpected turn. "Tell us about your family," Levin prompted the foreman. And in quiet response he shared: "Well, my wife and I have adopted five children who've lost their parents to opioid overdoses . . ." He mentioned how they continued to face the lingering problems of the children's prior neglect and abuse—the reality, for example, of their littlest one, who could not stop shaking. Sitting in that room, Levin says, she could physically feel the gut-wrenching shock wave as the group realized it had to reassess the man. "Because this is not the enemy," she explained. "Right? This man, who it would be much more convenient to think of as an uneducated problem, is doing something to make a difference—and everybody in this room is thinking, 'I couldn't do that.'" This was the moment Levin had hoped the trip would deliver, because "it removed certainty. . . . It just kind of blew the whole thing up." New questions poured into people's minds: "What is goodness? Who is a good man, a good woman? What is community? What is the worth of a child today, and a child tomorrow?" In the weeks and months that followed, Levin says, the group continued its work with a different understanding of the problem it was targeting—as she puts it, with a much greater appreciation of its complexity and a much deeper commitment to coming up with solutions that work for West Virginia and beyond.

Marilee Adams, who has thought more about the power of questions than most people, quotes in her bestselling book *Change Your Questions, Change Your Life* an observation by the cultural anthropologist Joseph Campbell. He said that "where you stumble, there your treasure lies." Campbell's *Hero's Journey* explains how from time immemorial people have told stories in which this happens. A turning point occurs when the hero, having reluctantly accepted a call to venture outside a comfortable routine, hits a big obstacle and must move to a new level of understanding and resolve. It's a good way to describe what happened to Levin's group in West Virginia, and to the other creative problem-solvers we will meet in pages to come.

I've already expressed the view that, if you want to increase the chances of coming up with a better question—reframing a problem you care about and putting yourself on the path to a better solution—you should spend more time in conditions where questions thrive. The previous chapter explored one of these conditions, a state of doubt about your rightness. This chapter will take us into the realm of the uncomfortable.

BEWARE THE BUBBLE

Is there anything more fundamental to human psychology than comfort seeking? Most of what we celebrate as societal progress involves the removal of discomfort-causing problems. Individually, we avoid situations in which we feel stressed—and with good reason: Stress is a killer. But in the modern world many of us have the luxury of insulating ourselves so thoroughly from stressors that we put ourselves at risk of adverse effects in the other direction. Untroubled by challenging experiences or information, we stop growing and learning. Our questioning capacity atrophies.

We often hear that privileged people now live in a bubble—with the implication that they must find ways to escape it. But it isn't only trust fund kids who cordon themselves off from too much of the outside world. Many deep forces are at work forming a bubble around all of us, in one form or another. It's hard to invite more uncomfortableness, whether physical, intellectual, or emotional, into our lives when we're busy and have the option not to.

The most acute form of isolation I have studied is found in the ranks of CEOs and other heads of large organizations, since they can rely on staff to gather and sift information.[1] These leaders are not more prone to comfort seeking than everyone else, I think, but they are under enormous stress and can work their way into feeling more entitled. Certainly they are surrounded by "gate-keepers" who see it as their job to protect the boss from sources of discomfort. Nandan Nilekani, the founder and former CEO of Infosys, told me the danger of this: "If you're a leader, you can put yourself in a cocoon—a good-news cocoon. Everyone says, 'It's all right, there's no problem.' And the next day everything's wrong." Or we can be thoroughly insulated by others, as Simon Mulcahy, Salesforce chief marketing officer, notes: "Many CEOs have this staff that basically creates a 'ring of steel' around them. They're all complicit in doing their very best to support the CEO, but they create an absolute cocoon, a vacuum of feedback. Then the CEO only gets presented what the direct reports tell him or her, and it leads to an incredibly stilted decision-making based on very nuanced feedback. Effectively, all of a CEO's decision-making powers get completely killed."

Thankfully, something remains within us that rebels against too much comfort—sometimes to extreme levels. For some reason, in Boston every January 1 (since 1909), hundreds of people go for a dip in a frigid Boston Harbor. At Zero Gravity, people pay thousands, or every once in a while get a "free pass" like Stephen Hawking did, to ride in the reduced-gravity aircraft that astronauts in training call the "vomit comet." Climbers keep summiting Mount Everest by the hundreds every year because it is there. They get more than bragging rights out of such experiences, since the other side of the uncomfortable coin is exhilaration. As people do these things, they often use the expression "It makes me feel more alive."

The same holds true for venturing into territory that is cognitively or psychologically uncomfortable, where science backs up that "more alive" feeling. Look at the brain scans of a novice engaged in an activity versus an expert, and you see neuronal fireworks going off for the new learner.[2] No wonder moving out of your element transforms you into a more active seeker of input: you become highly receptive, ears perked up, trying to pick up the scent. As you try to get your bearings in an unfamiliar setting, or to get on top of an unfamiliar situation, your instincts compel you to soak up all kinds of information via all five senses, and your mind fills with a flood of questions.

On a visit to the corporate headquarters of Twitter, I heard a perfect sketch of this process. I was meeting with Michael Sippey, who was Twitter's head of product at the time. (He has since launched his own start-up, Talkshow Industries, and is now VP of product at Medium.) As we sat in his beautifully appointed office looking out over his roof deck on a sunny San Francisco day, he talked about the importance of visiting customers in person: "It takes work, and it's hard. I mean, look at this space: no one wants to leave this and go out." A deliberate effort must be made, he said: "There are things you have to do to put yourself in that position [where] you can touch and feel what the customer is experiencing, and what their life is actually like."

Sippey spent the first five years of his career at a software start-up called Advent that came up with solutions for finance and investment professionals. He tells the story of how he and some colleagues first spotted a valuable opportunity. Across a series of visits with potential clients to get feedback about Advent's original product, he says, "we started to notice this pattern." In practically every one of these small investment firms, "there would be this one guy, with this big monitor, with Post-it notes stuck all over it." Finally, curiosity overcame them and they approached one: "Dude, lots of Post-its." What they learned by talking to him was that these guys were the traders responsible for processing buy and sell transactions ordered by portfolio managers. This one told them, "I've tried to do it a bunch of different ways with custom spreadsheets, but they all break. . . . So I make a trade, stick it on the monitor, make a trade, stick it on the monitor."

Sippey and his colleagues were incredulous. "You've got to be kidding me" was their reaction. And that, he says, "became our second product—a trade order management system." It's an experience that has guided Sippey's thinking about product innovation ever since. "How do you put yourself in the situation where you can ask the right questions?"

Too many leaders get their information catered—picked, prepared, and plated for them in the way they've already indicated they'll find palatable. To fight back, they need to get out into the field, gathering raw stuff on their own. Lior Div puts it this way: "I need to go to places that I'm not feeling comfortable. I need to try to push and find out where are the boundaries, so I'll know that 'oh, there's a blind spot there.'" Even when getting out doesn't deliver a brilliant new question, the outing can produce a valuable regrounding in an organization's founding purpose. When I spoke with Joe Madiath, who created the water-focused social enterprise Gram Vikas in India, he emphasized the motivational effects of going back to the communities he set out to serve. He told me that when he has spent too much time at headquarters, he begins to feel weighed down by bureaucratic concerns. His source of renewed strength is to get up and go back into the kinds of rural villages Gram Vikas helps with water and sewage solutions. For most executives, traveling a long, rutted, and dusty road to a place underserved by plumbing—and to stick out like a sore thumb there—doesn't sound like a lucky escape. But it's exactly the kind of trip that renews Madiath's sense of what he's on earth to do.

BENEFITS OF GETTING OUT OF YOUR COMFORT ZONE

Famously, discomfort spurs a lot of innovation. Problem-solvers habitually focus on pain points. Elon Musk, for example, was stuck in an epic LA traffic jam when he thought of the hyperloop—his vision of a huge pneumatic tube capable of carrying people at supersonic speed, reducing the time from Los Angeles to San Francisco to thirty minutes. "I was an hour late for a talk," he says. "And I was thinking, man, there has got to be some better way to get around." It's a classic necessity-as-the-mother-of-invention story.

But there are also more diffuse, indirect payoffs of finding yourself in an uncomfortable spot. When uneasiness puts your senses on high alert, that often puts you in a more mindful, attentive, and questioning mode. And at least three great things can happen in that state: you can be surprised, you can be distracted, and you can be wrong-footed.

THE ELEMENT OF SURPRISE

First, you can encounter the stimulating surprise of bumping into new things and new perspectives. You see and experience things you have never known or thought about. Novelty is all around you. This is why the executive team at the fashion company Kate Spade put a number of practices in place to keep their people from being bored—or boring. Mary Beech Renner, who is chief marketing officer there, tells me the "brand promise" Kate Spade makes to its customer matters: "We will inspire her to lead a more interesting life." For Renner and her colleagues, it follows that they had better lead interesting lives themselves. So they put together "team outings to gardens, art museums, baking classes—anything to create inspiration, to make sure that we ourselves are leading the interesting life that we promise." They convene regular "lunch-and-learn" gatherings with intriguing guests. Whereas some companies shift to half-day Fridays during the summer, Kate Spade observes them all year round, so people can soak up more of what their vibrant Manhattan neighborhood has to offer.

Meanwhile, Victor Hwang, Silicon Valley venture capitalist and now VP of entrepreneurship at the Ewing Marion Kauffman Foundation, advises entrepreneurs that they should "head into the weird places" to stretch their brains. Putting a slightly finer point on that, he outlines three ways to seek out the unusual:

> *Watch and listen to weird stuff. I enjoy watching obscure documentaries and listening to unusual podcasts. It's thrilling to find cool ideas lurking just a few clicks away.*
>
> *Walk in weird places. I take walks in hidden suburban neighborhoods, department stores, community colleges. When you're walking with no purpose but walking, you see things in fresh ways, because you have the luxury of being in the present.*
>
> *Talk to weird people. Striking up conversations with people who are different from you can be powerful. I still remember random conversations with strangers from decades ago, and how they shaped me.*[3]

For my money, Guy Laliberté has them all beat. Laliberté is the cofounder of Cirque du Soleil, whose spellbinding shows bring together aerialists, acrobats, stagecraft, and storytelling in wildly inventive spectacles. Laliberté travels constantly in pursuit of exotic and captivating inspirations—and has created the expectation that others at Cirque de Soleil will, too. To encourage reports from far and wide, the company's "Trend Group" now edits a regular feature in its internal newsletter called "Open Eyes." It is filled

A Bali beach beguiled my wife and me as ghost crabs kicked sand out to form perfect patterns around a wayward lightbulb.

every week with staff's "By the way . . ." observations about the places they visit in the course of their work and life, performing duties like scouting for new cast members. A submission might focus on an intriguing trend in architecture, fashion, music, or language—usually not directly relevant to the production in progress but, in a richly cultural enterprise like a circus, hard to call irrelevant, either.

By all metrics Cirque du Soleil is an exceptionally successful enterprise. Its show called "O," for example, has played to sellout crowds in Las Vegas for so many years running that by some estimates it is the single-highest-revenue show in the world. When I asked how R & D is done in such a place, the answer from CEO Daniel Lamarre was quick: "First and foremost, by Guy traveling around the world, and most of us traveling around the world, with great curiosity. . . . We're on the lookout all the time to see what's going on."

Back home in Montreal, Laliberté fights C-suite comfort in other ways. Lamarre told me about a surprising piece of news he got from Laliberté one day: "Daniel, I'm afraid we're getting a little bit too corporate and so I've hired you a new employee." Shortly after, a fully costumed and in-character clown reported to work at Cirque du Soleil's headquarters in Montreal. "Madame Zazou" spends a fair bit of her time staging entertainments and dispensing popcorn and, at a minimum, serves as a constant reminder to a professional headquarters staff that the whole point of their work is to stage circuses. More pointedly, she has full license to play the classic role of the court jester—for example, by "coming into our [executive committee] meeting and doing the introduction, and making fun of us." I've mainly described the act of moving outside one's comfort zone in terms of literally getting outside the office, but hiring Madame Zazou emphasizes that leaders can also invite disruption in.

Like Cirque du Soleil, Pixar believes in getting people out into the world and experiencing more than their computer screens. Pixar's product development process forces people out of their offices and out of the Pixar building—for example, to learn archery firsthand before getting too far in the animation of *Brave*. They go on "adventures" to experience new circumstances and ideas. For Pixar's 2017 hit *Coco*, in-depth immersion in Mexican villages and cities helped people grasp crucial elements of Mexican culture they would otherwise have missed. The filmmakers made trips to the southern Mexican state of Oaxaca to be able to create the town they call Santa Cecilia in the film, as well as to other places, like Santa Fe de la Laguna, a tiny town in the state of Michoacán where locals proudly preserve their heritage, including by wearing traditional Purépechan attire and crafting a particular style of pottery. Think of Pixar's approach as a form of creative anthropology, but it isn't only for classic "creatives." Many of the innovative thinkers I have met across the years count on being "out there" more than "in here" to surface their best questions and insights.

Rod Drury told me about a time when an intense effort to get out and interact with customers paid off directly in innovation. Part of his strategy to launch Xero as a seriously competitive threat to long-standing industry leader Intuit was to make sure he and his founding team spent serious time shadowing owners and managers of small businesses—the people for whom they design solutions. He says they visited with more than two hundred such managers while they developed their first-generation products, meeting them at their offices just as they arrived in the morning, booted up their computers, and poured their first cups of coffee. During this period of constant travel, Drury says he had an epiphany: "It was never about accounting software." He and his colleagues noticed that small-business owners were all in the habit of checking their bank statements online every morning to make sure there was enough cash to make it through the day. That simple observation, combined with insights gained from customer conversations about features they would use or ignore in a specific targeted solution, eventually led them to the bigger question in customers' minds: *Why can't we bring together all the data a small business gathers and needs into one aggregated environment?* That question, Drury said, struck him as "a once-in-a-lifetime opportunity," since they could "start connecting that data on behalf of our customers to do some amazing, magical things."

To Hwang's "weird people" point, the surprise that comes from leaving your comfort zone can come in the form of not just places but people with very different perspectives and cognitive styles. Bob Sutton makes this case convincingly in his book *Weird Ideas That Work*. Plenty of research shows that higher levels of creativity and innovation result from such interactions. Jeff Karp explained in an interview why he thinks this is the case. "There's tension when you have people from different backgrounds working together, because there can be some communication issues," he said. "But that struggle, I think, is a really great place to be, because it puts your brain in this kind of high-energy state. It keeps you very active and you're not *comfortable*."

For many people it's challenging to work with others who don't resemble them on multiple dimensions. Karp's point is that from that discomfort, catalytic questions arise and creative insights are born.

THE POWERS OF DISTRACTION

Second, breaking your routine causes you to stop doing whatever focused work you were doing. You become distracted—but often in a productive way. Your focus gets diverted from the problem you were hammering away at in whatever way you had framed it. Stepping away from intense concentration on a task puts your mind in a different processing mode, one more receptive to questions that have been lingering at the edge of your consciousness yet eluding you. You're not "working" in a traditional sense, and therefore not actively trying to go down the same problem-solving path you've been on. A new possibility for attacking the problem can creep into your thoughts.

Cognitive psychologists use the term "extra cognition" to describe what is going on here, and the classic example of it is the brilliant idea one gets in the shower. One creative thinker, the mathematician Henri Poincaré, was particularly apt to credit it with his greatest questions and insights. It was in a fitful half sleep, for example, that Poincaré came up with his first important discovery in the late 1870s. In his own words: "For fifteen days I struggled to prove that no functions analogous to those I have since called Fuchsian functions could exist. . . . Every day I sat down at my work-table where I spent an hour or two; I tried a great number of combinations but arrived at no result. One evening, contrary to my custom, I took black coffee; I could not go to sleep; ideas swarmed up in clouds; I sensed them clashing until, to put it so, a pair would hook together to form a stable combination." He reports that by morning he had solved the puzzle and "had only to write up the results, which took me a few hours." He continues:

> I then left Caen, where I was living at the time, to participate in a geological trip organized by the School of Mines. The exigencies of travel made me forget my mathematical labours; reaching Coutances we took a bus for some excursion or other. The instant I put my foot on the step the idea came to me, apparently with nothing in my previous thoughts having prepared me for it, that the transformations I had used to define Fuchsian functions were identical to those of non-Euclidean geometry. . . . I felt an instant and complete certainty. On returning to Caen, I verified the result at my leisure to satisfy my conscience.

The pattern continued, with Poincaré continuing to recognize how his best ideas seemed to surface in states of distraction. At one point, for example, he took up another class of problems and, disgusted at his lack of success, spent a few days at the seaside, where his thoughts turned to other things. "One day, while walking along the cliffs," he recalled, "the idea came to me, again with the same characteristics of brevity, suddenness, and immediate certainty, that the transformations of indefinite ternary forms were identical with those of non-Euclidean geometry." [4]

Recent research by Jackson G. Lu, Modupe Akinola, and Malia Mason adds some data to Poincaré's insightful self-awareness. In an experimental setting in which participants were asked to perform creative tasks, better results came with "task switching" because the break in concentration on the task at hand led to both more divergent and more convergent thinking. Interpreting their data, the researchers concluded that "temporarily setting a task aside reduces cognitive fixation." [5]

Like Poincaré, Ed Catmull grasps how crucial distractions create time and space for the mind to surface questions and insights that otherwise can't happen. He explained:

> When you don't know what the solution is, you actuate the initiative trying to address it. You move into a problem space full of unknown unknowns. Oh, I find it exciting. Fact is, something's churning, and I feel it inside, it's like churning, and very few people will not have conscious access to it. Sometimes something's going on and I can't interact with what's going on inside my head. My brain's working on it, and I'm not conscious of what it is other than the fact that it's going on.
>
> Decades ago I became very aware of this in graduate school. I was working on some problem with a new way of doing math for surfaces. (And it turned out to have been, over the long run, some of the most important work that I ever did [from] a technical point of view, although I didn't know it at the time.) But I remember working on this problem, and there was something happening in my head and I felt it. Like this deep visceral thing, this churning, it was like this grinder. And I didn't know what it was other than the

fact that my brain was working on the problem. I couldn't help it by going to the whiteboard, I couldn't do anything like that on a piece of paper. I'm just sitting there in this highly anxious state, and all of a sudden, boom, up it pops. And then I would write it down. It was like, "Whoa, that's a weird thing."

THE BENEFIT OF CONFLICT

The third benefit of getting outside your comfort zone is that it gives you the chance to experience unanticipated conflict. It forces you to come to terms with the fact that the way you have been seeing things is not the only way to see them. Creativity begins, write Jacob W. Getzels and Mihaly Csikszentmihalyi, when someone "experiences a conflict in perception, emotion, or thought," and that causes the person to articulate the conflict by formulating it as a problem. Robin Chase—who grew up in the Middle East and went to college in Swaziland before moving to the United States—comes to mind for me. In 2000 she founded Zipcar after she saw a version of car-sharing in Europe and recognized how Americans' unquestioning belief that everyone should own a car had created tremendous waste and misallocation of funds throughout society.

That is the most positive kind of conflict, because it involves being hit by an opportunity. More commonly, businesses have conflict thrust upon them as a new competitor poses a mortal threat or the inadequacy of the old way becomes downright painful.[6] This is what motivated a strategic change at SAP, Bill McDermott told me, when cloud-based solutions burst on the enterprise software scene. McDermott and his team became aware that the future of the business would live "in the cloud," but saw that the organization's DNA didn't equip it with the right instincts for selling on-demand software. Knowing that "we wouldn't be asking the right questions" to capitalize on a whole new realm of opportunities, he said, caused SAP to acquire SuccessFactors and Ariba.

Sometimes the conflict feels personal, and sometimes it is. In the last chapter I featured Jeff Wilke of Amazon, who thinks a lot about the mental models we carry around and how we go about refining them. He said this is done in two ways. One is by actively questioning what is really going on—in other words, operating on the assumption of wrongness and seeking out what you might be missing. The other is to experience some kind of crucible event that forces you to reckon with an unprecedented (at least in your experience) situation. That is a particularly acute form of uncomfortable, but one that leads to equally powerful insights.

Short of this, many of us feel discomfiture when we suddenly see an assumption we have been making or something we have been missing, and we feel awkward or guilty about it. This happened for Lindsay Levin's group in West Virginia. After the meeting with the miners, she says, a couple of her group recalled having been at a UN meeting where the closures of some large coal mines had been announced and the crowd erupted in boisterous applause. "I feel ashamed about that now," one of them said, thinking of the "whole load of people who lost their jobs." It wasn't that they no longer thought a shift away from coal was necessary, but more that "the mirror just came up," Levin said. For years they had castigated opponents for acting with no regard for the consequences of their choices. Now they saw how "profoundly disconnected" they were from the consequences of their own choices and actions. Levin noted that "what happens in those moments, in my experience, is that people then of course have a lot of processing to do."

Nick Beighton, CEO of the fast-growing online fashion retailer ASOS, told me about an encounter he had with an employee soon after his promotion to the top job that he found "quite uncomfortable." As part of a listening tour, he had scheduled a session with one of the company's merchandising teams, a group numbering about thirty. "You can ask me whatever you want," he invited them, "and I will answer it." When one young woman put her hand up, she questioned him about talent development. "Nick," she said, "you're not a product guy. How are you going to improve me as a buyer?" Beighton recalls how the question felt like a broadside. It was true, he was not a product guy. He was trained as an accountant and had been finance director of an entertainment company before being brought into ASOS as CFO. *Whoa!* he thought. This woman is "actually challenging my authority to be a chief exec of a fashion brand." That was an overreaction, he quickly realized, but the moment of discomfort focused him on what he came to see as "a great question." To my mind, Beighton's response to the buyer's question was also great: "Okay, let's talk about that. Don't expect me to know how to design a better dress, but do expect me to get the barriers out of the way to help you get to that product."

The truth that frontline workers don't often bring a sense of conflict to CEOs' lives is a simple one—so simple that a successful reality television series has been built around it. The entire premise of *Undercover Boss*, produced by Studio Lambert for UK and US audiences, is that when CEOs spend a few weeks walking in the shoes of their lower-ranked employees, they gain a whole new perspective on what should change. They lift the veil hiding a lot of what they don't know and sometimes don't want to know.

That was, for example, Rick Tigner's experience in doing the show. CEO of the California winery Kendall-Jackson, he donned a disguise to join laborers in the Sonoma County vineyard, and promptly started making mistakes. He managed to shut down a bottling line because he couldn't keep pace and had to hold his tongue as a delivery driver said some things that shocked him.

He appreciated for the first time the problems that arise when coworkers and supervisors don't speak the same language. He also grasped that for many employees who didn't speak English as a first language, the language barrier was the only thing keeping them out of managerial roles they were otherwise capable of performing. What he saw convinced him and vineyard manager Laura Porter that a program that might have sounded before like an expensive perk for the workforce—free, on-site English classes—was a needed investment in the business. Hundreds of employees subsequently signed up. (Kendall-Jackson also reimburses tuition for junior college and online classes for those who prefer that route.) In one of the show's scenes the CEO sees how his company's policy not to offer health benefits to all workers affects a model employee who is a mother of three. Reflecting later on the "rare perspective" he gained across two weeks of filming, Tigner explained, "I knew it would be a unique chance to learn, where I could see and hear things that I normally wouldn't, but I didn't expect the experience to deliver such an emotional impact as well."

What happened here was that a CEO who would normally have been excluded from the learning that comes in a spectacularly different setting was instead able to be fully present. Under normal circumstances he would have likely isolated himself, either by limiting his questions to matters he already saw as issues or by not going into the field at all. Just as surely he would have been isolated by others in their eagerness to shield him from information that might displease him or to focus his attention on issues they deemed most important. The good news is that there are many productive ways at work and in life to achieve greater presence that stop short of putting on fake beards and going incognito.

PRACTICES TO DO THIS WITH SOME DISCIPLINE

It's one thing to understand logically how uncomfortable conditions can yield benefits and another to actually seek them out or
create them. Let me offer a few suggestions to do both.

Live somewhere else far away. My research with Mason Carpenter and Gerard Sanders revealed that the more countries a person
has lived in, the more likely he or she is to leverage that experience to deliver innovative products, processes, or businesses. We
also found that companies led by CEOs who had tried out even one
international assignment on the way to the top office delivered
stronger financial results than companies whose CEOs lacked
such experience—roughly 7 percent higher market performance
on average.[7]

Related research with Jeff Dyer and Clayton Christensen found
that innovative leaders at all levels of an organization—in business, government, and social enterprises—were twice as likely to
come up with a valuable new idea if they had lived in more than
one country. The evidence is compelling and consistent on this
point (and also resonates with what my own family felt as we spent
over a decade living away, in England, Finland, France, and the
UAE). Immersing oneself fully in another culture is quite uncomfortable at times, but the result is seeing the world through
changed eyes—which can make all the difference when trying to
figure out a creative solution to a vexing problem.[8]

Take the scenic route. Fadi Ghandour is the founder of Jordan-
based Aramex, a global provider of comprehensive logistics and
transportation solutions. In the early years of the business, he
had an experience that changed his thinking—and it didn't happen purely randomly. Ghandour arrived in an Aramex hub city,
Dubai, at 2:00 AM for meetings slated to start just a few hours later.

He chose to skip the luxury car service from the airport and instead asked for one of the company's package couriers to pick him up in a delivery truck. For the duration of the drive to his hotel, he asked probing questions of the courier and listened closely to the man's answers. When the hot Arabian sun came up that morning, he called an all-person meeting of local management and made sure some couriers could be there, too. While the executives listened, he posed the same kinds of questions—and allowed everyone in the room to hear about operational issues that they hadn't known about.

Importantly, Ghandour set the tone of the gathering as one of mutual discovery. No one felt called on the carpet to explain why these problems had been overlooked and left for the boss to expose; instead, people were energized by the new opportunities to apply their collective problem-solving skills. Just as importantly, Ghandour underscored that this approach should become an ongoing way for executives—including him—to discover unknown unknowns before it's too late. He made it policy that executives periodically get out of their ergonomic office chairs and do trips with couriers. More recently, as his wealth has grown and he has become known as one of the most successful venture capitalists in the Middle East (in his role as executive chairman of the Wamda Group, a venture capital fund for technology-enabled companies in the Arab world), he sticks to the same routines. Every day he spends time talking with at least two of the entrepreneurs in his ninety-five-company portfolio—usually outside his office—learning about and helping to interpret what they are seeing in their markets.

Perhaps what Ghandour advocates doesn't sound so unbearable. It isn't. At the same time, if you are a CEO, ask yourself when you last made a decision resembling the one Ghandour made at the airport. In the midst of an exhausting month of travel, knowing you would touch down on the tarmac to find a slew of fresh messages and calls wanting responses, wouldn't you have had a town car waiting? As Ghandour told me, "If CEOs don't want to do it, they won't be pushed to do it." On any given day there is an excellent excuse to do otherwise. But still, he insists, "I would tell them: Just try it once. Go around asking questions, giving comfort. Just don't have too many people around you."

Closer to home, spouses and partners can take the same kind of approach to grasp the challenges each other faces. For example, when my children were young and my wife chose to be a stay-at-home mom, it was easy for me to have grand ideas about how the children could be better off. But it wasn't until I became a stay-at-home dad during a three-month sabbatical so my wife could finish up a teaching internship that I realized my bright ideas about child-rearing weren't exactly as bright as I thought they were.

Shake Your Entourage. Marc Benioff is my favorite example of this tactic, because the first face-to-face conversation I had with him happened when both of us were walking alone at the World Economic Forum Davos meeting and I recognized him. I have since learned that this is his habit wherever he goes, since the point of traveling all that way from San Francisco or Hawaii is to bump into people one could not or would not know to schedule. Later, when I mentioned this to a long-term Davos veteran, she told me she had noticed a pattern over the years. The leaders who move about surrounded by retinues are least likely to ask and be asked anything interesting—which she was convinced made them less able to change the world for the better. If you want your thinking to be challenged in productive new ways, you have to start talking to different people, ideally in different places. Someone once told me, "Talk to folks with voices spectacularly different from yours"—and those are the words I have used ever since to remind myself to do it.

Face Your Critics. At Cirque du Soleil, during the final stages of rehearsal of every new show, they stage a performance and call it the "Lion's Den." People involved in prior productions—for example, renowned shows like "Mystère," "O," and "Zumanity," all on the Las Vegas strip—are invited to watch a run-through and offer their feedback. This is as knowledgeable and tough a crowd as you could find. The *LA Times* talked to the director of the new $165 million budget Vegas show "Kà" just before it opened, and just before he was going to be thrown to the lions. "It's a very, very cruel thing," he told the reporter. But the reporter observed that he sounded, "despite his words, less fearful than eager."[9]

The "Lion's Den" is a dramatic example, but facing your critics is an everyday experience at Cirque du Soleil, according to CEO Daniel Lamarre. He told me it's a culture of constant internal debate because Guy Laliberté is "good at provoking us, all the time":

> *In a normal corporate world, we go into a meeting and you present your idea. I'm nice with you because I want you to be nice with me when I present my idea at the next meeting. Not at Cirque. At Cirque, we will debate to make sure that the best idea will prevail. It doesn't matter if it comes from me, or you, or Guy; that's not the point. The point is, let's debate the idea. I'm always surprised that we come from one direction and then, all of a sudden, it's something else that will come up. But the reality is you have to probably try ten or twenty different ideas, to get one good one to really go through the entire process.*

Head for the Cheap Seats. If you ever get the chance to talk with Michael Hawley, the founder of the popular EG conference, take it, because in my experience he draws on a great variety of experience to take a unique angle in any conversation. He once told me that, when the EG conference is under way, he likes to recede way back to the farthest wall of the room—to the "cheap seats." Most people, of course, prefer to sit closest to the action, where they hear every word, occasionally meet the presenter's eye, and feel especially drawn in. Hawley's thought is that, by going to the periphery, he is more likely to get out of his own inner circle. He'll be among the greater skeptics on the fringes. Note that the cheap seats are not just the farthest ones from the main stage of a building: they are also the closest ones to the world outside.

Years ago I had a conversation with an executive at the Swedish furniture company Ikea, and he told me how founder Ingvar Kamprad, even in his seventies, organized and attended conferences for teens as one way to stay close to the next generation. Though he grew to be one of the world's richest people, he never invested in a private jet, preferring to fly not just commercial but economy. Back on land, he favored public transportation. There is a famous saying in consumer goods: "Cater to the classes, dine with the masses; cater to the masses, dine with the classes." Kamprad was determined to defy that rule. He said in a *Forbes* interview in 2000: "I see my task as serving the majority of people. The question is, how do you find out what they want, how best to serve them? My answer is to stay close to ordinary people, because at heart I am one of them."[10] This is someone who was determined never to let the bubble form around him.

Don't overdo it. "Discomfort," of course, is a relative term. If your hope is to arrive at new questions—beyond "How did I get myself into this?"—things can't be so hard to endure that your mind shuts down to survival mode. For the most part, this was the lesson I took away from my trip to Everest Base Camp and the Khumbu Icefall, and in the following week of recuperation at home. Far from having questions arise that inspired new insights, I couldn't think clearly beyond my next breath. More useful to my everyday questioning capacity are my frequent travels, which shift me into a different mode where I am certainly not assured, but also not in danger.

Audit your comfort level. Whenever your goal is to change your behavior, whether it's to get out into unfamiliar environs more often or build any other new habit, a useful early step is to figure out your current baselines of related activity: What percent of your workday is spent outside of your office? Your building? Your organization? Your industry? Your city? Your country? Your continent? Your home? Your neighborhood? While you're at it: When was the last time someone asked a question that made you think twice, or even feel uncomfortable? When was the last time you asked one of someone else? Without turning it into an onerous task, figure out a few good, easily measured indicators—proxy measures for how you will venture more out of your accustomed routines. As in other areas of life, occasionally taking stock and seeing your numbers improve may even motivate you to do more.

THE DREADED COMFY CHAIR

Gary Erickson, the entrepreneur behind the Clif Bar energy snack and other organic food and drink products, is a great example of someone who believes in asking questions. "At Clif Bar," he writes in his memoir of founding the company, "I try to model the value of knowing nothing—of asking questions, avoiding absolutes, being humble, and seeking the wisdom of others—as a leadership and business style." He goes on to tell the story of a recent hire he made of a man whose prior managerial experience was with a big corporation. When the man asked for any advice on the transition, Erickson told him: "Ask questions more than give answers. Even when you think you have the answer, turn it into a question. You will find that there are ways we do things here that won't make sense to you, and you will want to change it. Figure it out first."

Where did he develop this high regard for questions? By hitting the road, traveling on the cheap around the globe. He pushed himself out of his comfort zones, and now he understands how it changed him. "My trip around the world humbled me," he writes. "I grew up believing that there were right and wrong ways of doing things, that much of life is black and white. My month in Israel and three months in India and Nepal deeply changed my understanding of the world and life. It was difficult for me to hold on to absolutes. Given the wide variety of peoples, cultures, religions, and beliefs that I encountered, I couldn't help but realize how little I knew. The trip freed me from feeling that I needed to have answers. It taught me to ask questions."

The message of this chapter has been the value of putting yourself, and possibly those around you, in the condition of getting outside your comfort zone so that you don't stay stuck in your comfortable ways of thinking about problems. But who really wants to spend time in a state of discomfort? Well, perhaps someone who cares about exercising their capacity to question. As Ahmet Bozer, former president of Coca-Cola International, put it, "Questioning muscles atrophy just like physical ones. Exercise, hard exercise, is the only option to keep the questions alive." Like acknowledging wrongness, experiencing discomfort signals to the brain that it must search for a solution. The discomfort might be small and chronic, or it might be acute and extreme. Either way, our minds are spurred to keep seeking something better and turning over the central questions of its source and resolution.

Like me, Erickson is a collector of other people's wise observations on questioning. He quotes a piece of advice, for example, from Wendell Berry: "Ask the questions that have no answers." His long experience as a globetrotter on a budget gave him a wealth of experiences and memories, but Erickson makes it clear that what he values most is how it piqued his curiosity. Coming home, he writes, "I knew that I could say, with Pico Iyer, '[The] point of travel for me is to journey into complication, even contradiction, to confront the questions that I never have to think about at home and am not sure can ever be easily answered.'"[11]

6

Will You Be Quiet?

A wise old owl sat in an oak.
The more he saw, the less he spoke.
The less he spoke, the more he heard.
Why can't we all be like that wise bird?
—TRADITIONAL NURSERY RHYME

I first got to know Sam Abell when I signed up for a one-on-one mentorship through the Santa Fe Photographic Workshops. I am a serious amateur photographer and knew I had struck a deep vein of creative gold with this arrangement. With thirty-three years' experience as a photographer for *National Geographic*—earning not one but two images in the magazine's "50 Greatest Photographs of *National Geographic*" exhibit—Abell is a master of his craft. But it quickly became clear that his ongoing mentoring would deliver benefits beyond photography.

Abell is unusually aware of how he does what he does. He frequently comments, "I'm a 'from-the-back-layer' photographer." What he means is that, when he composes a shot, he thinks about the layers from background to foreground and how they relate to one another. And while an amateur would likely seize on the obvious foreground subject—sometimes not even noticing what is behind it—he starts with the most distant part of the setting and builds forward from there.

Abell has figured out that the way to get a great photograph is not to take it but to make it. For him, framing his first photographs as a boy, this meant fighting his instinct to follow a moving subject with his lens. Instead he learned to follow his dad's advice: "Compose and wait, Sammy. Compose . . . and wait." Establish how you want those more static, background layers to appear, and—if you've chosen your spot well—the dynamic element you need to complete the image will eventually enter the frame. A woman will stride across the plaza. A bison will amble over the grassland. A sailor will toss a rope. The key, Abell learned, is not to chase its unfurling arc: "Let the rope come to you."

Perhaps this is more of a photography lesson than you expected from a book about questions. I share it to make a more general point. As I talk to many, many creative thinkers about their work, I have consistently asked: "Are there things that you personally do to create a context, or are there background elements in the environments you work in that cause you to find and ask more insightful questions? What are the things in your experience that help or hinder you in finding and formulating the right questions— questions that can unlock new answers you haven't considered before?" Over and over I hear that they don't try to force insight. Instead, they seek out or create settings in which questions more naturally arise, and in which they will be more likely to hear and engage with them. They compose and wait.

We've already explored, in the last two chapters, the first two conditions I've heard about: people putting themselves in states of feeling more wrong and more uncomfortable. The third condition is especially relevant to Abell's patient work. It's being more quiet.

Sam Abell

TRANSMISSION TROUBLE

Again, quiet is not the normal mode for a lot of us. As teachers, leaders, or parents, many of us operate in broadcast mode, seeing it as our role to proclaim phrases of inspiration, explanation, and unambiguous direction. The renowned CEO of Procter & Gamble A. G. Lafley has always liked to say his job is to keep repeating for his managers what the company's strategy is and to "keep it *Sesame Street* simple." That loud-and-clear transmission setting is a default for many, and for sound reasons. But as Lafley also well knows, it will never open a door for you and bring you face-to-face with what you don't know you don't know. It won't help you form your next strategy.

Meanwhile, being very vocal about your own point of view on a situation can prevent your detecting when others are not on board with today's plan. Linda Cureton is an experienced manager; she was chief information officer at NASA before leaving the agency and starting her own technology consultancy. She advises anyone running a meeting to table their "own excitement and criticisms until everyone has had a chance to formulate and express their ideas." But when she decided to write a blog post on that dynamic, the perfect example she found of this dead-wrong behavior was in her family. It was during a late summer vacation with family and friends in Jamaica, on a day when her brother—"the self-appointed leader" of the group—fell in love with the idea of having an evening bonfire. His plan had been sparked by a local "who served as our cab driver, tour guide, auto mechanic, caterer, escort, and hopeful bonfire organizer . . . ," Cureton writes. After presenting the idea with great enthusiasm to the rest of the family at breakfast, her brother counted heads and let everyone know the bonfire would cost only twenty dollars each.

Later, though, when he went around to collect, he was confused. Person after person opted out, saying they weren't interested. The truth was, Cureton reports, evenings were still too warm for a bonfire—and, on top of that, so breezy that everyone feared the fire could get out of control. Taken aback, her brother asked why no one had expressed these concerns earlier. She explained that it was because he had already "judged that it was such a great idea and no one dared to contradict him. He shut down the conversations about the heat and the fire hazard."[1]

It's a relatable story, not only because we all have family dynamics, but because it's easy enough to understand the brother's surprise. How many of us are similarly unaware of the subtle ways we prevent others from raising questions and sharing perspectives? What else might we be missing as we go through our days always bent on expressing our views and rallying support? Judging from conversations I have had with many people over the years, this level of self-awareness is usually hard-won. As Nick Beighton, CEO of ASOS, put it to me, "Observing and listening are two of the most underrated skills, and if I find myself doing too much telling, I'm normally doing the wrong thing."

If you want to create plans that succeed, you must tamp down the impulse to transmit and instead switch over to receiving mode for some significant portion of your time. I have heard about people creating these "more quiet" conditions for themselves in a few major ways: first, by listening better to others; second, by spending more time soaking up information in other forms; and third, by clearing their minds of the usual noise that fills them. Here are the key insights and practices I gathered about each approach.

LISTEN FOR THE UNEXPECTED

Listening is something that came up constantly in my interviews, and people often mentioned it as an admirable trait in others. Michael Hawley, for example, recalled his friendship with Steve Jobs. The two were very close, even living together for a time when they started the computer company NeXT. Hawley was at Jobs's wedding, and Jobs, he says, was "the only friend who knew when Nina and I eloped." He saw many qualities that made Jobs such an effective innovator. "But one of the things that always struck me about Steve," he says, "was how attentive he could be, even in chance encounters. He had a way of clicking in and engaging and applying all of his attention—in a nice way. It made people on the other end feel like there was a real focus there, which there was. Not many people are able to keep doing that." Andrew Gordon shared an anecdote about how he, in his early days as an animator at Pixar, personally experienced Jobs's focused attention. At the time, Apple was in the middle of creating the iPod. The two men were barely acquainted, but when they happened to get in the same elevator, Jobs immediately engaged Gordon in a conversation, inquiring about his tastes in music and listening habits. When the doors opened, Gordon realized how much, in that short ride, Jobs had learned about him.

I experienced a similar "clicked-in" engagement in the conversation I've already mentioned, when I first encountered Salesforce cofounder Marc Benioff. And when I asked him what his advice would be for anyone hoping for a breakthrough idea, he looked me in the eye and said one word: "Listen." Then he stood dead silent, waiting and watching to see how I'd respond. About to jump to my next question, I instead caught myself and listened for more. And over the next half hour I learned things I would not have thought to ask about regarding the art of inquiry.

We often teach and encourage young people to work on their debating skills and public speaking capabilities so they'll be able to make the case for something they care about when the time comes. I wonder, though, if we are not emphasizing enough how important listening is to achieving convergence on a good idea. Maggie De Pree, cofounder of the League of Intrapreneurs, is one person who learned this for herself in her student days. She tells the story of spending a few months at Nike as an intern, where she saw a positive change that could be made, and had the opportunity to present it to a vice president–level decision-maker. "I was fired up," she recalls. "I had the opportunity of my lifetime: to use my newly honed business skills to make a bad-ass business case."

Nike at the time was operating hundreds of company-owned retail outlets (now, in fact, they number over a thousand), but the light fixtures in them weren't very energy efficient. De Pree's idea was to replace them all. She had worked out how quickly the utility savings would cover the greater expense of the greener fixtures, and this seemed like one of those slam-dunk sustainability moves that would also benefit the bottom line. But minutes into her big meeting, she says, "what I discovered is that the guy in charge didn't see this exciting opportunity in the same way as I did. In fact, he didn't seem to see an opportunity at all . . ." He brought up various numbers she had left out of her calculations. For example, he explained that lighting is a science in retail design; messing with it has direct impact on sales. Meanwhile, the company, like any vibrant retailer, was in the habit of refreshing its store designs frequently, so a five-year payback on the higher cost of the fixtures was too long a time horizon.

Somewhere in the midst of this meeting, De Pree says, "it struck me. I wasn't making a business case, I was making my case. I was using my own lens to determine what was important to the business without really listening to what mattered." It was only when she stopped selling and started listening that she realized she had framed her case with the wrong question. The important thing for Nike wasn't how it could save some pennies per day on electricity. To get buy-in, she should have presented an argument for how it might stake out a leadership position in sustainable business practices. "This was a company that had been a trendsetter since the 1970s, and was used to creating waves not chasing them. . . . [T]heir brand integrity was riding on their ability to get it right." De Pree took an enduring lesson away from the experience: when you're working hard to make a case for a change, you can "get others to do some of the heavy lifting by observing how they frame something or what resonates for them." The key is to "take time to listen to people and understand their needs, priorities, and motivations.[2]

SILENCE YOUR OWN VOICE

Deval Patrick, the former governor of Massachusetts and now an executive at Bain Capital, is a huge believer in "the power of the pause." When I asked him what practices he routinely uses to uncover the unknown unknowns in his world, he allowed that it "might be too grand to make it sound like I have actual *disciplines*, but one thing I notice is how we all seem to feel like we have to fill up the space between our comments." Checking that impulse to jump into a pause has repeatedly benefited him. For example, he says, if someone is "having a real tough time telling the boss that something isn't going well, if you wait a beat or two, it's like they take a deep breath and then they go ahead." A simple pause is rewarded with "layers of valuable information."

That is great advice, and an important question about such pauses is: What is your own mind doing during them? Are you busily constructing how you will phrase your next utterance, which will ideally be so incisive it will bring matters to a close? Or are you imagining that some critical insight you need is trapped for the moment in the head of the person you are talking with, and it is your mission to coax it out? Simon Mulcahy tells me he has learned to remind himself to do the latter: "This is sort of background music playing all the time: *Don't tell. Ask questions. Don't tell. Ask questions.*"

One of the more brilliant people I have ever talked with on the subject of listening is Tony Piazza, who makes his living as a high-stakes mediator. Since 1980 he has helped people involved in over four thousand different disputes come to terms. Clients who come into his office are typically there because they have reached a serious impasse where two sides have staked out very different positions and dug in deep. Almost always, the main order of business is to reframe the fundamental questions participants came in with. Most are in a state of outrage over what they deeply believe is right and wrong. Piazza knows this must shift to the question of what realistic options there are to end what has become a protracted, painful situation. Typically he has one day to work some kind of magic.

I learned of Piazza's deft mediation from an attorney I know, Claude Stern, who first engaged him to help on a case in 1989. In Stern's words:

After I made my opening plenary session presentation, where the parties and the lawyers are all physically present, I was so blown away by the fact that Tony not only repeated back the words I said, but with the precise inflections and emphasis. He's an artist at that. What that verbatim and precise mimicking does is, the person who has spoken, who has presented, and his or her client who are present at the mediation, are immediately validated. The lawyer and the client believe: "You're really listening to me" and therefore Tony earns tremendous credibility.

Then, after the lawyer's presentation, what Tony does is, he'll say, "I just have a couple of questions," and emphasize that "the purpose of my questions is not to embarrass or humiliate. I'm going to simply ask questions." And then he asks questions that show the vulnerability of the position that's being asserted. They're not mean-spirited or aggressive. They're simply questions, the purpose of which is to suggest to the lawyer and client, "perhaps you can explain more about this" or "it sounds like what you're focusing on is this."

Tony goes through that same process with the other side when they complete their presentation. So, at the end of the mediation plenary session, the vulnerabilities of both sides are identified—

and that's how the case eventually, at the end of the mediation session, settles. Tony settles cases by showing each side their vulnerability, increasing their risks, so they come together because each side is interested in minimizing its downside risk. That's the entire approach.

When I had the opportunity to meet Piazza in person, his point to me was that if magic does happen, it's not because there is a magic formula. There are many books and seminars on how to be a negotiator, and he has read his share of them. Most attempt to provide a standard toolkit or repertoire of tactics to use in different types of situations. But Piazza says that schooling oneself in that kind of playbook can impede resolution more than facilitate it. "Any time you come in with assumptions about what is going to get someone from state A to state B, then you're setting in motion a cascade of bad things," he says. That's because, by devoting part of your brain to analyzing how the behavior of people in the room maps to a common pattern, "you are in some sense typecasting the people" rather than respecting and listening deeply to them. "You're off in your 'fellow brain,' referencing your toolkit there and trying to apply it to 'problem/situation number D-5.' But you are separating yourself from them with the mere process of going through this kind of analysis."

Piazza's goal is always to "minimize the amount of separation—because it's within that space of separation that the collisions occur that fuel the process of fighting." But the separation he is thinking about isn't only between the warring parties. Mediators have to shrink their own distance from the parties, and that means "diligently, zealously letting go of your preconceptions in order to be present with people." Only then will the use of, say, Socratic questioning yield the unpredictable breakthrough the mediator can use to disrupt entrenched positions. If what you are asking in the room is based on your assumptions, what you hear in reply is likely to be "an echo of your own thoughts." But at that point, Piazza says, "to call them Socratic questions is almost insulting to Socrates."

GET READY FOR SURPRISES

Biotech entrepreneur Hal Barron, now president of research and development at GlaxoSmithKline (having held similar roles earlier at Calico and Hoffman–La Roche), also flags the problem of listening with assumptions about what you are about to hear. He says, "The most important thing is to genuinely, actively listen. When I say actively listen, I mean, when you start to tell a story in your head, that's a form of *not listening*. You have to clear your head of the stories and you have to really open your ears." His use of the word "story" here is interesting: it implies that there is a narrative structure you have already settled on, so that you are sure of what will come next—and therefore that is what you hear. "As long as you're truly listening as opposed to fitting what they're saying into your story," he says, "then you ask good questions. Because you're not really sure what the story is yet, so you *have* to ask good questions."

Barron cares about this subject because he has seen the power of asking the right question many times, and he also believes it's a skill that should be consciously cultivated. When I made a reference to managers who are more answer-centric than question-centric, he said it wasn't as simple as believing one of these was better than the other. "It depends on the job and stage in your life and what you're trying to do." When a person is young or just embarking on a path, they succeed on the basis of being an individual contributor and being "the smartest person in the room." People know how to operate in that mode of having all the answers because, Barron says, "it's a phase that most of us got trained for." But as you advance in a field and have the opportunity to lead others and have much more impact, your focus has to shift to "making *other* people the smartest in the room, with good questions." The problem is "there's not a lot of training on that next phase. It's usually just that you see inspiring leaders working that way and realize, 'Yeah, I want to do that, because I see the impact.' You have to find somebody who does it well, and watch."

Scott Di Valerio, former CEO of Outerwall and now COO/CFO of Spiceworks, is also adamant that, to listen effectively, you must clear your mind of your expectations about what you are about to hear. He reminds himself constantly to "listen to understand" versus "listen to defend"—an approach he learned long ago from his wife. It is all too easy for assumptions about what someone believes, or memories of what they said or did in the past, to get in the way of real understanding of what they are truly trying to communicate.

Beyond preparing to be surprised, some people proceed with real *eagerness* to be surprised by the person who has their ear—to the point that they encourage and help them get their point across. Daniel Lamarre told me about one of the "most amazing qualities" he sees in Cirque du Soleil's founder Guy Laliberté: it is his tendency, when someone utters some crazy idea in a meeting, to urge that person to say more—at a moment "where most people would just hit the brakes." Everyone else in the room might be highly skeptical and ready to dismiss the person's line of thinking, he says, but Laliberté persists: "Okay, keep going. I'm not sure about it, but keep on going."

I heard an echo of this approach in conversation with Infosys cofounder Nandan Nilekani. As a person in high demand for giving guidance on many fronts, he knows how hard it is to spend much time in a quiet mode. It's "one of the big challenges business leaders have," he says, since much of their job requires "talking about what's to be done." But this makes it all the more important to work deliberately on listening skills. Nilekani tries to pay special attention to the nonverbal cues that make up so much of face-to-face interaction. Above all, he urges going into a conversation with strong optimism that something valuable will come out of it. It is his experience that "when people are talking, even when quite a few things they say are not useful, there's always one nugget of value in what they're saying that's pretty good." What a waste of everyone's precious time if that nugget goes unnoticed.

It's important to remember that if you don't go actively looking for surprises at work and in life, surprises will sooner or later sneak up on you. Being on the hunt for them is the best way to see the unseen before it's too late.

BECOME APPROACHABLE

One last theme in my interviews related to listening is about something that actually comes first in the process: for you to gain opportunities for listening, others must see you as approachable. And approachability can be compromised by things you don't intend or think much about. Take the obvious example of electronic devices. If, in the moments when you could be available to someone nearby, you promptly pull out your smartphone and start tapping away—or put in your earbuds and close your eyes—you will cut yourself off from untold encounters in which you might have learned about something you didn't know you didn't know.

If you set your mind to it, there are many ways to enhance your approachability. When Nick Beighton arrived at ASOS, he was glad to join a fashion company in part because he had always been something of a clotheshorse. He loved his beautifully tailored suits and collection of elegant neckties. But ASOS is all about street wear, and the millennials who make up the majority of its workforce dress more like hip-hop artists than attorneys. It wasn't long before he ditched the carefully curated wardrobe, Beighton told me. Other than a few favorite suits he would still use at special events, he "sold them all on eBay." Wearing them to the office was setting him apart too much, and putting up a silent barrier.

Lior Div agrees that approachability is a product of "everything that you are doing: the way you dress, the way you look, your body language, the way you approach people, and the way they see you treat everybody." He joked that probably "if you are even using the word 'approachable,' it means that you have failed. Because it needs to be so much a part of the DNA of everything that you are doing that you don't need to talk about being approachable. You *are* approachable by nature."

A similar perspective came from General Stanley McChrystal. He recounted to me a time, years before he became a general, when someone referred to him as arrogant. The person pointed out that he rarely talked to people, particularly peers, when he entered a room. General McChrystal admits that—as a self-described introvert—he has rarely felt comfortable in cocktail party settings, and his reflex is to clam up. It took this difficult feedback to alert him to how his actions—or rather inactions—were negatively impacting others' perceptions of him.

Prompted by that long-ago criticism, General McChrystal to

this day tries to remove barriers between himself and others, including quite literally by getting out from behind his desk and sitting with a guest in another corner of his office. Other leaders do the equivalent by silencing cell phones or making regular forays beyond the executive suite. Simple gestures like these signal willingness to engage fully in dialogue and make everyone more comfortable sharing their thoughts. They are acts of empathy that lay a foundation for new ideas to develop.

ACTIVELY SEEK PASSIVE DATA

At ASK, a small but lively gathering about asking the right questions hosted by the MIT Leadership Center in 2017, Clay Christensen told the rest of us that to be first to see disruptive opportunities—where the right questions present themselves—we should be "actively seeking passive data." He defines passive data as the information you need that "has no voice or clear structure or champion or agenda." It won't, in other words, push its way through to you because someone has already decided it's important and figured out how to present it in a structured way. It is "just unfiltered context. It's always present, but it isn't loud." It is up to you to cast about for it, to try to trip over it, to soak it up.

Say, for instance, you're an aspiring entrepreneur, or part of your job is to come up with new products and services. You'd like to give the world something truly innovative that it never saw coming. But how do you sense a need for something that doesn't already exist? There are no statistics being compiled on it, since you're not surrounded by consumption of it but by nonconsumption. Good luck designing a market research survey to tell you what must-have thing doesn't exist and how much people would pay to get it.

But if you recognize that your surroundings, and other places you could explore, are rich with passive data, you can actively work to tune into it. You might pick up on a customer's frustration with a regrettable tradeoff, or become aware of a technology being applied in a different business sector that could be brought to bear on yours. Because "passive data does not broadcast itself loudly," Christensen says, "you have to seek it out, put clues together." By engaging purposefully with the messy context of real life, and not sitting back, waiting to be served up neatly organized analyses, you might come up with the reframed question that will yield the novel solution people need.[3]

Christensen's comments on this subject remind me of a great observation by Peter Drucker that "innovative opportunities do not come with the tempest but with the rustling of the breeze." And they have made me more aware that not all listening involves just a person trying to convey information. There is more to cultivating the condition of "quietness" than learning not to dominate a conversation. It's important to stay in receiving mode more broadly, picking up on all kinds of weak signals at risk of being drowned out by noise. This is the core message of "mindfulness": the way of going through the world that Ellen Langer and others advocate.[4] This is not the place to try to do justice to that body of research, but the basic idea is to take things that have been part of your life's backdrop and pull them to the forefront of your mind for a time.

It's an approach that my MIT colleague Ed Schein, for one, has called "far more powerful than mantras or meditation." He recalls talking to Langer about the case of someone who occasionally experiences arthritis pain. When the pain flares up, the person is acutely aware of what they are experiencing because it is not their normal existence. But her question was: "What about when it isn't hurting? What's happening then?" It was a question that had real power for Schein because he suddenly recognized "how you wipe out three-quarters of what's happening to you because you don't treat it as relevant." Being mindful means paying more attention to the things you don't normally notice, the things you take for granted, and the questions you stopped asking long ago. It is, in short, the opposite of being mindless.

SILENT MODE THINKING TIME

It's also important to carve out time to think deeply in quiet solitude—in effect, to listen to your own thoughts. Recently I found myself commiserating with a C-suite leader from a European-based retail company who had been "caught thinking." It was a classic stock-photo moment. She was leaning back in her office chair, looking toward the window, and seriously pondering a strategic challenge when her boss, the CEO, walked by and noticed her "doing nothing." He put his head in the door and asked, "What are you doing?" Startled out of her ruminations, she simply said, "Thinking." His next comment—"And when will you start *working*?"—said a lot about the kind of ship he was trying to run. My reaction to the tale was to shake my head and say, "Unbelievable!" But she seemed resigned, saying, "Trust me—it was and is quite believable."

Several decades ago Henry Mintzberg, a renowned leadership scholar based at McGill University, studied the daily work patterns of CEOs. His analysis showed that the average time spent per task during a day was nine minutes. Yes, the senior leader was spending, on average, only nine minutes focused on a particular task before moving on to the next one.[5] Now fast-forward to 2017, when researchers at Harvard Business School studied 1,114 CEOs in six countries and found an even lower rate: only 5.3 minutes on average spent per task during a day.[6] Meanwhile, the pace of work also seems to increase for people in lower ranks as demands to do more with less keep ratcheting up. Put simply, people everywhere, from the tops to the bottoms of most organizations, are less and less able to get serious thinking done.

One mark of creative questioners is their insistence on somehow finding a way to take time, clear their minds, and reflect deeply on unresolved issues, often in solitude. I regularly ask students in a class or participants in a conference: "Where are you physically located when you get your best new ideas?" Almost always it's a space where their thoughts can go uninterrupted, such as on a plane, riding a bike, or in the shower. During the years that my family lived in France, we had a home with an inherited name, "La Solitude," sitting in on the edge of the Trois Pignons Forest near Fontainebleau. And it was a place made for solitude, even when there were extra people around. Our houseguests often commented on how it evoked reflection about work, and even more often about life.

READ DAILY, READ DEEPLY

When I asked my graduate school mentor Bonner Ritchie—to me, hands down the best questioner on earth—how he fueled his ability to see things from different perspectives, he simply said, "I read books." What more proven way to impose a period of silence on yourself and focus on information intake? Not surprisingly, it came up with others as well, such as eBay founder Pierre Omidyar and VMware cofounder Diane Greene. Ed Catmull is a great reader of nonfiction in particular, from the classic works of great historians to the newest titles relating to brain science. Books like these bring him information he wouldn't ordinarily pick up in the course of his day, but that could spark a line of thinking related to a challenge he is actively trying to solve.

The benefits of reading deserve a few more lines, because while many of them have to do with the prose form itself, others have to do with the frame of mind adopted by the reader. Regarding the format, it is generally the case that ideas that have been wrestled into prose are more organized and more clearly articulated than they would be in spoken speech or other grammar-defying formats. Writing is an efficient mode of delivering large amounts of information with minimum ambiguity. I'm sure this is why, at Amazon, managers insist on prose reports and other communications regarding proposed actions as opposed to, for example, presentation decks full of bullet points. When people there talk about Amazon's culture, they often mention its "writing and reading orientation."

Many times, too, a well-crafted piece of prose explicitly names the question it is attempting to answer. Authors often set the context by explicitly naming the questions they are out to address and why those questions are the right ones—despite how others have framed matters in the past. (Recall Malcolm Gladwell doing this in Chapter 1.) It models the catalytic quality I have been describing: an intriguing question is articulated, the reader is invited to engage with it, and the exploration is off and running.

Just as important, on the other side of the equation, is that the person settling in to do some serious reading puts him- or herself into a condition of expectant learning. And because a piece of reading material requires no immediate response, they can receive more challenging ideas without feeling compelled to react on the spot, and can take more time to consider them. If someone is provoked by content, they have time to process it. If they are confused by content, they can reread it or refer to other sources. Many of the same benefits come from watching a documentary, online talk, or live lecture. But the time commitment involved in reading a book, and the full attention demanded by the reading process, might bring with it a greater commitment to engaging with the ideas. It may not be the extrovert's way of stumbling over new questions, but it accomplishes the task of creating productive solitude.[7] In such contemplative moments, Intuit cofounder Scott Cook's motto "Savor the surprise" seems perfect, because that's when the best new questions—and answers—surface.

CLEAR YOUR HEAD AND HEART

One final category of quietude advocated by many people, like Marc Benioff, Maureen Chiquet, Ray Dalio, and Oprah Winfrey, is the formal practice of meditation. Ed Catmull does this every morning, spending about an hour at it soon after he wakes up. He is a student of Buddhist philosophy. He has even gone on "silent meditation retreats." In these ten-day sojourns into "noble silence," participants are guided through a process that allows them to focus their minds inward for long periods of time, beginning with the single-minded contemplation of breathing, and to heighten their ability to detect the sensations to which they have been oblivious. Why do this? As with so much of Buddhist teaching, the hope is to gain a greater ability to walk away from the attachments we have picked up in life that, without our consciously noticing, are causing us suffering and holding us back. People say that this disciplined immersion into quietness and stillness causes them to question what matters on the deepest possible level.

It can also build habits of mind that are more conducive to creative thinking. In a conversation with Disney Animation's senior VP of production, Ann Le Cam, the topic turned to Catmull. "I remember sitting with Ed when he first came to Disney Animation," she told me, "and as he learned about some process here, he would always ask, 'Why do you do it that way?' He would ask these big questions, followed by these huge silences. He would just sit there and look at you. And you start talking and start filling in all the blanks." When he's the recipient of a question, Catmull also pauses to reflect on the response he might have offered off-the-cuff, and works to take it deeper. It marks enough of a difference from the usual cadence of conversation that people are a little thrown off by it, and then impressed to "feel like there's really some thought going into it." As one Pixar animator put it, "It's, like, a meditative thing."

Catmull is hardly alone as a leader who is responsible for managing a creative enterprise and who has found it valuable to meditate. Marc Benioff also does it on a daily basis, and specifically with a hope to quiet the noisy signals in his mind so that he has a better ability to pick up on subtle signs of change in the world. As he describes his approach, it begins with gratitude and acknowledging what he is thankful about, then proceeds to forgiveness and putting out of his mind what has bothered or disappointed him. He owns up to his anxieties and then deliberately sets them aside. By clearing his mind of all these matters that would otherwise consume his thoughts, he opens it to new perceptions and ideas—signals that would normally be overwhelmed and drowned out. Meditation is a practice with known physiological effects. Studies have shown, for example, that it lowers blood pressure and rate of respiration. But the evidence is strong that it boosts creative thinking as well by creating the space for new questions and insights to arise.

THE SOUND OF SILENCE

This chapter focused on the third of three conditions I find creative people seeking out in their lives and organizations. Call it the sound of silence. For many, it is the hardest of all the conditions to maintain.[8] Operating in receiving versus transmitting mode is not a natural act, especially for many high-energy people. It's a condition that must be deliberately, constantly, and actively reinforced for catalytic questions to surface.

People with made-up minds who brook no questions are undeniably loud. They assert their views and cease to listen, seeking no further input. Questioners, by contrast, work to turn up their reception more than their transmission of information. Some do this for themselves as individuals, through practices like meditation and improving listening skills. Others do it for groups they are part of, or groups for which they serve as leaders, by putting new processes in place and cultivating new norms.

Successful individuals, teams, and organizations actively frame the background conditions that allow creative thinking to flourish and be heard. Having composed those steady-state layers deliberately (think conditions of being more wrong and uncomfortable), they can then wait—impatiently, perhaps, but with the confidence that some fleeting, highly valuable insight will materialize. Most important, when that compelling element crosses their line of sight, they will see it for what it is: a flash of brilliance that deserves to be captured and that justifies all the work that gave it a proper "background" setting. That is what they are working for.

They compose and wait.

Quietly waiting for people in Jerusalem.

Quietly waiting for a boat on the Seine.

Quietly waiting for a rogue wave on Boston's North Shore.[9]

7

How Do You Channel the Energy?

The people who are able to transform their questions and
ideas into actual accomplishments are the people
who really uplift society.
—MICHAEL HAWLEY

One day in 2002, Rose Marcario, at the time a financial executive
working in a private equity firm, was sitting in a limousine, stuck
in New York traffic. She had come to town to raise money for a new
investment round, and as the limo slowed to a halt she sighed in
frustration. Glancing out the window, she saw the problem: it was
"this person crossing the street, who obviously had some kind
of mental problem. . . . The person was kind of wavering in the
street." Marcario's own mother had struggled with schizophrenia,
so she recognized the signs well enough, but as seconds dragged
by, she was losing patience. This person was "making me wait,"
she later recalled, and "I had to get somewhere!" A moment later "I
saw myself in the window of the car." Barely recognizing her own
tense, irritated face, she asked the driver to pull over and got out
of the car. "I walked to Central Park to get near some nature, and

I just reflected," she says. "Is this what I've become? Is this what success is?"[1]

That's the kind of question that could be catalytic. Everything could change from that moment. But others of us have had moments like it—times when we felt overwhelmed, or glimpsed the possibility of a better us—that didn't end up changing anything. We got distracted, or realized that change would entail sacrifices and hard work. We let the mood pass. Marcario didn't. She actually did quit her job. She then spent serious time figuring out what work would align with how she wanted to go through the world. She made a major change, eventually accepting an offer to join Patagonia, a firm committed to sustainability, as its chief financial officer. Within five years she was CEO, the job she still holds today.

What was different for Rose Marcario? The simple answer is that she managed to capitalize on that moment, find the motivation in it, and channel that energy into action. She followed through to the point that new insight was converted to new reality. And only by doing so was she able to realize the potential value of her question.

Asking the right question itself is always critical, whether we're talking about transformation at a personal level or at the level of an entire society. Lisa Jardine, author of *Ingenious Pursuits*, a history of the scientific revolution, puts it this way: "Advance in any field has always been preceded by a sudden leap of the imagination, which is recognized for its brilliance by the participating group, and galvanizes them in their turn into further activity."[2] But as the quote implies, the question is only the beginning. It is the key that unlocks an answer, but it usually takes more effort to get to that answer—and still more effort to put the new solution into place.

To use my favorite metaphor, the question is catalytic: it lowers barriers to thinking and sends energy down a different path. But that energy still has to be connected to some engine of change. It has to be managed and sustained. This is, I think, part of why questions and questioners don't get as much credit as they deserve in the processes of creative invention and personal change. For every one that ends up driving a difference, there are dozens that sputter out. We've all seen people who raised perspective-altering questions but didn't push for implications and answers. By failing to deliver on their promise, they left everyone more disappointed than if the questions had never been raised at all. And in the meantime they may have delayed other action and wasted people's time.

This chapter will share what I've learned from the people who are giving questions a good name: the ones who are channeling the energy and converting inquiry into insight, and insight into impact.

ESCALATING THE QUESTIONS

I began this chapter with Rose Marcario's anecdote in part because, as I write this chapter, Patagonia is on my mind. I have just been talking to people there about the company's history. It began when Yvon Chouinard, an antimaterialistic surfer and rock climber, became an accidental businessperson. The question that development raised for him was his alone: *How can I make a living without losing my soul?*

That question turned out to have a lot of juice in it, and he could engage with it for many years. He figured out how he could reconcile his pursuits and reframe what it meant to do business so the tension wasn't so intolerable. But as the company he founded grew, the next related question loomed: *What kind of organization does a leader who cares about that tension build?* The results of his thinking on that matter are captured in his 2005 book, *Let My People Go Surfing*. His intent in writing it, I suspect, was not to get himself on the bestseller list but to force himself to figure out what he really believed, and to explain it.[3]

At the same time, larger tensions were developing that had to be confronted. Chouinard's company was founded on his love of the outdoors. What if it was, through its rapidly growing manufacturing and distribution operations, damaging the environment? How could that be minimized? The organization was energized by that question and made great progress over many years on the herculean task of moving to organically produced fibers.

Then the company's ambitions—and questions—escalated further. Beyond having less negative impact on the planet, how could it manage to operate a net-zero impact? And, for that matter, not just no negative impact on the environment, but none on society? How might it even get to the point of having a net-*positive* impact? It was now stepping up to a point where it was questioning the very assumption that society must make painful tradeoffs to have thriving businesses.

Patagonia was still small, however, in relation to the giants of the apparel industry—a fairly minor player in a huge industry. It was getting its own house in order. Was that enough? People inside the firm started to question what difference that could make in the context of a globalized business sector mostly moving in the opposite direction. How could its influence spread to other players, many of which were its direct competitors? This was pushing things rather far, even for Patagonia veterans. In some consumers' minds it was an important point of differentiation for the company that it operated so sustainably. Talk of broader influence raised a fair question: "What if other companies do follow our lead—and as a result, we lose that competitive advantage?"

To me, this was one of the most interesting points in Patagonia's history because of the way that question got flipped: "What if they *don't*?" others in the company responded. "If we really want to protect the environment, isn't it a good thing if others emulate us? In fact, what if we at Patagonia were to give away our knowledge of how to be more green? What if we actually helped competitors who wanted to do the same?"

It was around this point that Rose Marcario joined Patagonia. She was very attracted to the firm's questions as more meaningful and aligned with her priorities than the investment sector's short-term focus on the next quarter's bottom line, where, as she puts it, "earnings per share are like a chain around the neck." Her decision to join Patagonia signals that a questioning company has an additional advantage: it can attract talented, problem-solving people. Marcario is now leading the charge on the next escalation of the question: "How do we make it uncomfortable for other businesses *not* to follow us?"

No wonder people at Patagonia continue to enthusiastically pursue answers to its original catalytic question: How can I make a living without losing my soul? It's the gift that keeps on giving. As I pore over the transcripts of conversations with many senior leaders there, it is not that any single questioning practice or creativity discipline jumps out as essential to fueling and sustaining the energy. Rather, it's a set of core cultural values and actions that keep questioning—and answering—alive.

These were evident in my conversations with Dean Carter, for example, who is Patagonia's vice president in charge of human resources and shared services. He told me about the company's pioneering decision to do away with bell-curved performance ratings in employees' annual reviews. It's a trend that has caught on in many other companies since, but at Patagonia it was the outcome of deep questioning about what performance management should be trying to achieve.

Carter really won me over with his explanation of another employee-serving decision: to open a daycare center on-site at headquarters. It would be hard to say this was an obvious decision. After all, how many other companies have them? But in retrospect, Carter says it should be obvious to everyone. Before coming to Patagonia in 2015, he worked in HR elsewhere and was very attuned to the problem of employee engagement. The polling firm Gallup annually gauges whether US workers feel engaged in their work, and year after year the numbers look dismal. In 2015, under a third of workers said they were engaged, versus 51 percent who said they were not engaged, and 17 percent who said they were actively disengaged. So Carter, along with every other HR head of a major employer, had been trying to figure out: *What can we do to make the work more meaningful to people?*

After working at Patagonia for a few years, he told me, he was downright embarrassed at how narrowly he used to think about this and other HR issues. Gesturing toward the hallway where an employee was just that moment pushing a stroller with a toddler in it, he said, "A big part of the embarrassment has to do with that little buggy. After twenty years of doing HR, the simple answer to engagement—and gender parity, too—is right in there." Frame the question about on-site daycare in these terms, and it turns out "it's such a ridiculously simple answer," Carter exclaims. "Had I known that, I would've been advocating for it a long time ago!"

I have spent time inside many companies over the years, and I must say that this is a truth-seeking place. Its people honor "radical transparency" inside and outside the company, to such a level that it's like an extreme sport. They hire people predisposed to solve problems, hunt down the truth, act independently, care about people, and make a difference. Then they back up those extremes with values and actions that say *We mean it,* knowing that some long-term interests, causes, and commitments will have short-term costs—and being fine, very fine, with that.

Coming back to Rose Marcario, something I heard from Matt Dwyer, Patagonia's senior director of materials innovation, makes me think she will take care to sustain all this. Dwyer is a very experienced scientist, and always ready to challenge the status quo on methods and materials for, say, durable water repellence. "Rose embodies more than any leader I've met the ability to ask uncomfortable questions—and call people out if the answer doesn't make sense," he said.

> I mean, she'll do it in a way that's loving, but it's uncomfortable. That's the only word there is to describe it. The longer I'm here, the more I am trying to emulate that—because I always try to get there, but typically not in as direct a way. I'll ask two or three questions, where she can ask the one—and make it uncomfortable, get to the root of the issue, and move on—either to fix it, or just say, "Hey, this is something that's just a critical fail, and we can't move forward." She's so efficient at doing that, and she's not afraid.

Patagonia's way of channeling the energy that was unleashed in the first instance is to keep looking for the next, bigger implication of the question it is solving. This is a company that keeps finding questioning handholds and footholds to reach new heights.

CASCADING THE QUESTIONS

Hyatt Hotels' recent success, meanwhile, has been a story of starting with a big and abstract question and driving it downward, finding a way to concentrate the energy it created and drill down to impact. The big, vague question started like this: "The major decisions in hotel management tend to be driven by considerations of operational efficiency. But shouldn't we be looking at them more through a lens of customer experience?" And in that realm: "What are we missing?" A new chief innovation officer was hired in 2011: Jeff Semenchuk, who brought with him a strong belief in the "design thinking" approach to innovation.

It started with what I think Clay Christensen would describe as "actively seeking passive data." Of course, Hyatt has loads of data—active data, that is, from analyses performed on its millions of transactions and marketing touch points with guests around the world. But active data only reflects the questions you have posed in the past. Somehow it had gone unremarked in recent years that a big demographic shift was under way in Hyatt's customer base. As Semenchuk explains, "We realized that 37 percent of our guests globally were women and that number was growing as a proportion of our overall guest stays. And we just hadn't been paying attention to it. This was a real opportunity to say, 'Well, are there some different needs unmet or otherwise for women guests, and if so, what are they and how could we address them better?'"

The initiative Semenchuk kicked off to correct for that has become one of the company's favorite examples of how "Hyatt Thinking"—its tailored version of design thinking—can yield breakthroughs.[4] Its process begins with a resolve to "listen and learn." Semenchuk's team started talking to women, many of whom were businesspeople booking single-occupancy rooms.

What was their experience of traveling? When they arrived at their accommodation on the road, what made them happy or unhappy? In some ways, Semenchuk says, this was "the hardest thing for a lot of our colleagues to do—to look at a focus area and not jump right into solutions." They had to instead "start by asking questions." The remainder of Hyatt's innovation method involved defining needs, brainstorming, prototyping, and testing, but in this first stage, it was all about empathizing with real people and soaking up that passive data—and honing the questions that would energize all those later phases of work.

Moving on to "define needs," Semenchuk's team sifted through interview notes to find major themes. Two were most prominent. The first was that women often felt trapped in hotels when they were traveling alone. Many felt awkward stepping out for solo meals and vulnerable taking in the neighborhood on their own. They tended to spend much more time confined to their rooms than men did. This made for a lonely experience, and—considering that, given the traditional demographic, those rooms had been designed in the first place with men in mind—that extra alone time indoors held little charm. The second finding reflected the fact that most of these solo travelers were businesspeople, who often had colleagues on the road with them. Teams often needed to touch base on their work, but it felt wrong to go to a colleague's hotel room to confer. At least two big needs came into high relief then: women travelers wanted to get out of their rooms more without feeling awkward and vulnerable, and they wanted neutral ground for impromptu meetings.

Once the team had defined these needs, the next phase of work could move to the questions of how to solve them. Brainstorming sessions were held, but the planning of them raised its own question: Who should be at the table? Semenchuk says that, for example, "if it's an arrival opportunity or a front-desk thing" under consideration for change, "typically only front-desk people would be involved in solving it. What we said was, 'You know what? Why don't we invite a housekeeper in? Why don't we bring in a director of finance? Why don't we ask a waiter . . . and a couple of external people—maybe somebody that works in a different industry who has done analogous work?' In the brainstorming, we really try to get a diversity of perspectives, because that's when we get the richest ideas."

Now it was time to prototype the most promising ideas coming out of the brainstorming. Which were most promising? Semenchuk says a number of questions helped identify them: "What's going to be easiest to do? What's going to be hardest? What's going to be most transformational? What can end up making us the most money? We considered a whole variety of criteria to choose some ideas, and then we said, 'Now let's prototype them.'"

The whole idea of prototyping as practiced by design thinking and lean start-up adherents is that it should entail the use of "low-fidelity" solutions that improve across many iterations based on feedback from real customers. That posed its own challenging question to the Hyatt organization. Could it stand to expose real customers to half-baked ideas? How could it contain the risk to the customer experience and brand that comes with that? Semenchuk tells the story of the first "Escape Bar" prototype it threw together, with the Hyatt Regency O'Hare serving as a "lab hotel." When his group approached managers there with their idea, they were willing but saw it as a three-month project that would require architects and cost perhaps $50,000. "We said, 'No, let's just go into the storeroom and see what furniture is lying around and we can pull out and start using now,'" he recalls. "They were mortified. But within a day we had an Escape Bar and guests just started flocking to it." The innovation team was able to allay the hotel manager's fears by being upfront with guests. They approached guests and told them, "This is an experiment. Can you give us feedback? And, by the way, it didn't cost us anything, so don't worry—you won't hurt our feelings. How can we make it better?" Feedback from those guests not only contained good suggestions, it showed they actually enjoyed the experience of trying something new and having the chance to weigh in. Gradually Hyatt's people have come around to the new question posed by prototyping and are now engaged by it: "How can we put in place the simplest functioning solution, involving minimal cost, that will allow us to learn?"

Finally, the testing phase of Hyatt Thinking poses its own questions: "How do we prove whether this change is worth rolling out or not? Does this really move the needle on hotel performance?" Anyone who has worked in performance measurement knows the whole kettle of additional questions these open up. The follow-ons begin with "Which needle?" Is the right focus on guest satisfaction ratings, repeat business, overall revenues, or perhaps that ultimate barometer, bottom-line profitability? Scmenchuk says Hyatt uses "a variety of ways to measure the impact of things, from revenue to cost savings to net promoter score," and won't roll out new ideas until at least one hotel has declared success and has the data to prove it.[5]

To me, the Hyatt story is about the power of questions. It consists of a team beginning with a big, energizing question and channeling that energy to achieve impact as quickly and surely as possible. Whereas across Patagonia's long history we can see the escalating impact of a great initial question, here we see a cascading one, from a broad objective to focus more on customer experience all the way down to the tiniest operational details of implementing a specific solution under that banner.

Both of these cases show the kinds of initiatives that give questioning a good name. They challenged assumptions in important ways, got large numbers of people to see things differently as a result, and produced results that made everyone feel they were better off than they had been before. Question-driven successes like these make it easier for organizations to keep questioning.

MANAGING THE EMOTIONAL ARC

Questions that reframe things and show new paths to solutions are exciting. They produce a positive boost in mood. This is something that has been evident even in the very small-scale setting of the Question Burst—the brainstorm-for-questions exercise I described in Chapter 3. One great thing about its contained and controlled conditions is that they make it easy to collect data about emotions before and after an intense questioning period. More than 80 percent of the time, the effects on mood are positive after just one round (and even the holdouts are often able to see a boost by simply repeating the process). People feel better able to take on the problems that have had them feeling stuck.

We also know this anecdotally. Every story we hear in which someone asks a new question that opens up a new insight has that moment of joy, whether it's a climactic "Aha!" or "Eureka!" or a more subtle form of intrigued engagement ("Gee, that's funny . . .") that eventually yields a better answer. Even questions that don't immediately unlock answers hold the power to spark our imaginations and give us reason to hope.

That positive emotional response in turn unleashes energy. This we know from a large body of psychological research. A great variety of studies have shown how positive mood fuels creativity.[6] When people are happier and more hopeful, they are both more motivated to think creatively and more cognitively capable of doing so. Participants in creativity studies who are in more positive moods are able to make more creative connections, and to think across broader categories.[7] The other side of the coin is also true: people in negative moods are more likely to miss interesting solution possibilities. One recent experimental study, for example, focused on people experiencing stress and found them less able to generate the kinds of unusual ideas and configurations that subjects in creativity studies are typically prompted to come up with by being supplied with disparate materials. Greater stress, the authors concluded, leaves people with greater "intolerance of incongruity" and therefore causes them to "develop mental rigidity."[8]

Engaging in category-expanding, assumption-challenging questioning therefore produces a double boost in mood. It is an inherently hopeful activity that is then further energized when a novel question offers some glimpse of a new solution approach, perhaps a new angle of attack on a problem that had begun to seem intractable.

But there is also a danger here: that this burst of positive energy may give way to a trough of frustration even worse than what existed before. This can happen if the solution possibility turns out to be a false lead or ushers in what turns out to be a long slog of hard work full of setbacks and short on interim rewards. These are the times that separate great leaders from not-so-great ones, as my MIT colleague Andrew Lo knows. He asked the question: Is there a better way to finance the drug discovery process? Risk is a huge roadblock to funding. Could financial engineering reduce the risk and bring more money into the space and ultimately bring cures to patients sooner? He has suggested that a large "megafund," consisting in large part of long-term bonds issued by financial-portfolio companies, would help fund languishing projects while providing a safer investment option for large institutional investors and money managers.[9]

That is an energizing question for the people who work with Lo. But making progress also means moving quickly beyond the posing of the question. "It's not enough to have a vision," he said. "One has to be able to map the individual contributions of the team to that vision. In other words, it has to be a *realistic* vision as opposed to a pie in the sky, and part of the challenge is to understand just how much you can expect from your colleagues. Sometimes they don't even understand how much they're capable of, and so being able to develop that sense of accomplishments, goals, and abilities is really the key to putting it all together." When a great question transitions into a multiyear effort to devise the answer, it's the job of the project's leader to keep reinfusing the team with positive energy.

Research by Teresa Amabile and Steven Kramer is important to cite here. It shows how vital it is to people's ongoing engagement in a task to have the feeling of making *progress*. By the way, by publishing this research, the scholars themselves put a beautifully reframed question on the table for anyone leading a team expected to produce creative work, such as a bunch of software developers working on an innovative application. If those managers thought that the question to focus on was "What rewards should I dangle to get more good work out of people?" this research suggests they should think again. The better question is: "What more can I be doing to facilitate the team's progress and minimize its setbacks?"[10] The fact that people want to do good work should be assumed and the attention shifted to what's making that unnec-essarily hard for them.

When it comes to managing the emotional arc of getting from an inspiring question to a viable answer, one objective is to get the maximum distance out of that initial question's energy burst. Try not to let it diffuse in too many directions. I think this is what Hyatt has done effectively. Semenchuk, who recently left Hyatt and is now CEO at Yaro, told me it was important to have a pro-cess that channels people's efforts, even though it's "sometimes counterintuitive to people exploring innovation. They want to go really broad. But what we've learned is that you have to pick some focus areas, which may be emerging opportunities or problems we need to take on." The pursuit of the opportunity/problem that more guests were women business travelers featured many points at which collective energies were focused.

Bob Sutton and Hayagreeva "Huggy" Rao have studied the whole class of problems they label as "scaling" opportunities, where some new practice has been adopted in one place and the ques-tion arises: Could this be done more broadly? In a sense it is the foundation question of any "change management" process, since the basic need is to get people to adopt a better way of doing things that they were not initially involved in creating. Their advice for energizing that process is to go out to people with a one-two punch of "hot emotions and cool solutions."[11] Both are essential to the scaling process, since without the hot emotions people won't be inspired to go through the motions of the solution that has been arrived at. And without the cool solutions, all that hot emotion will be wasted, like so much fuel spilled on the ground, without being channeled into productive action. This is what is happening a lot of times when great questions fail to produce great answers. The

positive emotion and energy they create at the outset is not channeled in any disciplined way.

However, there is another way to keep a question-inspired initiative moving forward. Rather than depend on the initial big
question's ability to create all the momentum, people can keep
injecting new bursts of energy with follow-on questions that are
themselves energizing. This can happen at any level. It is something I do for myself when I am working on a problem and can feel
my energy flagging. Those are the moments when I decide to take
four minutes and do a Question Burst. It's what Patagonia is doing when it looks for fresh ways to reengage with its fundamental
meaning-of-life question. And in the context of Hyatt's initiative
to improve the experience of women traveling alone, this was a
great benefit of all the questions that came up in the phases of its
process. All individually intriguing and assumption testing, they
kept fueling positive energy and motivation. The emotional arc of
the effort never took a nosedive from which it couldn't recover.

It is not for me to say how, in your own efforts to use questions
to inspire transformation, you must manage the emotional arc
you will experience. My intent here has been to make you aware
that it exists and will play a key role in your success. Know that it
has a tendency toward peaking early with a rush of enthusiasm,
and plunging thereafter, if it turns out that the door unlocked by
a question has not been flung wide open but only cracked. When
that happens, and it is clear that the new pathway to a solution,
while more promising, may be long, give real thought to how
you will keep recharging your efforts. If you were assuming that
getting to a breakthrough solution was as easy as reframing the
question, revisit that assumption. How exactly you should manage
the emotional arc is a question you will have to confront—and it
might prove catalytic in itself.

WHAT A GREAT COACH DOES

This is a good point to bring in the role of coaching—and I use the term broadly to include everyone from sports coaches to executive coaches to life coaches. Helping clients manage their emotions and energy is a big part of what coaches in all these realms do.

I went to the coach to the stars, Tony Robbins, to get his perspective on this. Robbins is a larger-than-life character. He has written multiple self-help bestsellers and routinely speaks to audiences numbering in the thousands, even tens of thousands. On an individual level, he works with people who have a lot of energy (and many of them, a lot of money) and who want to channel it to accomplish the most.

It turns out that much of what Robbins does is focused on questions—not just in the sense that he asks them, as of course he must to understand who his clients are and what they hope to accomplish. The point of his work is to help people understand the questions that are unconsciously driving their thinking. As he puts it, "The only way to get new answers is by asking new questions, and the quality of your questions determines the quality of your answers—and so, that is the foundation of everything I do."

Questions are important "because questions control what you focus on." Robbins notes that it's easy enough to manipulate someone into switching their focus however briefly. If you ask them, for example, "What's really lousy about your life?" then even though up to that point they might not have been bothered by much of anything, their brains will focus on that and start generating answers. Likewise, if you ask "What are you grateful for?" or "What are you excited about?" their focus will shift accordingly. If you want to cause a shift in someone's mental or emotional state, he notes, you can do that with a question "faster than anything else." There are only two ways to change things for people, he explains: either you change their external environment or you change their internal environment. A coach's focus is on the latter, and "I can shift what's happening in your internal environment by the question I ask and the way in which I ask it." The thing to note is that all these questions have presuppositions built into them—that there is something lousy about life, for example, or that you are in some way grateful.

Robbins starts from the position that "everyone has what I would call a primary question, a question you ask more often than any other question in your life." Using himself as an example, he says, "The number one question I'm asking is: How can I make it better? And it is obsessive, it's driven, and I ask it all the time." That makes perfect sense: he is, after all, an icon of self-improvement. But as he tells the story, he wasn't aware that he was being driven so thoroughly by this question until well into his career—and much less had it occurred to him that it wasn't the same question that drove others. Since then, his early work with a new client is very focused on finding out what theirs is, and to what extent it might be holding them back. The big concern is that the question guiding them, almost always subconsciously, has negative presuppositions built into it. "That's the biggest energy killer in the world," he believes, and in that case some work has to be done on the question. He has a process he takes people through to uncover this and address it. Drawing an analogy to the old computing expression "Garbage in, garbage out," he says, "Your brain is the same: if you ask a lousy question, you're going to get a lousy answer."

Once Robbins has helped a client identify that primary question, then they have a foundation for the client to make many other decisions—for example, about the best uses of their time.

QUESTIONING CAPITAL

My conversation with Tony Robbins happened courtesy of Marc Benioff; the two have been friends for years, and Benioff credits his conversations with Robbins for many improvements in his habits of thinking. It wasn't until I spoke with Robbins myself, however, that I made a connection between Robbins's focus on questions and something I have heard Benioff talk about more than once. He notes that some people have more "innovation capital" than others. Talking about the need for his Salesforce organization to keep coming up with new and valuable ideas, he said, "I can't do it all. I don't have all the ideas. That isn't my job. My job is to build a culture of innovation. That's something that we try to enforce. We encourage it. We value it. We notice it. We compensate for it. We require it." But he also acknowledged that innovation is not something an employee can simply be trained how to do. It isn't only a skill set. To lead a transformational change, they must also have gained credibility with others. By getting things done in the past that bucked the status quo, met with resistance, and worked out well, they have to have built up some innovation capital.

The related observation I can make is that some people's questions have more catalytic effect than others'. While we might like to think that a brilliant question could arise from anywhere and light a fire under people, many of us have noticed the reality that the same question posed by two different people creates very different responses. Some of this is just positional power. Perhaps you have sat in a meeting where one of the more junior or marginalized participants attempts to make a point and is not heard—only for the same point to be made later, to great effect, by someone more established in the power structure of the place.

And sometimes the key to a question's force is the background of the person giving voice to it. For example, in 2018, Larry Fink wrote a letter to the CEOs of companies his investment firm Black-Rock holds shares in. Since the majority of the money BlackRock manages for its clients is invested in index funds, trading collectively in thousands of companies, this was in effect an open letter to the management of publicly traded companies. The letter generated a lot of buzz because of the hard questions Fink put to the group. What were they doing to fight the crippling effects of the stock market's fixation on short-term share price gains? How did they intend to keep earning the "license to operate" they had been granted by societies expecting them to be wellsprings of life-improving innovations and good jobs?

The thing is, none of these questions were new in the least. Legions of activists and scholars concerned with corporate social responsibility have been asking them for decades. But Fink's voice had special force. As Judith Samuelson of the Aspen Institute put it, "When the head of BlackRock, the largest investor in the world, says that companies must produce not only profits, but contributions to society, it sends a powerful message."[12] It's hard not to recall the biblical story of Saul on the road to Damascus having the vision that converted him—a cruel persecutor of Christians in the earliest days of the Church—to Christianity himself, and indeed becoming Saint Paul. It is the story that gave our language the phrase "the scales fell from his eyes." As a pillar of the community he was speaking to, who has now decided to challenge its ways, Fink has a level of questioning capital not many can match.

It may not be welcome news that the same question coming from different mouths gets less respect, but one thing we can take away from it is that part of the positive emotion and energy generated by a great question must be people's level of belief that something could really change as the result of it. What I would propose that the more energizing people have is greater *questioning capital*. Whether they deserve to have it is a different question. A better question still is: How could those of us who lack questioning capital gain more of it?

We know how questioning capital gets lost. It dwindles away like so much cash at the blackjack table when someone's questions do get noticed, but then end up going nowhere. That person does not apply the extra energy required to pursue the pathway their question cracked open or isn't able to recruit a sufficient number of others to the cause. Worse, there are people who make it to senior ranks in organizations without having accumulated any questioning capital at all. Bill McDermott of SAP explained to me that this is the downfall of many an executive:

> *It's like "So-and-so was great all twenty years of their career. But when they got to executive vice president they just fell apart. What happened?" Well, they didn't just wake up and turn into a loser. What happened is the things that got them there couldn't get them here. They're not able to handle the next rung in the ladder because they don't know what questions to ask. They don't know how to take a difficult situation and bring it to its knees with questions.*

McDermott's comment suggests that questioning capital translates to leadership capital, and it is a point he doubled down on in another part of our conversation. He told me: "What kills leaders is that they don't scale, because more senior people don't respect them and don't want to work for them. And the reason that senior people don't respect them and don't want to work for them is because they just give orders. They don't ask questions." Ray Dalio, one of the world's most successful hedge fund investors (he founded Bridgewater Associates), lays the same kind of stress on questioning strengths. When he decided to share his management philosophy in the recent book *Principles*, his advice on hiring was not to choose someone because their skills fit the immediate job but someone who you want to "share a long-term mission with." Above all, he writes: "Look for people who have lots of great questions. Smart people are the ones who ask the most thoughtful questions, as opposed to thinking they have all the answers. Great questions are a much better indicator of future success than great answers."[13]

By the same token, though, the main way to build questioning capital is to build that track record of seeing and seizing on the right question and seeing it through to impact. And so now let me bring this back around to the work Tony Robbins and other effective coaches do. To me, his service to clients is largely about helping them build their questioning capital so that they can be more effective in whatever pursuits they choose.

LEARNING TO TELL THE TALE

If you are hoping to recruit others to the pursuit of answers raised by a novel question, one particular skill worth cultivating is storytelling. Good stories are a way to keep showing how a problematic situation gave rise to an energizing question, and why it would improve life in some meaningful way to pursue that question to its solution. A storyline links the problem perceived to the problem reframed and creates momentum toward the problem's resolution.

Perhaps it should not surprise us that transformational leaders are so often good storytellers. In an earlier chapter I described a decision Fadi Ghandour made after a long day of travel to skip his car service and instead hitch a ride to his hotel with one of his company's low-ranking delivery drivers. The conversation the two of them had on that late-night ride opened his eyes to some problems he hadn't even known to ask about, and when he woke up the next morning he decided immediately to take up those new questions and bring about a change for the better.

There is a coda to that story. Evidently the news made the rounds that Ghandour had done this, and in subsequent travels he was surprised to hear people bring it up. The same happened with some other actions of his that struck employees as unusual, like the time he was touring a warehouse and, in the middle of a conversation with another executive, grabbed a nearby broom and swept up some debris he noticed on the concrete floor. Gradually stories like these became part of his personal mythology, and he was smart enough to spot their value in helping to shape the organization's culture. Stories don't tell people explicitly what to do. Instead, they invite them into imagined scenes where they can think for themselves what one might and should do, and leave them to consider how that carries over to other situations.

There is considerable science behind why storytelling engages our attention so well. Research by neurobiologist Paul Zak, for example, shows that when a speaker uses character-driven stories with emotional content to make key points, listeners understand those points better and recall them much longer. He writes that "in terms of making impact, this blows the standard PowerPoint presentation to bits."[4]

One reason it does this is because storytelling raises questions in the mind of the listener or reader and leaves them there to be considered for a while, if not indefinitely. One of my favorite people to talk to about the craft of storytelling is Andrew Gordon, who was an animation director at Pixar for many years and is now head of animation at Illumination Entertainment. On one occasion when we spoke, he had just been to a talk by Mo Willems, the children's book author responsible for *Don't Let the Pigeon Drive the Bus!* and its many hilarious sequels. Some of what Gordon heard was "really eye-opening" for him, such as the distinction Willems drew between the visual controlling idea for a book and the central idea of its story.[15] Especially interesting was that Willems "doesn't want to give the reader all of it. He wants to give them 49 percent—not even 50—so that they have to figure out: What is this book really about?" One online reviewer might declare that the book is "about working with your friends and never giving up," while another says it's "about knowing when to give up." Gordon laughed with appreciation. "That is perfect. . . . They're figuring out what *they* get out of it, right?" In a similar way, at Pixar, he said, "When we're doing a story, there are a lot of different ways that we are asking questions."

A well-crafted story engages grown-up minds in just the same way. It pulls them in, engages their empathies, and leaves a lot up to them as to what they will make of it. What else can explain the phenomenal success of the TED talk format? In these brief seventeen-minute presentations, speakers have learned to make heavy use of stories and narrative arcs. "Unlike challenging explanations or complex arguments, everyone can relate to stories," TED CEO Chris Anderson writes.[16]

One of the popular TED talks in business innovation circles is Doug Dietz's account of how he and a group of others came to collaborate on a new approach to medical imaging in hospital pediatric wards. As Dietz tells the story, he had been working as an industrial designer at GE Healthcare for many years, designing medical devices including magnetic resonance scanners. But across those years, he had never been in a pediatric ward and seen one in action. When the day finally came that he visited a hospital site, he recalls, "I see this young family coming down the hallway and I can tell as they get closer that the little girl is weeping. As they get even closer to me, I notice the father leans down and just goes, 'Remember we talked about this; you can be brave.'" It was in this moment, filled with empathy, that Dietz saw the setup from the young patient's eyes. "Everything was kind of like, beige," he says, and the combination of dim lighting and warning stickers posted on the walls and machinery created a sense of foreboding. Then there was the machine itself, Dietz's baby, which "basically looked like a brick with a hole in it." His experience only went downhill from there that day. But, as bad as it was, the observation left him with the profound sense that he should be doing something better for these young patients. What would a better designer do?

My own awareness of where the story picks up from there comes from Kathleen Kapsin, director of the Pediatric Radiology Department at the Children's Hospital of Pittsburgh. She and her team were aware of problems that needed to be solved. Kapsin told me that it often took multiple tries to get images at the quality level physicians needed to make diagnoses and treatment plans with full confidence. The problem was that, in contrast to adult patients, it was hard to get children to remain still. They were hard to calm down long enough for the imaging machine to do its slow scanning work. The obvious solution seemed to be to push machine vendors like GE for ever more sophisticated technology capable of getting that image faster, between squirms. That, of course, had the downside that it would undoubtedly make for a much more expensive piece of equipment, and the decommissioning of a machine that had been expected to last many years.

One day the problem got reframed, and the insight hit. What if instead of making images faster, they could get kids to stop squirming? Why did the kids do that, anyway? Soon enough, through observations like the one Doug Dietz made on his visit, that question was answered: because the kids were scared. So what could be done to make that brick with a hole in it less terrifying?

To say that the solution—to create the distraction rooms that are now so widespread in pediatric wards—was born in that moment is true, but at the same time makes it sound like it was implemented in an instant. In fact, there were many months of work ahead for Kapsin's team and their many collaborators, including Doug Dietz and his design team at GE Healthcare. The solution they ultimately created transforms those clinical imaging rooms into colorful adventure stories that kids play-act their way through. The time they spend in the imaging tube is a moment in the storyline when they, as the heroes, must be quiet and still. They are in a pirate's cave. Or in the shadow of the dinosaur. It's like magic. The images turn out fine. The child is happy. Some even ask, at the end of the adventure, "When can I come back?"

Themed signs show children on several adventures throughout the Children's Hospital of Pittsburgh.

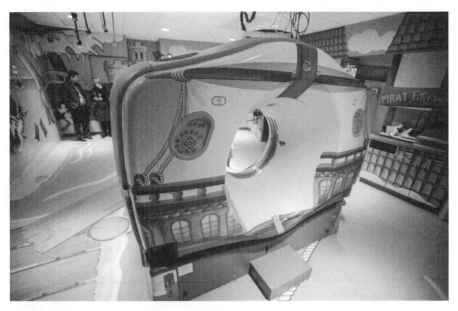

Kathleen Kapsin, director of Pediatric Radiology, guiding the adventures at the Children's Hospital of Pittsburgh (background on the right)

The Pirate Island Adventure combines a treasure chest of surprises with a monkey that swings to finish off a room full of positive distraction.

8

Can We Raise a Next Generation of Questioners?

Once you have learned how to ask questions
—relevant and appropriate and substantial questions—
you have learned how to learn
and no one can keep you from learning
whatever you want or need to know.
—NEIL POSTMAN AND CHARLES WEINGARTNER

Isidor Rabi won the Nobel Prize in Physics in 1944 for his discovery of nuclear magnetic resonance, the fundamental discovery that enabled the new scanning technology of magnetic resonance imaging. He worked on the atom bomb during World War II and after the war helped set up the research laboratories in Brookhaven and the European Organization for Nuclear Research (CERN). All in all, it's quite a résumé. Years later an interviewer asked him if there had been something special about his upbringing. "My mother made me a scientist without ever intending it," he mused. "Every other Jewish mother in Brooklyn would ask her child after school: 'So? Did you learn anything today?' But not my mother. She always asked me a different question. 'Izzy,' she would say, 'did you ask a good question today?'" Rabi credited his career to the habits he gained as a result. "That difference—asking good questions—made me become a scientist!"[1]

Our entire society will benefit to the extent that we intentionally raise more good questioners. This means building a set of mental habits and behavioral priorities in our youngest citizens that is best established—or at least not nipped in the bud—in the setting of families and homes. But this questioning skill set must also be taught and encouraged in schools, workplaces, and communities. It is a set of keys to better leadership and more creative breakthroughs that mentors, role models, and heroes can bestow on the less experienced people they influence.

Most of the great innovators I have interviewed during the past decade had the unusual benefit, in multiple stages of their lives, of being around adults who taught them the act of asking and gave them opportunities to engage in the act of creation. They learned in the way all generations learn from their elders, but in their cases those elders put a clear emphasis on the value of inquiry. My contention is that, if we can collectively do this for more of our children, students, and young colleagues, we can give our world the gift of more creative minds like Isidor Rabi's. What would it take to raise a whole generation of good questioners?

SCHOOLED IN QUESTIONING

Let's start with school practices, since that is where the mind typically goes first when wondering how to improve how and what people learn. Dan Rothstein and Luz Santana are big believers in a certain kind of educational reform. At the outset of *Make Just One Change* they are absolutely straightforward about their thesis.

This book makes two simple arguments:

- *All students should learn how to formulate their own questions.*
- *All teachers can easily teach this skill as part of their regular practice.*[2]

That is my kind of book on the topic of classroom improvements, and Rothstein and Santana are not alone in emphasizing questioning.[3] In Chapter 2, I noted the large body of research showing how little of it goes on in the average educational setting—whether we're talking about grade school, high school, college, or workplace training sessions. Recall James T. Dillon's observation, for example, that students who give voice to their curiosity got all sorts of negative reactions from both teachers and classmates. The lesson they took away from the experience was "Don't ask questions."[4] Scholars monitoring other classrooms and arenas of learning and decision-making have consistently come to the same conclusion: creative inquiry is an innate human behavior that gets actively suppressed and shut down in schools. And thus children grow into adults who take pride in having better answers but don't think to ask better questions.

Thanks to this ongoing line of research, school leaders today are frankly much more aware of the value of cultivating questioning skills. Unfortunately, it seems to get harder and harder to bring about change in educational systems. Mark Zuckerberg discovered this when he saw the results of his $100 million gift to the Newark public school system. In fact, the gift he announced in 2010 was matched by local donors, so the amount poured into the system was $200 million. Many smart consultants were brought in and changes were devised based on the best current methods. Everyone's intentions were good. The upshot, however, was that the infusion of cash barely moved the needle. Worse, students' math achievement slightly declined.[5]

My point in bringing up this high-visibility disappointment is not to conclude that we should abandon all hope of change on the public schools front. It is more of a suggestion that the most direct route to change may not be the top-down one of policy change at the institutional level. Perhaps this campaign to teach kids to question can succeed better as a kind of social movement in which individuals resolve to take action in all the ways they can have impact personally.

When I talk to teachers who are attuned to the need to develop students' questioning skills, they tell me about the low-cost, no-tradeoff ways in which they keep a spotlight on generative questions while covering the required curriculum to equip students for accurate answers on standardized tests. Here are a few practices I have seen, offered in the spirit of inspiring educators' own thinking, rather than in any attempt to be exhaustive:

Drawing on a Box of Questions. The Workshop School is an award-winning district high school in West Philadelphia that was specifically designed by a nonprofit organization to operate differently from typical schools; I will discuss the merits of its project-based learning model later. But some of its practices could fit easily enough into any classroom. Take, for example, the routine that is built into "circle" time each day when students discuss school and community problems to which they could try to come up with solutions. The workshop maintains a box of questions from which, in classic "job jar" fashion, one slip is randomly drawn every day. The students all respond to it. Even more important, the students are the ones who *add* to it. It's expected of them as learners to spend some time figuring out what they should be asking.

Noting the Question That Produced the Answer. Every fact that is taught in schools began its life as the answer to a question. Every formula started out with someone's need for a better way to solve a problem. It takes very little extra time for a teacher to frame a piece of information with this added historical context. To be sure, not every fact cited requires an origin story, but occasionally highlighting the great question that gave rise to an enduring answer delivers real benefits. It makes the answer more memorable by showing why the insight was important enough to arrive at in the first place, and it underscores how many of the facts schoolchildren learn in the future will come from fresh questions asked today. Similarly, in history lessons, teachers always name the person who came up with an invention or breakthrough insight and how things changed as a result—but they shouldn't leave out the crucial part where a different question was asked that led to it. Why did people in the time of Copernicus not know the sun was the center of the planetary system? How did he come to question the Earth-centric model, and how important was his question to opening up new pathways for understanding? By teaching the lesson as a narrative in which posing the question marks the turning point, teachers can make it clear that great insights in the past have always sprung from assumption-challenging questions, and will always do so in the future.

Increasing Wait Time. One classroom dynamic that teachers can easily become aware of and alter is wait time. Mary Budd Rowe was the first education scholar to note that most teachers don't wait long enough after asking questions to allow students to respond thoughtfully. What do you suppose she found to be the average wait time after a teacher's question? It was one second.

Clearly, that is not enough time to engage a student's higher cognitive faculties; it is only appropriate for retrieval of facts stored in memory. In studies Rowe conducted, a simple increase in wait time from one second to at least three seconds was associated with dramatic boosts in students' language and logic capabilities.[6] The big takeaway from this work is not that teachers should ask the same kinds of fact-retrieval questions, of course, and simply wait a few beats to call on someone. Longer wait times call for more thought-provoking questions, and vice versa.

Consistent across the studies of classroom questioning is the frequency with which teachers ask questions. They tend to be incessant, in the range of fifty to a hundred questions per hour. The use of questions in classrooms has long been, as Karron Lewis puts it, "to ascertain whether or not they were learning the book content and to see if students were paying attention in class." But this means that "teachers largely have been asking the wrong questions. We have been focusing primarily on questions regarding the specific information students possessed rather than questions to promote learning."[7] In fact, double damage happens here by neither serving the student's immediate learning need nor modeling to a young mind a questioning approach that, once internalized, will serve them well in the future.

Celebrating Questioners. A school is a social community as well as a learning institution, and students are acutely aware of who among them is succeeding. Doing more to praise and reward the students who ask good questions can change how many get asked. As I write this, a group of students who survived the February 14, 2018, mass shooting at Marjory Stoneman Douglas High School in Parkland, Florida, is making a very prominent show of asking questions: they are doing it at the level of the national conversation about gun control, with obvious conviction that their voices should be heard. No one in their school system is demanding that they take fewer days off from regular classes and come back and cram for their AP exams. It's an extreme example, but instructive. Scaling back from there, do students in other schools feel empowered to ask questions about the issues that affect them most, or perhaps challenge a lesson they suspect is not telling the whole story? As Sophie von Stumm and her colleagues write, schools "must early on encourage intellectual hunger and not exclusively reward the acquiescent application of intelligence and effort. . . . It is not only the diligent class winner who writes an excellent term paper but also the one who asks annoyingly challenging questions during the seminar (a habit that is, unfortunately, not appreciated by all teachers)."[8] Along the same lines, Christopher Uhl and Dana L. Stuchul write that "encouraging students to become fearless questioners means applauding them not so much for the correctness of their answers as for the audacity of their questions." They conclude that "transforming the contemporary classroom's pervasive fear of questions and preoccupation with answers into a school culture that celebrates and delights in questions is a monumental, yet utterly worthwhile, task."[9]

Orit Gadiesh, chairman of Bain & Company, is "always asking a hundred questions" because she knows that is the only way to solve a vexing challenge at work or in life. She learned this lesson early on when growing up in Israel. Her father was "curious about a lot of different things and would rather listen than talk," while her mother was "always asking questions about anything that she thought was interesting." Gadiesh came to see herself as "naturally curious" before ever stepping into a school. From her first class onward, she constantly put her hand in the air, asking not just one but often two or more questions on any topic. By the end of eighth grade her questioning skills were so sharp that her homeroom teacher wrote, "Orit, always ask those two questions, and even a third and a fourth question. Don't ever stop being curious." Throughout her career (early on in the military and afterwards in consulting), she has always known that asking the right questions is the only path to creating value—real value—at any level and in any role.

Leaning on Ed Tech to Achieve Answer Recall. It's possible in the age of e-learning tools to have our cake and eat it, too, when it comes to standardized test preparation, according to Ann Christensen, president of the Christensen Institute, and her colleagues. Probably the biggest thing that should be challenged at the system level in our schools is the "batch processing" model we use to advance age cohorts through grades. But even within that antiquated model, it is possible for a teacher with thirty students to provide more individualized instruction through technology that can easily detect where a given student struggles and what content he or she has already mastered, and respond accordingly. To the extent that classroom teachers employ e-learning tools to do test prep, they can free up time for personalized attention to higher-order learning skill development. Unburdened by the need to bring a whole classroom to the point of answering a set of closed-ended questions, the teachers can start acting as the Sherpas on learning journeys and stop feeling like the yaks.

Shifting to Project-Centered Learning. In mentioning the Workshop School earlier, I made passing reference to its commitment to project-centered learning. This is hardly a new idea; it is central to long-established pedagogies such as the Montessori method and the curriculum of International Baccalaureate schools. And it has everything to do with cultivating student curiosity. As Angeline Stoll Lillard writes about Montessori's system, it is "open enough to allow the evolution of interests and learning to happen organically. The Montessori teacher is not supposed to plant questions in the children, but only to stimulate their imaginations, such that children develop their own questions." She presents ample research showing that "learning based on such interests is superior to learning that has its roots in the interests of others."[10] In the study Clay Christensen, Jeff Dyer, and I did a decade ago, we found that about half these adult innovators had attended schools where learning was project-centered. Many others had parents or grandparents who encouraged challenging projects or were involved in community efforts that created that kind of space outside of school.

This is a harder change for a classroom teacher to effect without school system air cover, for sure. More commonly we see special schools set up in which these methods can be piloted. High Tech High, for example, was founded as a charter school more than fifteen years ago, thanks to a grant from the Bill & Melinda Gates Foundation, because many Silicon Valley employers believed a project-centered approach would do a better job of preparing the talent needed for innovation. It has since grown into a system serving over five thousand K–12 students in thirteen charter schools across three campuses. The point is for students to choose projects that are inherently interesting but require mastery of various learning concepts to complete. Having chosen the project, they are more motivated to do the learning, and the relevance of what they are learning is clear.

But it is useful to reflect on the beginnings of the Workshop School, which had its genesis in an after-school program where Simon Hauger invited kids to come work on cars. The program was called EVX and was specifically focused on installing hybrid systems in older models. Hauger recalls that for the students who participated, "suddenly there were these real problems that were driving the academic learning after school. What struck me is that the kids at school were learning more in my afterschool space than in my class."[11] This is the perspective that might inspire individual teachers who can't reinvent whole school systems. Some of them might win grants to create extracurricular programs based on project-centered learning principles. Just as important, the many who are already involved in after-school activities—the theater and band directors, prom committee advisors, sports coaches, and more—might see those activities with fresh eyes, as platforms for student learning about the power of questions.

Again, it is not the case that educators are actively against the notion that students should learn how to formulate their own questions, or don't believe it is possible to teach this skill as part of their regular practice. Awareness is growing that, as measures of whether students are really learning, questions are the answer.

One bright spot I noted recently is the essay prompt now included on the "Common App"—the standard application form accepted by virtually all colleges and universities in the United States. The key part of the application that allows a student to show the quality of their mind beyond standardized test scores and GPA is the required short essay. Among the thought starters provided by the application designers is this new option: "Reflect on a time when you questioned or challenged a belief or idea. What prompted your thinking? What was the outcome?" It's a great signal to students that, by the twelfth grade, many of them have experienced this already. What a pity, though, for those who, at the end of their high school careers, are considering that possibility for the first time.

Put simply, challenge-centered learning matters at school, work, and in life. Peter Diamandis, founder and chairman of the XPRIZE Foundation and cofounder and executive chairman of

Singularity University, knows this well. He was asked at a recent Innovation Partnership Program (led by Kian Gohar, executive director): "What matters in the future of education?" His response was telling, especially as the father of two young children. He said, "What I want to teach my kids is how to ask the right questions and how to keep being passionate about challenges. That's all that matters in the future in education because standard models of rote memorization won't matter. You're going to have intelligence systems that will help you with that. So how do you ask the right kinds of questions about the things you're passionate about, to do inquiry and exploration?"

WHAT AGE CAN YOU START BEING AN ARTIST?

In my experience, the settings that have been specially designed by educators to encourage students' questioning are nothing less than inspiring. Take, for example, Room 13 International, a model of after-school activity that began quite accidentally in Scotland in 1994 and has spread globally since. The original Room 13 was the classroom made available to an artist in residence named Rob Fairley who had been hired on at Caol Primary School under a one-year grant. Fairley was especially effective because he not only helped the kids with their art techniques, he emphasized how to think. Making art, he urged them to recognize, was not a means of reproducing what was in front of their eyes—it was a way to investigate it, and to produce something new. When the year was up, the students wanted him to stay, but that meant finding a way to fund the arrangement. Their decision to set up their studio as a business, where proceeds from sales of their work would cover the cost of materials and instruction, was a stroke of genius.

It made for a project-centered learning experience on a whole new level. Room 13 is student-led, and the artist in residence is its employee. Students make up the management team that makes day-to-day decisions on how to pay the bills.

A big turning point happened in 2004, when a documentary created by Room 13 students in partnership with a filmmaker aired on Britain's Channel 4. It was called *What Age Can You Start Being an Artist?* It happened that Rod Wright, a director of the global advertising giant TBWA, was tuned in to that channel and saw a connection with his own deep interest in developing the creative potential of children growing up in poor communities around the world. Wright was soon in touch with the ten-year-old managing director of Room 13, pledging the funds for her and her classmates to expand the concept much further.

Artists at heart from Room 13 in Kewtown Primary School, Athlone, Cape Town, South Africa.

A management team "to do" list—including a reminder to prepare the presentation for the Scottish parliament and to follow up on the open "assistant treasurer" position—in Room 13 Caol Primary School, Caol, Scotland (founded in 1994).

A "Help Wanted" ad created by kids for kids in Room 13 Caol Primary School, Caol, Scotland (founded in 1994).

Haroon Collier (far left in the back), artist-in-residence at Kewtown Primary School, often spends evenings and weekends here, without pay, to give kids a safe harbor.

Today there are about seventy Room 13s worldwide, from Africa to China to the United States. Room 13 arrived in North America when a nonprofit arts organization called Light Bringer Project established one in South Los Angeles in 2008, followed by more in California. Others have cropped up in North Carolina, Indiana, Missouri, and Colorado.

In Room 13, artists learn to pay even better attention to the world around them. When visiting studios in South Africa, I noticed how much children's artwork reflected sounds heard, images seen, and things witnessed that might horrify adults. Marie Jamieson, managing director for TBWA South Africa, recalls one such example:

The first picture that really screamed at my soul was by a young artist from Soweto; his name was Nzakho and he was thirteen years of age. It was oil on canvas and was simply a picture of a middle-aged African man with a big paunch pulling up his trousers, doing up his zipper. In big letters the message on the picture is simply "Let's Stop Rape Please." That picture lives with me. It is in my office, and anytime when I am running and at my wit's end and I am stressed, and I have got to do something or I have to give back, that picture is my reason for being involved in Room 13. It's a thirteen-year-old boy who is crying out to stop rape in the community. He told me that it was not something he had experienced directly but he was screaming out loud to put a stop to this in his community. That is the voice of Room 13.

With full awareness of how difficult the kids' everyday challenges can be, artists in residence not only help young people see

BOTTOM LEFT Effortless concentration and energized focus by students in Room 13, Sapebuso Primary School, Soweto, South Africa.

We are all works of art in progress, as John Hunt detected while watching this young man in Room 13, St. Martin de Porres High School, Soweto, South Africa. John Hunt

their world better through all five senses. They help them make better sense of what they observe, by transforming insights into powerful art about themselves. John Hunt, creative director TBWA, shared one student's moving experience:

One conversation with an artist sticks out the most and I have a photo of the mosaic here on my wall. He had been doing a paper collage for months and months and months. He had been coming in every day and did very little each day because he was meticulous about how he built it. I watched him trying the pieces of light brown and then dark brown paper torn from old magazines, all with such precision that I had to talk to him. He was very friendly with a big smile and I said, "How long have you been doing this?" He said, "Seven or eight months," and I said, "Wow." Then I said to him, "Do you know who this is? Do you know who you are building, the face?" And he said, "No." And I'm thinking to myself, "Really?" I had my cell phone with me and took a picture of him and laid it beside the mosaic; he was building himself, and it seems crazy, but he didn't know it. I'm not a psychologist, but it seemed like he was building himself piece by piece—but how, without a picture of himself? Perhaps that was why it was taking so long. Or perhaps he simply didn't want to finish himself quite yet.

EXTRACURRICULAR QUESTIONING

If Room 13 and other extracurricular activities are creating better spaces for questioning in schools, plenty of other organizations are aiming to do the same off school grounds. I spoke with Betsy Bowers when she was at the Smithsonian Early Enrichment Center in Washington. She now manages the Lakewood Heritage Center outside Denver (a museum of the twentieth century that consists of fifteen acres, several historic buildings, and a collection of over 35,000 artifacts). She told me, "There's still some occasional controversy about whether a museum is an appropriate place for a child under the age of six." But she and her colleagues feel strongly that they can make an important contribution to learning. "I feel like museums have this capacity, with their authentic objects, and their interesting displays, to inspire questions in really exciting ways," she said.

Cirque du Soleil is pursuing a similar line with its Cirque du Monde initiative. Set up as the organization's humanitarian arm, this program was created in 1994 to train children internationally as street performers. The point is not to grow Cirque's next generation of elite performers; it is to use circus arts to bring a sense of purpose and discipline to at-risk youth, and to provide a setting in which people from very different backgrounds collaborate and learn to trust one another.

One thing I want to underscore is that Cirque du Monde is itself the result of a reframed question. Most people involved in running circuses are asking themselves: What would it take to create an even greater circus event? It's the mission that drives Cirque du Soleil every day. But Cirque du Monde asks: How could the staging of a circus event help people who might otherwise be struggling in society? In this reformulation, the circus is not the end but the means—a tool for achieving social change. That reframing of the question has unleashed a tremendous amount of energy. To date, Cirque du Monde has pursued its implications in more than ninety projects around the globe. And beyond Cirque's own efforts, the concept of "social circus" has taken hold in other settings. Cirque du Monde doesn't see this as threatening competition—it sees it as thrilling contagion. On its own website, it maintains a map of social circuses around the world, which continue to proliferate. Daniel Lamarre, CEO at Cirque du Soleil, summarizes Cirque du Monde's unique impact as "using circus art as a way to intervene with youth at risk, improve that, and help make it a snowball effect around the planet towards that end."

While teaching social entrepreneurs at INSEAD in France and the UAE, I learned of many other organizations, including the Real Ideas Organisation, Dreams Academy, and the Partners for Youth Empowerment (PYE), that encourage and educate young people to take on projects of real consequence. Junior Achievement has always had the mission to prepare young people to start the new businesses society needs. Its signature program is a fifteen-week project to create an entrepreneurial venture. In 2019 the organization will celebrate one hundred years since it was founded by business leaders Horace Moses of the Strathmore Paper Company and Theodore Vail of AT&T. My initial insight into the program came from getting to know the amazing Soraya Salti, who led INJAZ Al-Arab, the Middle East/North Africa region of Junior Achievement Worldwide. This part of the world is afflicted with the highest levels of youth unemployment—a problem that produces the worst ripple effects imaginable—but before her very untimely death in 2015, Salti was able to leave her profound mark on this world. Her expansion of INJAZ into fifteen countries, reaching more than 1 million youth, made her the first Arab woman to win the Skoll Award for Social Entrepreneurship.

What does her work have to do with raising questioners? As she explained it to me, pretty much everything. Salti recognized that the young population of the Middle East and North Africa were being terribly under-equipped for the world of work by education systems that assumed their best job opportunities would be in government agencies. To make the marks and pass the examinations required to gain those jobs, they were drilled in "rote memorization" of facts and were not encouraged in the least to take note of the changing world around them. That kind of education might have prepared them for jobs that involved adhering to protocols and making decisions only within tight parameters. But the demographics of the region created a youth bulge that meant there were millions more job hunters than there were government jobs on offer. And the destructive irony was that, as the region's average education attainment rose, its population only became less fit for employment in the private sector.[12] By putting together the public-private partnerships that could bring Junior Achievement's educational offerings to these countries, Salti made young people capable of more than spitting out good answers. They were—and still are, thanks to the foundations she laid—learning to ask better questions by building their own businesses.[13]

A DIGITAL HEAVEN FOR QUESTIONING—OR HELL?

One big question regarding the mental habits of the rising generations is: What is the digital environment doing for our questioning powers? Is it good or bad? All the screen time that children have today is a big natural experiment. Will they turn out to be the greatest generation ever in terms of their ability to frame catalytic questions? Or the most stunted?

In some ways, the digital world is a questioner's nirvana. We have all become accustomed to posing questions to Google, and we are well rewarded for that impulse with (usually) good answers. Our volume of questioning rises steadily as a result. We are often less inhibited in the questions we pose in Web chat sessions and forums. This is something well observed in very different parts of the world.

Dhirendra Kumar works at Value Research, a stock advisory company. Based on its experience of fielding questions from small investors through its website, he has concluded "a web chat is a very different forum for asking and answering questions." He has done his share of Q & A sessions at live events for investors, and he thinks the people posing questions online are the same kinds who attend those. But on the Web, he says, "because they are essentially anonymous and don't have to interact with each other, people ask questions much more frankly, being less apprehensive about appearing to be novices." Another effect of that lack of inhibition is that they tend to pose "more spontaneous kinds of questions."[4]

Meanwhile, Doreen Kessy, who interacts with a very different clientele, looks forward to the same lifting of inhibitions. Kessy is one of the cofounders of an educational television series in Tanzania. Called *Ubongo Kids*, it teaches math lessons by putting its animated characters into situations where they must solve problems. Most interesting, it allows for viewers to interact with what they are watching using their mobile phones. If they answer a multiple-choice question via SMS, they get feedback and encouragement from the show's characters. In its first six-month season in 2014, *Ubongo Kids* reached over 1.4 million unique viewers and its impact on math learning outcomes for Tanzanian primary school students was measurable. But Kessy sees many more opportunities for *Ubongo Kids*, including serving the mothers of those children, who often don't give voice to their questions.

Some of the women's questions are straightforward, life-and-death matters: "What are the symptoms for malaria? How do you have a healthy diet? Is it okay to give a newborn water? How does birth control work?" But Kessy notes that "many communities across Africa are incredibly conservative, and it may be deemed inappropriate for girls and women to ask questions regarding sensitive subjects like reproductive health, sex, religion, politics, and societal norms." She sees digital technologies as the key to empowering women to ask away and better protect their health and well-being.

Tony Wagner holds a fellowship in innovation education at Harvard—that there is such a fellowship is in itself a good sign—and he founded the Change Leadership Group at the Harvard Graduate School of Education. He consults to schools and foundations, including as an advisor to the Bill & Melinda Gates Foundation. He started his career as a high school teacher and did a stint as a

K–8 principal. His experience told him that "questions are stifled by teachers believing they have to 'cover' so much or prepare kids for tests and so have no time for questions. I think this response does serious damage to kids' curiosity." After reading *The World Is Flat*, by Thomas L. Friedman, he asked himself, *So what must we do differently to prepare kids for a "flat world"?* That inquiry led to three bestselling books tackling the question. Wagner is convinced that the overall effect of the new digital environment on young learners is a good one. In *Creating Innovators*, he writes that "the result of this new form of learning is that many of our youth, whom I call the Innovation Generation, have extraordinary latent talent for— and interest in—innovation and entrepreneurship, likely more than any generation in history." He explains why that would be the case: "On the Internet, unlike in their daytime classrooms, young people act on their curiosity. . . . [T]hey 'google stuff for fun' and love following hyperlinks to see where they may lead." They have, he concludes, "learned to create, connect, and collaborate on the Internet—far more so than they are ever allowed to do in school."[15] To take online learning deeper, he suggests that teachers (and I would add, parents) have their kids keep a question journal and then make time periodically for kids to research their questions.

On the other hand, the digital environment can also be toxic for questioning, and concerns about its effect continue to grow. My friend Tiffany Shlain, for example, is about as digitally hip as they come (as is her husband, Ken Goldberg, a professor at UC Berkeley in the field of robotics and automation). Quick to recognize that the Web would be a transformational force, she was founder of the Webby Awards and the cofounder of the International Academy of Digital Arts and Sciences. But even she does not want it shaping her children's thinking and conversational habits too thoroughly. Her family observes a "technology Shabbat"—a day of rest each week from devices when they will be completely present for visiting friends and each other.

What are they taking a break from? Largely the world of social media with its armies of trolls and venters. Think of the person posting comments avidly on a site like Facebook or Twitter, or responding to news stories published online, and you don't picture someone who is open to assumption-challenging questions. It isn't the image of the person trying to discover they are wrong. They are not getting out of their echo chamber. They are certainly not being quiet. And those are the postings with someone's name and face attached to them. In the case of anonymous or disguised postings, social media undermines questioning, not because there are no questions posed on it, but because so many of the questions are posed with belittling and abusive intent, especially for teenagers in today's world.

As in perhaps every other area of life, the digital influences on questioning would appear to be a mixed bag. Instant connectivity to the world's information sources is a priceless and positive development, but don't expect the Internet, left to its own devices, to raise a new generation of better questioners. The important question to consider is: Is this technology helping me and those I love to embrace conditions of being a little more wrong, uncomfortable, and quiet? And if it isn't, consider changing the conditions.

QUESTIONING BEGINS AT HOME

Parents and caregivers, more than anyone, must take responsibility for raising children to question creatively. Habits of mind get established very early in life, as much work by neuroscientists is revealing. This is not to say that new habits can't be established later, but the opportunity to shape how the brain will respond to information is greatest in childhood. If we want to raise a generation of better questioners, we should try harder to influence what happens at home.

The power dynamics discussed in Chapter 2 certainly infect households, and in too many homes children are discouraged from asking the questions that could open up new possibilities for health and happiness. Contrariwise, almost every creative thinker I have interviewed, when I have thought to bring up the topic of their childhood, has told me how their curiosity was actively fueled early on.

Diane Greene, for example, who cofounded VMware, told me about being raised near a bay, with "a father in love with sailing," and being given free rein to "go on incredibly independent adventures" in her rowboat. Growing up on open water helped her learn that "if a puzzle can't be solved one way, there's always another. It's just a matter of navigation." Debbie Sterling, founder of GoldieBlox, had an upbringing full of international travel thanks to her father's work and was constantly having her cultural understandings challenged. Mir Imran's parents encouraged him to tinker, create, and take apart whatever he was interested in. Over time they ended up buying two of anything complicated to allow him to take one of them apart. He went on to medical school, then to found nineteen companies, and at last count had some 140 patents to his name.

Imran's story reminded me of Amazon founder Jeff Bezos's memories of summers spent on his grandfather's farm in Texas. Bezos said his creative and "extremely self-reliant" grandfather once bought a tractor that didn't work expressly to give himself and young Jeff a problem to figure out together. Over the course of those endless summers, Bezos came to realize that his grandfather was "really focused on solving problems" and "had an optimism that he could solve problems even in areas, like veterinary work, where he had no training." Bezos emerged from the experience with a "relentless problem-solving self-reliance" that serves him, and Amazon, well to this day.[16]

Of all the people I have talked to about their upbringing, Carrie Schaal may have had the parent most determined to build her child's questioning skills. Schaal, by the way, makes her living today as a corporate educator at AstraZeneca, working to train its oncology sales teams. Her father was a lifelong educator. "I would say he's the person who probably taught me best how to question," she told me, "because anytime I went to my dad with a problem, he would never solve it for me. He would only ask me questions." You may be imagining, as I did, that her father was simply throwing out a few helpful pointers, but evidently it went further than that. "There was a time when I was probably ten years old," she recalled, "when I said: 'Dad, I just want the answer. I don't want you to go through Bloom's taxonomy!'"

Schaal laughs now about the occasional irritations of growing up in a household that thought so hard about questioning. "I just need the answer," she would protest, "Should I keep going out with this boy or not? Like, I don't need an evaluation or a synthesis question here—just give it to me." But today she applies all those questioning habits in her work and, in retrospect, she admits: "That was a great, great gift."

David McCullough, in his biography of the Wright Brothers, mentions Orville Wright's reaction when a friend commented that he and Wilbur were great examples of how far a person "with no special advantages" could go in America. "But it isn't true to say we had no special advantages . . . ," Orville responded emphatically. "[T]he greatest thing in our favor was growing up in a family where there was always much encouragement to intellectual curiosity."[17]

Just as often in my interviews, if I am talking to people who have children themselves, I hear about their eagerness to pass along questioning habits to members of the next generation they love most. Bea Perez, for example, is someone who has always struck me as a great questioner in her role heading up sustainability initiatives at the Coca-Cola Company and as a leader who creates good questioning spaces for her teams. Knowing she also has two school-age children, I couldn't resist asking: "Are there any things you do with intentionality to help them become better questioners, or to keep their questioning spirit alive?"

Sure enough, there are things she does. The one I will pass along is the rule in her house that anyone can "call a family meeting" at the dinner hour to get help in thinking about a topic of concern. When a dinner has been so designated, "my husband and I don't talk first," Perez told me, "we go from youngest to oldest." In one "table talk" session she related, it was the littlest who had a social situation at school to sort out. After she described it, it was her older brother who spoke next, and his job was to raise some questions to provide ways of thinking more deeply about the problem. Then Perez did the same, and finally her husband. Each question prompts some discussion, but it is up to the person who calls the meeting to get what they need from each segment and decide when to move on to the next person. Frankly, I was astonished to hear of such a thoughtfully crafted practice to turn dinnertime into an opportunity to both solve problems and cultivate questioning skills. And such an easily copied one—which is why I happily share it here.

Also easy enough to copy is Michael Sippey's habit in reading to his kids. He told me he deliberately chooses book series about kids similar in age to his, but very dissimilar in circumstances, so that the tale he's telling will raise "a lot of questions about how they lived, about politics, about why they are going West . . ." The series he was reading at the time happened to be the *Little House on the Prairie* stories by Laura Ingalls Wilder, and it had led to a "great multi-month conversation about the history of the United States, about settlers moving West, about what it must have been like to live in that time." Almost all parents read to their children, but this is a parent giving a little extra thought to his reading choices because he also wants to give his kids the habit of questioning.

Finally, when I asked Lior Div of Cybereason whether his own intense introspection as a learner affected what he teaches his kids, he said, "The answer is yes. It's about failure. It's about encouraging them to try, and not to give them the answers. To teach them to ask the questions. Because if you give people answers all the time, especially kids, then they start to get used to just waiting for the right answer. The thing is they should understand from an early age that there is not one right answer. There are different answers and different ways that can lead you to achieve what you want. If you can teach them that, then it's very enabling."

THE CAMPUS CHALLENGE

"Most people never encounter much thinking in a typical introductory college course. Instead, their professors feed them a plate of well-barbequed facts to memorize, never offering many hints about how these morsels had been cooked, how anyone came to believe them, how anyone had tackled ill-structured problems." So claims Ken Bain in his account of higher education and what the best college students somehow manage to do.[18] "Introductory courses rarely offer mysteries, reasoning opportunities, or challenges other than the necessity of stuffing it all in your brain before the exam," he continues. "Students typically develop little understanding of how the discipline raises and answers questions. They seldom examine messy, complex questions or even hear how anyone else does so."

Many are shocked about the state of campuses today, in which students seem incapable of engaging in civil discourse. Competing ideas are sometimes kept from being uttered at all, let alone engaged with. Is there anything that can be done to take students past the age of eighteen and turn them into more creative and productive questioners? I believe the answer is yes. All hope is not lost if the child has not learned early.

Owen Fiss, the longtime law professor at Yale, published a career-capping book in 2017. Called *Pillars of Justice*, it devotes a chapter each to thirteen lawyers who influenced his thinking—and, not incidentally, also left their marks on the world. The portraits he paints have as much to say about great leadership and inspired teaching—and the crucial role of asking questions in both—as about the evolving legal doctrine of the civil rights era.

Take, for example, his account of how he was mentored by Harry Kalven, a leading light at the University of Chicago Law School—an apprenticeship that started when Fiss joined its faculty in the summer of 1968. As Fiss describes their interactions, they always began with a question, which grew into an "intense, all-absorbing" dialogue as the two walked through a nearby perennial flower garden and along the Chicago lakefront. "His method was conversation," Fiss writes of Kalven:

> *He would manage to find in the words of the apprentice glimmers of insight, which he would then restate in terms so eloquent*

and profound that they deepened understanding and encouraged further inquiry and comment. The apprentice felt obliged to say more, to think harder, to look at the problem from a new perspective. The conversation became an escalation of insights. That was the core of my apprenticeship with Harry. It was one of the most extraordinary experiences of my life, and it revealed the special qualities of the master.

Fiss concludes that "Harry Kalven was a genius, a completely original intelligence . . ." Whether the two of them were discussing a recent Supreme Court decision, a political event, or the future of legal education, he says, "My view of the world would almost always change." Perhaps you've had your own great teacher that, on reflection, you realize had a knack for "escalating insights" by asking questions—and, even better, encouraging you to ask better ones yourself.

Owen Fiss makes clear that, as well as knowing his share of inspirational thinkers, he has also experienced the corrosive effects of bad teaching. He tells the cringe-inducing story of a professor in his first year at Harvard Law, back when a class of about 125 students included only three or four women:

Now and then students volunteered a comment or posed a question, but for the most part Leach conducted his classes by calling on students to recite the facts of a case or answer a question he put to them. At the beginning of the course, though, Leach announced that he would not call on any of the women students on a regular basis. Instead he would designate one or two "Ladies' Days," during which the women students, and only the women students, would be called on.

To this day, it rankles Fiss that he and his classmates didn't object on the spot to this obnoxious marginalization. Instead, "we said nothing, not a note of disapproval, not even a whimper." If Kalven's effect on his students was an escalation of insights, then this man's was just as surely a degradation of them. I suspect it's no coincidence that the other aspect Fiss recalls about him is his stunted form of questioning.[19]

Teachers who make good use of questions—the kinds that challenge assumptions and draw others into intense, all-absorbing dialogues—produce protégés who don't hesitate to defy traditional thinking themselves. Whether it's an outdated preconception that needs to be confronted or an outright prejudice, the person who rises to the occasion will be someone who transcended the traditional student role and learned how to question.[20]

My MIT colleague Robert Langer, the health care technology innovator who has been called "the Edison of medicine," has similar goals on the educational front. In a recent interview he said: "When you're a student, you're judged by how well you answer questions. Somebody else asks the questions, and if you give good answers, you'll get a good grade. But in life, you're judged by how good your questions are." As he mentors his students and postdocs, he explicitly focuses their attention on making this all-important transition, knowing "they'll become great professors, great entrepreneurs, great something—if they ask good questions."

NEVER TOO LATE

Finally, a few words for managers, who also have their vital role to play in raising the next generation of high-impact questioners. People often arrive in workplaces without strong questioning habits. But any job change plunges a person into active learning mode, as they come up to speed on "how things work around here" in the new place. In that state, they can be shaped by their bosses' and colleagues' influence—in fact, there is no escaping that they will be shaped by it. What can you do to make it more clear to all your colleagues that questioning is valued?

First, think about the conditions you create or contribute to—which is the overarching theme of this book. I mentioned earlier the marketing agency TBWA's support of Room 13. That company's emphasis on encouraging creativity in children is of course connected to its own imperative to be creative in its own work. John Hunt, the company's worldwide creative director, decided that in the spirit of the Room 13 kids he would produce a creative product himself and channel the proceeds to their organization. The result is the book *The Art of the Idea*, and Hunt says he wrote it for two reasons: "First of all, I noticed there were certain 'patterns' around situations where ideas seemed to float or sink. I'd always thought having an idea was a purely intuitive moment. So the observation that different things could be conducive to an idea, or block one, intrigued me. And, secondly, I wanted to explain that ideas do not have a hierarchy, nor do you have to be blessed in any special way. Anyone can have an idea."[21]

Since realizing this, Hunt has tried more deliberately to create those settings in his own office that are conducive to ideas—or at least don't block them—and to signal his expectation that everyone should be contributing them. Having this mindset causes him to commit micro-encouragements that ultimately, collectively, do more to build the culture than any formal practices.

You can do the same by, for example, speaking up in support of the questioners among your colleagues. Don't do this only in private solidarity with the brave soul who asked a question you did not dare to. Support that person—and the others asking good questions you hadn't thought of—in the moment and in the open. Others in the room are taking note of whether and how that act will be acknowledged. Convey quite explicitly, as Walt Bettinger does at Charles Schwab, that it is everyone's job to be probing matters like "What's broken around here?"

You can also make it a habit to expose your team and colleagues to thought-provoking stimuli. For that matter, do the same for your clients. At EY, the global professional services firm, the power of questions has become a theme that informs everything from the firm's internal leadership development to its client service methods to its multimillion-dollar brand campaign. Perhaps you have seen its ads in airports and major media, all of which feature compelling photographs and headlines in the form of questions. A typical one: How Do You Steer the Business When AI Is Running the Ship? Recently I have gotten to know the marketer behind the "better questions, better answers" campaign, John Rudaizky, and heard how its ambitions go far beyond the usual advertising slogans.

When Rudaizky joined EY, the firm had just adopted a tagline of "Building a Better Working World," which its new chairman, Mark Weinberger, did not see as just a marketing promise to customers. It was also a message to the firm's own professionals who, like all workers, want to know that their work is meaningful. This is what great advisors to global businesses do, he wanted them to understand: they cause their clients' organizations to be better managed, helping the "working world" to be better. And by increasing those clients' capacity to do good work, they cause the world to be "better working." The cleverness of a tagline that could be read in either way was irresistible. Rudaizky's task was to take it a big step further and communicate just how EY professionals do that.

He found his answer in questions. "In talking to people it soon became apparent," he says. Great consultants don't just provide answers to the questions clients ask, or solutions to the problems their clients have identified. They help the client arrive at better questions which, if they could be answered, would make a much bigger difference. "Every problem we help solve for a client helps our working world get better," he says. "Question by question, answer by answer, we can ladder up to build a better working world."

An important thing to note is that EY is also redefining what a great advertising campaign should accomplish. Rather than just changing the market's perception of a company, it should change how the company's people approach their work. It can get them using questions with each other more. As Mark Weinberger put it to me, "Instead of saying, 'Go do A, B, and C,' it's better to say, 'This is my outcome I'd like to achieve—how would you go about doing it?' and then enter into dialogue." In his own experience, Weinberger says, "It's amazing how much better project work, even from young staff people, you get back when you ask them instead of telling them." It can also get them rethinking how to serve clients. "Where the rubber hits the road for this campaign," Rudaizky muses, "is that our practices are using it directly, by going in and reframing the questions with their clients." He offered some examples of "early adopters" of the new brand promise—among them, a partner named Pamela Spence who won a groundbreaking project for EY "because the client asked one question and she reframed it into a better one."

In your own work with colleagues and clients, you can have a similar impact on the perspectives of those around you. Think about using a version of the question box at the Workshop School—a thought starter at the beginning of meetings to get

"Breathtaking" is how I describe Innovation Realized, an annual EY client retreat Gil Forer and his creative team deliver (in collaboration with C2), where multisensory spaces and experiences—including Question Bursts—spark catalytic questions and insights about key global challenges.

Sitting in chairs suspended thirty feet off the floor is a perfect place to discuss strategies for breaking down glass ceilings and building up gender parity in c-suites and boardrooms around the world.

EY works hard—at Innovation Realized and beyond—to cultivate creative conditions where anyone can choose to ask better questions and, hopefully, shape a slightly wiser world.

people thinking bigger about the job to be done. Or include an article in the prereading that they wouldn't normally run across but that offers an analogy or explains an important, gathering trend. Maybe organize a visit to a customer site or bring in a guest speaker. Or keep a question journal as a leader, as Richard Branson, founder of Virgin Group, has done all his life, and draw on it to spark conversations. Whichever provocation you choose, the key is to debrief afterward: What did gaining that information or perspective suggest in terms of questions we should be asking—and answering?

It is critical, too, that people in your organization see good questions spurring real follow-up. Ultimately they know that their creative input isn't valued if nothing ever happens as a result of it. Make sure that enough of the questions they raise are pursued to the point of producing new insight and true impact—and when impact is achieved, tell the story of how a reframed question unlocked that opportunity for value creation. In fact, whenever you are celebrating a breakthrough, trace it back to the question it constitutes a better answer to—and tell its story in a way that highlights why that was the right question to ask.

Model the questioning behaviors you want to see by visibly engaging in them yourself. A good friend of mine has been a C-suite executive at a Fortune 50 company for many years, and we have often talked about the value of raising fresh questions to arrive at better answers. She has done much to create a sense of safety in her teams, encouraging them to challenge assumptions. But recently she told me about how she felt she had failed them. "I was doing the same kind of questioning with the people above my level, but never felt I should do it in a group setting, in case it was perceived as aggressive." Obviously her own bosses were not taking the same care she did to signal that such questioning was welcome and expected—but the realization hit her that whether she held her tongue wasn't only up to them. By failing to model for her team that a manager should be free-thinking and curious in the company of higher-ranking executives, she now thinks she undercut the habits she was trying to instill in them—at a time when the company needed all the creative thinking it could get.

Mike Inserra of EY raised a very similar point in our conversation. His own observation is that the younger generations in the workforce tend to be "much more free to offer up their perspective"—at least at first. The problem is that "more seasoned folks then pick and choose where they share those questions" beyond that initial conversation. The fact that some of their challenges to the system end up going no further is not lost on the junior employees. "I think that's why some of the younger folks do then end up hesitating to offer up their questions more publicly. It's because they feel the leaders hesitating to do that same thing."

EXPECT DIFFERENT QUESTIONS

Progress in any generation is driven most by the members of that generation who are able to frame and focus on the right questions for their era. The issues that consume our attention today are not ones that captivated our parents and will not be the most riveting ones for our children. The implication is that, as we raise a new generation of questioners, we are also raising a new generation of questions. Some of them will be hard for us to see as better ones, or as important reframings of matters we have already figured out for ourselves.

I have always loved how Antoine de Saint-Exupéry expresses this tension in *The Little Prince*. In that classic children's story, the narrator makes a kind of apology for having deduced that the Prince came from the tiny asteroid B-612:

> *If I have told you these details about the asteroid, and made a note of its number for you, it is on account of the grown-ups and their ways. When you tell them that you have made a new friend, they never ask you any questions about essential matters. They never say to you, "What does his voice sound like? What games does he love best? Does he collect butterflies?" Instead, they demand: "How old is he? How many brothers has he? How much does he weigh? How much money does his father make?" Only from these figures do they think they have learned anything about him.*[22]

To an older generation, a younger generation's questions can often just seem like the wrong ones to ask. And thus we have too many children living in home environments where questioning is shut down. Too many school systems and communities are structured to silence their voices.

My own campaign to change the state of questioning in our society is what I call the 4-24 Project. It's a quiet but sustained effort to keep growing a community that has committed to set aside just four minutes every twenty-four hours to engage in focused questioning. The four-minute commitment is based on the Question Burst methodology I explained in Chapter 3, since it can accomplish a lot in that amount of time. But that particular exercise doesn't have to be a daily approach, and it is probably better to mix things up from day to day in terms of just how the question generation is done. Conveniently, four minutes a day adds up to one day per year devoted to deliberate, creative inquiry—not too much to ask, especially of someone already motivated to enhance their creativity and find fresh answers to vexing problems.[23]

We need to have more faith that by allowing more questions to be raised, by giving voice to the voiceless, we will benefit from many better questions among them. Some challenges and opportunities will be bigger and more broadly inspiring than others. Most important, we must recognize that the world's biggest problems remain to be solved and that solving them absolutely depends on the next generation asking better questions. Will our human minds be equal to the challenges? We turn to that subject next.

9

Why Not Aim for the Biggest Questions?

I wrote the song "Show Me" as a prayer to God
asking simple, honest questions about life and death
and why there is so much **suffering** in the world.
As I grew with the song I realized
I shouldn't limit these questions solely to God;
I should ask those questions of others and of myself.
—JOHN LEGEND

For Gary Slutkin, the question that would energize two decades of groundbreaking work came in the late 1990s. He was living in Chicago, having come back to America after years in Africa working to stop the spread of infectious diseases. By this point, gun violence had become a fact of life in Chicago's toughest neighborhoods. Slutkin noticed how many initiatives and crackdowns had failed to disrupt the cycle of murderous retaliations on the streets. One day it struck him that the flaws in these particular solutions might not be the problem. Maybe the fundamental nature of the problem needed radical redefinition. What if the shootings were cast as a *public health* phenomenon rather than a criminal justice challenge? Could thinking about the measures one would use with, say, cholera, possibly lead to more effective interventions? In short, was gun violence literally contagious?

For the field of psychology, a transformative question took hold when Martin Seligman became president of the American Psychological Association. Before 1988 virtually all well-trained psychologists focused on attacking the roots of mental disorders and deficits on the assumption that human well-being came down to the absence of these negative attributes. Seligman reframed things for his colleagues in a speech at the APA's annual meeting. What if, he asked, well-being is just as driven by the *presence* of certain *positive* elements—keys to flourishing that could be recognized, measured, and cultivated? In other words, what if psychologists shifted their focus from the *wrong* to the *strong*?

The modern environmental movement had its start in the questions Rachel Carson somewhat reluctantly decided to put into the public's mind. In the 1950s, Carson was a trained biologist who had turned her hand to writing engaging books and articles to introduce the wonders of the oceans to popular audiences. But in the course of researching and writing her sunny explanations of ecosystems, she kept hearing about and seeing the damage of pesticides, foremost among them DDT. She published *Silent Spring* in 1962 to challenge the notion that humans should try to dominate nature by the use of chemistry. "Can anyone believe it is possible to lay down such a barrage of poisons on the surface of the earth without making it unfit for all life?" she asked. And: "We are rightly appalled by the genetic effects of radiation. How then, can we be indifferent to the same effect in chemicals that we disseminate widely in our environment?" Carson was fond of writing in the form of questions, and by asking them she catalyzed the actions of millions.

Some questions, in short, are bigger than others. This book began with the observation that new questions are the (often unacknowledged) parents of novel insights, in business and also in many other settings. The work of the book has been to impress upon you that this is a skill you can acquire. And it is a skill we can collectively pass on to the next generation. All of this has led up to the message of this chapter: that part of becoming a greater questioner is developing the capability, and the temerity, to frame questions of larger scope. The bigger the problem or opportunity in the world, the bigger the insight we need—and the bigger the questions we should be prepared to ask.

TO ASK A MIGHTY QUESTION

Definitely, some people are better than others at asking big questions. Elon Musk comes immediately to mind. In the first conversation I had with him, the subject turned to his rare feat of building several highly valued companies across completely different industries. His first start-up was Zip2, offering software for the Web. PayPal is a financial services company. Tesla is an automotive manufacturer. SpaceX builds reusable rockets. The Boring Company is a transportation infrastructure company. How could the same person provide leadership in all these realms?

Musk highlighted two aspects of how he approaches problems in general, and hinted at a few other keys to his ventures' success. The first thing he mentioned is something I've already noted in Chapter 1: his belief in going back to "first principles" to find better solutions. It means recognizing that, with regard to any problem, there are assumptions that have grown up over the years as to what can be altered versus what is simply reality that must be accepted. Second, Musk noted that many fresh solutions are the products of cross-fertilization of ideas from different domains. "A lot of people who spend a long time trying to figure out how to solve tough problems in one industry don't ask, 'Well, is there some way we could apply that solution to a different industry?'" he noted. "And that can be really, really powerful."

As for what he hinted at, his comments when I asked about the Hyperloop were revealing. Musk himself marveled at how that notion took off. It began with an offhand remark he made on a stage in Santa Monica. "I was trying to explain why I was so late for the talk, and I said that we really need new forms of transport—and that 'I think I have an idea for a new form of transport.'" In truth, that idea was little more than a whim, as described earlier. He had literally just envisioned the concept within the previous hour. But immediately "the Internet wouldn't let me go. I got hounded constantly: 'What is this idea you said you would tell us about?' I'm, like, 'Aw, man.'" He told us his initial version of how it could work didn't actually hold up, and the concept had to be reworked. When he arrived at a feasible version, he "wrote this paper with the support of some of my colleagues, and published it, did a Twitter link, and did a half hour of press Q & A." Hyperloop, in other words, was not overhyped. "So, yeah," he concluded, "anyway, that's what happened there."

Wait a minute, though. Could we probe a little further into what happened there? Because I think there are a whole host of reasons Musk's question translated so quickly into action. First, Musk had once again targeted a big problem. He gets this. "I think it speaks to the fact that the general public really wants radical improvements in transport," he mused. "I think that's why it caught the popular attention." Even though he wasn't trying to promote it at all, the question was so energizing to others that they pulled more commitment out of him. Herman Melville declared in *Moby-Dick*, by way of explaining why he wrote it: "To produce a mighty book, you must choose a mighty theme."[1] The same goes for producing mighty questions. If you raise one that goes to the heart of a problem that many have and hate, your influence can be enormous.

Second, when that interest was ignited and many others took up the question, Musk was willing to engage with it seriously. He didn't back away from it as a flight of fancy or beg off on the (reasonable) grounds that he was running two big companies already. He stayed on the task of turning it into a viable if still audacious idea—a process in which many more questions had to be asked and answered.

Third, the reason that so much interest was excited by his comment is because Musk has visibly followed through on plenty of questions he has raised in the past. He made it clear in our interview how strongly he believes that people have to earn the credibility to take on big jobs. He demands this of others. When we asked about traits he hires for, he said: "I really just look for a track record of exceptional ability. . . . And I actually don't care if they graduated from university or even high school, they just need to have solved hard problems." He demands the same of himself. He won't ask investors to put their money into something he hasn't already prototyped to the point that he has managed to "iron out all the wrinkles and have something which can be commercially built at a low enough cost for people to afford." This is the kind of credibility that adds up to the "questioning capital" I talked about in Chapter 7. You build it with the questions you not only ask but pursue to impact.

Finally, a person's questioning capital increases when it's obvious they want to engage others in the quest. (You might recall the quote from Elie Wiesel that began this book. Questions are matters we *quest* after.) Again, we were talking to Musk that day because Tesla had come in at the top of a rankings exercise. It was the kind of moment where he could have reveled in the experience of trouncing the competition. Instead he talked about the joys of influencing them:

> *Tesla's really the company that got the car industry to reconsider electric vehicles—because they had abandoned electric cars after California changed its regulations. GM recalled all of their EVi electric cars and crushed them in a junkyard. Nobody was making electric cars. So, when we came along and made, initially, the Roadster, that got GM to make the Volt. And when GM announced the Volt, then Nissan felt confident enough to go forward with the Leaf. And so, we basically got the whole ball rolling on the electrification of cars, albeit quite slowly. But it is rolling. I think that's pretty important.*

Elon Musk is one of those problem-solvers who loves to talk about the power of questions. On various occasions he has recalled reading *The Hitchhiker's Guide to the Galaxy* by Douglas Adams when he was around fourteen years old and taking away "an important point, which is that a lot of times the question is harder than the answer. And if you can properly phrase the question, then the answer is the easy part." That is a tender age to arrive at the realization that being able to summon up accurate answers will take you only so far. Today, Musk applies his prodigious intellect to summoning up better questions—questions that will knock down assumptions and channel energy into new pathways of discovery. Why is he so much more capable of this than most people? In large part because he started early and he kept at it.

LEARNING TO LIVE THE QUESTIONS

There is a passage in the writings of Rainer Maria Rilke that goes directly to the distinction between focusing on questions versus answers. It goes like this:

> *Have patience with everything that remains unsolved in your heart. Try to love the questions themselves, like locked rooms, or books written in a foreign language. Do not now look for the answers. They cannot now be given to you, because you would not be able to live them. And the point is, to live everything. Live the questions now. Perhaps then, someday far in the future, you will gradually, without even noticing it, live your way into the answer.*

Recently, in the *New Yorker*, Andrew Solomon took a hard look at those words. "The insight is tremendous, but he has it backwards," he declared. "Belief in answers can get you through your early days, while the belief in questions, which is so much less tangible, takes a long time to arrive at. To know more is simply a matter of industry; to accept what you will never know is trickier. The belief that questions are precious whether or not they have answers is the hallmark of a mature writer, not the naïve blessing of a beginner."[2]

I'm not sure Rilke has it wrong. He did, after all, pen these words as "Advice to a Young Poet," so presumably his objective was to share wisdom he had gained as a mature writer and would himself have liked to have known as a naïve beginner. But I agree with Solomon's observation that people tend to "live the questions" later in life. I saw evidence of this so many times in my interviews with people late in their careers.

I think many of them take on bigger questions at a point when their mastery of their trade is obvious. At this point they are not only supremely capable craftspeople, they are also reflective about their work to a level they have never been. That reflection brings them to considerations of the larger purpose that their craft—which has become core to their identity—fits into. Take Tony Piazza, for example, the expert mediator we first met in Chapter 6. Having spent thirty-three years honing his talent, he told me this: "I've belatedly realized what I want to do when I grow up—which is to try to see if we can take something that we've learned from doing this and add a little bit more efficiency to the process of resolving disputes that devolve into violence, up to and including armed conflict." He has launched a nonprofit on the question of how far his techniques can go in "stopping other kinds of fights."

The founders of Handspring Puppet Company, the creative forces behind the London and Broadway theatrical hit *War Horse*, provide a perfect example of this late-but-not-too-late reflection. For most theatergoers, *War Horse* was a first introduction to Adrian Kohler's and Basil Jones's artistry, but in reality the duo had been staging highly original and impactful puppetry productions for decades already when it debuted in 2007. For them, *War Horse* marked a turning point in a more personal way. "*War Horse* was the first play in thirty years that we didn't perform in," Jones told me. "And two things coincided at that time: one, we were writing a book [*Handspring Puppet Company*] about our work, and two, we were for the first time becoming 'directors of puppetry' rather than performers. And we suddenly had to think very analytically about the work that we were doing, and answering the question: 'Why puppets?'"

Jones laughs that this was a question he had never considered engaging with before:

I used to find it irritating, questions like a journalist asking a dancer: "Why dance?" It's like, "It's what I do." But actually, it's a very good question, because we had to start to answer the question: "What is the offer of puppetry?" We have now written about that, and we are very much clearer about what the offer is—and are quite evangelical about it. Because I think it is an incredible, nascent art form that actually is being used very powerfully, but remains almost invisible.

One thing Jones talks about is that puppets bring vital parts of the human experience onto the stage that have historically been "completely left out of the canon of theater writing." Because it wasn't possible to have babies or small children—or certainly animals—perform reliably on stages night after night, playwrights left them out of the plot. Another powerful effect of puppets is that they can serve as "emotional prostheses." Someone who has been through a traumatic experience "can talk to others about that trauma through the prosthesis better than they can talk about it as themselves," Jones has observed. "Talking about the hurt of having your father in prison, for instance, and what that means to you. If you're using a puppet, it's easier to do it."

What became clear to me as we talked was the strong theme running through all of Kohler and Jones's projects. From working with township children in South Africa (where they grew up) in the aftermath of apartheid, to creating theatrical productions centered on animals—and, for that matter, to living openly as gay men for the past forty years in parts of the world where doing so was dangerous—they have sought ways to give voice to the voiceless. I wasn't surprised to hear of their establishment of the Handspring Trust for Puppetry Arts, a nonprofit organization focused on identifying, mentoring, and championing the next generation of puppetry artists in the rural areas and townships near their Cape Town factory. I am also not surprised to see that the company itself has grown to a full-time staff of over twenty people plus numerous performing artists. Thinking about the bigger questions your work responds to has a natural effect of expanding its scope, too.

STEPPING UP TO THE BIG PICTURE

The fact that Kohler and Jones found themselves engaging with bigger questions about the purpose of their work after they moved into less hands-on performing roles is a common phenomenon— or, I should say, common among people who actually succeed as leaders. Often the ones who don't make it fail because they can't rise to that level of examining the questions, versus the solutions, that their organizations should focus on. It is probably not a coincidence that the business leaders who are most renowned as visionaries and motivators of others are entrepreneurs—and in particular the people whom the Ewing Marion Kauffman Foundation calls "high-impact entrepreneurs," who capitalize on technology breakthroughs and create industry-disrupting solutions. People like Steve Jobs, Robin Chase (Zipcar), Anne Wojcicki (23andMe), Diane Greene (VMware), and Jeff Bezos (Amazon) started out asking challenging questions and have the questioning capital to keep doing so.

In some ways it is more interesting to see when someone who has inherited their managerial role figures out how to pivot from providing smart answers to posing smart questions. Abigail Johnson, CEO of Fidelity Investments, impresses me in this regard. I have had some exposure to the questioning culture she is cultivating because Fidelity has made use of my Question Burst exercise along with other methods of surfacing and challenging assumptions. Johnson is a true believer in laying more emphasis on questions throughout the organization. She says it doesn't happen automatically at Fidelity. "Throughout our company's history, we have generally been action-oriented," she explained. "We identify a customer issue, produce metrics verifying the problem, and then move into problem-solving mode. It's hard to have the patience to spend time brainstorming about customer needs when we have an apparent problem staring us right in the face that we could be fixing instead." But, she says, "the process of asking questions helps make sure that we haven't missed a larger, more fundamental issue that could be impacting the customer experience."

Part of Johnson's task, as she sees it, is to "set the stage" for others to think more expansively and welcome creative questions from their colleagues. As part of this, she emphasizes psychological safety. In her words: "One of my responsibilities is to create a supportive environment where Fidelity leaders are comfortable and confident asking uncomfortable questions about Fidelity's business strategy, culture, and customers." It is vital, she says, "that everyone knows that there is no intent to find someone or something to blame. The point of catalytic questions isn't to try to identify the culprit for some past mistake or transgression. The idea is to get beyond what first appears and instead to really probe the root issues."

Johnson also recognizes that she herself is in the ultimate position in her company to give voice to the questions she wants to inspire people's best thinking. She has given careful thought to this and lays out the questions in four basic areas. The first is the continual downward pressure on prices and revenues in the investment industry. What is working and what do we need to update or change? The second is the need for greater speed and agility. "Gone are the days of large-scale, multiyear, overly complex projects," Johnson says. How can we move more quickly by using customer feedback all along the way to make course changes and adjustments? The third is the fact of constantly changing regulations in the business and markets where Fidelity operates. How do we anticipate, prepare for, and adapt the customer experience, not just to comply with new regulatory regimes, but to deliver an exceptional customer experience? And the fourth is the impact of changing demographics. For example, what different expectations, as customers and as employees, do millennials and Gen Xers have?

CEOs of companies the size of Fidelity have insanely big jobs, and the hardest part of doing those jobs is figuring out how to allocate their finite time and attention. Where will it have the most positive impact on the future of the company? My observation is that top executives' legacies come down to whether, across their tenures, they have been able to spot the moments when big change is called for—what Intel's Andy Grove famously called the "inflection points"—and marshal the energies that only they can marshal to bring about the transformation. They get the questions right.

Time will tell if Abby Johnson is focusing her organization's best thinking on the right four areas, but, to my eye, the questions she is asking achieve the right balance of open-endedness and focus on the job to be done. More generally, I couldn't agree more with how she sees her responsibilities as CEO and prioritizes the allocation of her attention. She is very focused on the threats inherent in what Fidelity and its competitors "don't know they don't know." And she is creating the conditions that will get to the right questions, and the right answers, first.

IN THE BUSINESS OF QUESTIONING

Back in 1994, Peter Diamandis had a problem to solve. He wanted with all his heart to make a trip into space. But space exploration was only for astronauts, which Diamandis was not. He was someone who, with good friend and business partner Gregg Maryniak, had just been trying to start a satellite-launching business, and even that space-oriented venture was going nowhere. There would seem to be no hope of fulfilling his wish.

It happened that Maryniak was browsing in a bookstore one day and spotted Charles Lindbergh's classic account of his historic flight across the Atlantic, *The Spirit of St. Louis*. He bought it as a gift for Diamandis, to encourage him to keep working toward his pilot's license. Before then Diamandis had vaguely known that, back in 1927, Lindbergh had beaten out other pilots who all wanted the bragging rights of being first to fly nonstop from the United States to Europe. Until he read the book, however, he didn't know there had been prize money at stake. Lindbergh's account made it clear that the impetus for his and others' attempts was the $25,000 prize offered by New York hotel owner Raymond Orteig.

The question hit Diamandis immediately: *Why don't we have a prize for space travel?* Was that the missing element that would galvanize the growing community of space entrepreneurs—that is, all those private-sector concerns with capabilities that could be applied to the mission of putting paying customers into space? And thus the "XPRIZE" was born. That *X* was initially a placeholder while Diamandis and the small team he assembled got the word out about the idea and sought the equivalent of an Orteig to put up the biggest chunk of the sponsorship money. Eventually they found those generous donors in Anousheh and Amir Ansari and the prize was dubbed the "Ansari XPRIZE"—the *X* was retained because by then the prize had already created a lot of buzz under its working title. And the *X* lived on, since the success of that first competition inspired Diamandis and his team to replicate the prize model at least a dozen times more. It became a question in itself: What other big problems are out there that seem like they are on the cusp of being solvable, only lacking the excited effort that a competition could spur?

Perhaps you remember how that first competition turned out. Having been announced in 1996, it was able to award its $10 million purse just eight years later when SpaceShipOne, the entry financed by Microsoft cofounder Paul Allen and designed by aviation innovator Burt Rutan, fulfilled its requirement: that a nongovernment organization must launch a reusable, manned craft, with the equivalent of a three-passenger payload, into space twice within two weeks.

The story has been broadly published, but I wasn't aware of the details till I visited XPRIZE's offices in Culver City, California, courtesy of Kian Gohar, whom I had met in a photography workshop some years earlier.[3] When he showed me around, there were mementos everywhere of the prizes offered and won over the years—for "earth exploration, ocean exploration, energy, environment, education. All areas where there was an opportunity to solve big problems using this appeal to crowds." Another big award, for example, had recently gone to a team of five health scientists and medical doctors. A "great thing about them," Gohar told me, "was that they were a team of five brothers and sisters who experimented in their family basements." This was the Qualcomm Tricorder XPRIZE, inspired by the device used by Dr. McCoy in the original 1960s *Star Trek* television series. "We asked," Gohar says, "how can we create a handheld consumer device that can diagnose major diseases to democratize access to health care?" It seemed

SpaceShipOne inspires anyone at XPRIZE to push questions and insights to the edge of the possible.

Stepping into the unique XPRIZE Science Fiction Advisory Council space with my guide for the day, Kian Gohar.

Dead center is a replica of the *Star Trek* tricorder—from the original series—
that inspired the Qualcomm Tricorder XPRIZE.

obvious how valuable such a thing would be in rural areas of the
world, and even in areas well served by health care institutions, if
people wanted, for example, to access the technology in the middle
of the night. That competition was launched in 2012, awarded in
2017, and—assuming the winning team's device goes through the
FDA's regulatory approval process smoothly—will be ultimately
be available for consumer purchase.

Soaking all this up, it occurred to me that Diamandis and his
team are professional big-question askers. Their organization is
built-to-purpose to do exactly that, and they spend a lot of time
thinking about how to do it well. One especially intriguing feature of their approach, for example, is that they have assembled
"an advisory council of science fiction writers to help us ideate
about how the future can look; we work with this council to come

up with creative ideas that can really push us." They also hold annual "Visioneers Summits" where people with a lot of questioning capital—think James Cameron, Larry Page, Anousheh Ansari, will.i.am—are convened with the XPRIZE Board of Trustees to consider anew: "What are the big problems in the world that we should try to solve? And how can a prize model be used to solve them?" They draw up "road maps" for the challenges cast at the highest level. These exist so far for combating climate change, achieving sustainable housing, providing access to education, and getting humans to Mars. The road maps essentially break these huge questions into component questions that can be the basis of interim prizes. Figuring out the right level to pitch a prize at is, I would say, the greatest competency the XPRIZE Foundation has built. It can't constrain the solution by making unwarranted assumptions about the shape it will take; it must strike teams and donors as something that is achievable within a reasonable time frame; and the prize must be sufficiently motivating to lure many great minds away from alternative uses of their talents. Of course, the criteria for winning must also be crystal clear and objective. For the Tricorder challenge, for example, the winner was defined as the first device to diagnose ten major diseases as accurately as a room of fifteen board-certified physicians.

Think of the XPRIZE Foundation as being in the business of asking big, and you start to realize that they are not alone. There is, in fact, a growing industry focused on the crucial work of posing catalytic questions. Companies like InnoCentive and NineSigma exist solely to manage the crowdsourced competitions that engage outside innovators to solve companies' R & D problems. Similarly, they have focused on how to do that well and gotten very good at question design, both from the standpoint of what will produce the most innovative solutions and what will engage the broadest participation.

Within this same industry—or perhaps, more accurately, ecosystem—I would put the MIT Media Lab. This renowned nexus of innovative, systems-level thinking is just footsteps from my office in Kendall Square. On a recent visit there I talked with director Joi Ito about the lab's projects and purpose. In a nutshell, he told me, the point of it is to "create a place where we're constantly questioning, and creating the conditions for serendipity." With staff, students, and researchers together numbering somewhere around eight hundred people, he called it "this little ashram of questioning." The term seems apropos, given the semiannual events the lab hosts for its corporate sponsors who trust the lab to "explore those areas that wouldn't otherwise be explored." Twice a year, he says, "a thousand people from the companies come and they all click into this mode where they're exploring, they're open, people are being experimental, and it feels okay."

Here, too, very serious thought has been put into the question of how to ask bigger and better questions. Central to the lab's work is the constant interchange between people with real responsibility for creating solutions in the real world, and people who know the theoretical and cutting-edge capabilities of technologies. Getting quickly to prototypes—or "demos," as they have always been called at the lab—is also a core tenet, because it allows for better collaboration in multidisciplinary teams. "If you're envisioning an educational robot and you have a developmental psychologist, a mechanical engineer, and a computer scientist working together, they can't talk to each other theoretically very well," Ito explains. "But make a robot, which everyone can see, and suddenly it becomes rigorous."

There are many methods and norms that have been developed over the thirty-year history of the MIT Media Lab—it was founded in 1985 by Nicholas Negroponte and Jerome Wiesner—to make it more capable of asking the right questions. I will highlight just one more here—an organizational practice—just because I loved hearing about it. The lab routinely recruits for the academic position it refers to as "Professor of Other." The point is that there are always a few very capable scholars in the world trying to pursue big questions that don't fit neatly into currently established disciplines. If asked to designate their field on a form, they would have to check the box labeled "other." Ito says these people are not "without" disciplines: they are "anti-disciplinary." The message this search puts out to the vast population of academics who would like an appointment at the MIT Media Lab is, in Ito's words: "If you can do whatever it is you hope to do anywhere else, you shouldn't apply for this. If you could get funded by anyone to do it, this is not for you."

The proliferation of entities like the Media Lab, the XPRIZE Foundation, the crowdsourced innovation platforms springing up, Google's "moonshots" unit (curiously also called "X"), and more is an exciting development. These organizations are creating more discipline around the art and science of asking big questions even as they are making the world much more aware of the power of raising them.

ASKING THE BIG SOCIAL QUESTIONS

The same can be said for the rise over the past couple of decades of what is known as social entrepreneurship. Enterprise builders who are more oriented to impact than to profit are putting many of today's biggest social questions on the table in ways that make more people engage with them.

For many years I have known a couple, Mark Ruiz and Reese Fernandez-Ruiz, both of whom are social entrepreneurs who learned to "live the question" early in life. Reese is the force of nature behind Rags2Riches, which empowers community artisans in the Philippines to create fashion and home products and get them to global markets. Since she was a little girl, Reese tells me, she had a very strong and visceral reaction to any injustice she witnessed, so it makes sense that she would help the laborers and vendors around her by creating what she describes as a "level playing field." But she also credits her questioning impulses. When she was in university, she and her friends were dismayed by the poverty they saw around them, but "some of us would tell ourselves that, you know, many people are poor because they are not working hard enough." Rather than simply accept that, she reasoned, "If you create a level playing field and everyone has the same opportunity, that's how you'll *know* if it's because they're not working hard enough." In retrospect, Reese says, "I didn't have a lot of assumptions about people who are in poverty, but rather I would always ask: Why? Why are they this way? What would their reaction be if we created this?"

Her questioning instincts were just as vital to helping her persevere with a project that took much longer to get established than she imagined upfront it would. "It took us about four years to get the trust of the artisans," she recalls. "And if you're somebody who wants to do good, that is a surprise: 'Oh, why aren't they trusting me? I'm already doing them good. Why aren't they reciprocating?'" But that is not a productive line of inquiry, she stresses. Instead, "the right questions to ask are: What have they been through? What made them distrustful?" Taking that perspective allowed her to accept that a trust deficit built over generations cannot be erased in a year. "Those questions helped shape Rags2Riches and still do now," Reese says. "If I had jumped to conclusions, we wouldn't be here now."

Mark also launched a social enterprise, at around the same time that Rags2Riches was founded, on the similar theme of leveling the playing field for commerce. He had been working at Unilever, learning about marketing channels, and as part of this had met with owners of "sari-sari" stores—the tiny, convenience-oriented shops that number perhaps half a million in the Philippines. "The question I had when I was studying them was: How come there are so many of them?" he recalls. "And only very few that are able to really grow?" Working at Unilever, he also saw the level of service the multinational provided to its biggest customers, such as Walmart. So he wondered: "How could we provide for these small sari-sari stores what we're able to provide for our largest customers: that kind of care, that same attention, that kind of energy?" He refers to these now as the "genesis questions" that led to his founding Hapinoy, a nonprofit that exists to "empower the marginalized last-mile micro-retail sector of the Filipino economy." Its work is all directed at giving those merchants the benefit of the efficient distribution channels and effective business development strategies that only large-scale retailers had access to before.

One of the things I admire about this couple is that, not only are they big questioners, but they are self-aware questioners. For example, when I asked Mark about whether their efforts complement each other, he talked about a tendency in himself to ask more "cold, logical" questions about how operations could be improved, while Reese moves more easily toward questions calling on emotional intelligence. He is always asking how Hapinoy might make a change to boost the incomes of its shop owners, many of whom are mothers trying to earn cash to help struggling households. "But Reese always goes beyond just income augmentation to ask questions about what her community really values and how to improve their wellness." Rags2Riches, he says, "has a quality-of-life program that I would never have been able to conceptualize because, to be honest, I don't have that orientation. But she does."

In telling Mark's and Reese's stories, I know that I am focusing on a microcosm of a very big and vibrant world of social entrepreneurship, but I think the themes here resonate broadly. The rise of social entrepreneurship can be equated with the rise of bigger questioners. We live in an era when more people seem eager and able to take on challenges of vast scope. More people, too, seem to yearn for that sense of large purpose. As Mark did, they look around themselves as they work in jobs with narrow definitions of success and they ask: *Is this all there is?* They look at colleagues whose questioning powers have been diminished, not built, by their work environment and they ask: *Is this what I want for myself?* And to a larger degree than in the past, they don't stop at those potentially dispiriting questions. They don't resign themselves to "lives of quiet desperation." They translate their questions into a serious sense of resolve and find their ways to energizing answers.

BIG MEANS FUNDAMENTAL

Another, probably more accurate way of saying "big questions" is to refer to them as "fundamental questions." The most significant, potentially transformative questions are the ones that go back to first principles. Thinking about them this way makes clear that not all "big" questions are on a planetary scale. They can be transformative at a more local level, such as in a single community, or a single company, or for a single individual.

Joan LaRovere is a pediatric cardiologist at Boston Children's Hospital, and it's more than a full-time job. But early on in her career she also cofounded the Virtue Foundation, an organization dedicated to humanitarian relief around the world. The foundation had its start in LaRovere's realization that medical and other supplies sent to aid-recipient nations were not finding their way to the areas of greatest need within those countries. They tended to swamp the urban areas to which they were shipped, leaving people in more remote and rural areas high and dry. The solution, LaRovere and her cofounder Ebby Elahi realized, was to get finer-grained data about incidences of problems and map the territories to guide aid activities better.

This is great work for the world, but as I talked to LaRovere about it, it was clear that she sees it as great work for her soul as well. Years ago, LaRovere realized that it wasn't sufficient to focus on how to succeed in the material world on its own terms. Her transformative question, given her belief that there is a deeper dimension to our reality than this material one, is: "Where am I preparing to go?" That might sound like a big, spiritual question—and it is—but it actually provides very practical guidance to LaRovere in her daily work and life. "When you start living your life that way and start thinking that way, you take care to protect that, and you nurture that, and you feed that, and you grow that through all of your life experiences," she explained. "Then you start asking with each thing that you do, and all the interactions that you have: Is this good for my soul, or is it bad for my soul? Is this getting me closer to the human being that I want to become?"

I thought about LaRovere's question when I heard about the initiative Oprah Winfrey has embarked on. She is calling this year (I write this in early 2018) "the year of the big question." What does she mean by that? "Every person has their own big questions that no one else can answer," she explained at the outset. "And this year we will pose twelve of them, one every month. They are all questions I've thought about deeply and know my answers to. I also know my answers will keep evolving."[4] The interesting thing about Oprah is that her unique personal brand allows her to address the gamut of her fans' lives, from their personal struggles with relationships and health issues to their interest and activism in national and international causes and social movements. From her book club picks to her investment choices, she has the power to influence millions. In her year of big questions, she has been using that influence to urge people to focus more on the questions they should be asking of themselves and others, at all levels.

In a sense it is no surprise that Oprah is a believer in the power of questions. She has been interviewing personalities in live settings since she was a teenager; by the last episode of her daily television show, she had racked up 4,589 shows and over 37,000 one-on-one, on-air conversations. "One lesson I learned from all my years of interviewing," she says, "is that the key to getting the answers you need lies in asking the right questions." Conceivably she has asked more questions than any person on earth. But I think her urging others to get clearer on the big questions in their lives has more to do with how she reframed her own life with one. According to Oprah, she had a life-changing epiphany after reading the book *The Seat of the Soul* by Gary Zukav. "The chapter that stirred me most," she writes in an introduction to that book's twenty-fifth anniversary edition, "was the one about intention." Prior to that, she says, "I suffered from the disease to please. . . . I was a slave to the needs, wants, and desires of others. I would say yes when I seriously wanted to say no." Her breakthrough came, she says, when she recognized "that my intention to be liked was causing all the requests. . . . That was an aha moment! When I changed my intention to be about doing what I wanted, what I felt was worthy of my time, the effect automatically changed."[5]

From that time on, Oprah says, she made it her practice to ask all the guests invited to appear on her show, "What is your intention?" She wanted to make sure that her understanding of that guided the questions she would pose to them. Probably, for many, it was the first time they had been asked that, and they benefited from being forced to think about it. Now Oprah is asking the same question of all the rest of the world she reaches because she knows by her own experience that simple inquiry yields significant impact. In her words, "Ask the right questions, and the answers will always reveal themselves."

Some of us are in the habit of asking bigger questions than others, but the message of this chapter is that all of us could be asking bigger ones than we do. This is the great payoff from becoming more aware of and more adept at questioning. It allows you to take on the problems that matter most.

Some of that will involve questions about your own life's purpose. You don't want to be one of those people who, as Joi Ito puts it, "work their asses off on some path only to suddenly, when they have a moment to pause and become aware, realize they've been on the wrong path." To avoid that, he says: "I think it's an important thing to be constantly checking in to see whether you're actually doing the things that matter to you." And some enhanced questioning power will allow you to take on the problems of the wider world.

Ideally, in a life more focused on arriving at the right questions, and not just the best answers, you will be able to combine both. As Reese Fernandez-Ruiz says, "The question driving me has evolved throughout the years. It used to be finite and time-bound—like 'Lift five hundred artisans out of poverty'—and that was great. But I realized that finite and time-bound goals should be milestones, not my reasons for being. Powerful questions should be long-term, enduring, and strong enough to survive and surpass setbacks, delays, pain, disappointments, and failure."

EPILOGUE

WHAT WILL YOU ASK OF YOURSELF?

The questions which one asks oneself begin, at least, to illuminate
the world, and become one's key to the experience of others.
—JAMES BALDWIN

I now believe that all of us have keystone questions guiding us
through life—whether or not we are consciously aware of them.
They are the deeply established questions we ask of ourselves
in the attempt to be our best selves. I've heard about these many
times in conversations with people who have for whatever reason
sought to understand their own motivations more deeply. People
who have spent time clarifying their purpose have often distilled
it down to a compelling motto of some kind, or declaration of intent.

Some are more imaginatively expressed than others. I have
always loved the story that author Robert Fulghum tells about
attending a two-week cultural seminar in Crete organized by
Alexandros Papaderos—a man who personally did a tremendous
amount to reconstruct a positive relationship between that country and Germany after the horrors of the Second World War. Fulghum was so inspired that, as the "Any questions?" moment came
at the end of the last session, it struck him as reasonable to ask:
"Dr. Papaderos, what is the meaning of life?" Papaderos didn't

laugh at what many others would consider a clichéd, unanswerable question. He knew the answer—for himself, at least. After scanning Fulghum's face for assurance the question was in earnest, he fished out his wallet, produced a small mirror that he kept in it, and quietly explained its significance:

When I was a small child, during the war, we were very poor and we lived in a remote mountain village. One day, on the road, I found the broken pieces of a mirror. A German motorcycle had been wrecked in that place.

I tried to find all the pieces of the mirror and put them together, but it was not possible, so I kept only the largest piece. . . . I began to play with it as a toy and became fascinated by the fact that I could reflect light into dark places where the sun would never shine—in deep holes and crevices and dark closets and behind walls. It became a game for me to get light into the most inaccessible places I could find.

. . . As I became a man, I grew to understand that this was not just child's play but a metaphor for what I might do with my life. I came to understand that I am not the light or the source of light. But light—the light of truth, understanding, and knowledge—is there, and that light will only shine in many dark places if I reflect it.

I am a fragment of a mirror whose whole design and shape I do not know. Nevertheless, with what I have I can reflect light into the dark places of this world—into the dreary places in the hearts of men—and change some things in some people. Perhaps others may see and do likewise. This is what I am about. This is the meaning of my life.

Gaining a sense of purpose like this allowed Papaderos to create a life that had real impact. Every day brought the question implied by it: *What dark place will I find today in need of light, and how will I manage to reflect some into it?* This led him to the very big answer that he should join forces with Crete's Bishop Irineos to build a vibrant academy of learning dedicated to the spirit of reconciliation—the site of the conference Fulghum attended. And it also led him to every day's small answers, like his choice to tell his story to Fulghum in that moment.[1]

I think it's a wonderful thing when someone perceives and articulates at an early age the question that drives their journey of discovery through life. Steve Jobs had this benefit, as he explained to the 2005 graduating class at Stanford: "When I was 17, I read a quote that went something like: 'If you live each day as if it was your last, someday you'll most certainly be right.' It made an impression on me, and since then, for the past 33 years, I have looked in the mirror every morning and asked myself: 'If today were the last day of my life, would I want to do what I am about to do today?' And whenever the answer has been 'No' for too many days in a row, I know I need to change something."

Lior Div told me: "For me it was from an early, early age that I realized that I need to be happy because I will never be satisfied. Every time that I'm doing something, I want to see again the boundary instead, where I can push it more. Can I push it a little bit and achieve something that is bigger than I've managed to achieve till today? This is my inner motto."

Sara Blakely, founder and CEO of Spanx, shared that when she was growing up, her father often asked a question at dinnertime: "What have you failed at this week?" She describes his encouragement to Blakely and her brother to take more risks as "a gift" because it made her understand that failure is not a matter of outcome. Rather, "failure is not trying." (Similarly, Tiffany Shlain has always remembered and thanked her father for telling her: "If you're not living on the edge, you're taking up too much space.") I've already mentioned Blakely's work to pass along her father's question to everyone who works at Spanx. "It's really allowed me to be much freer in trying things," she says, "and spreading my wings in life."

Many people arrive at the right question to guide their daily actions only after they are struck by a sudden awareness of being guided by a wrong one. Walt Bettinger, the CEO of Schwab, told me a story of how this happened to him in college. Determined to succeed in the world of business, he had focused relentlessly on mastering the frameworks and formulae in his management classes and making top grades. In his third year he even doubled up his quarter hours to graduate early and was still making all As. But the last test of the last class was the undoing of that perfect grade point average. It was a strategy course that had met two nights a week, from six o'clock to ten o'clock, in a nondescript wing of the business department. After nearly every class in that ten-week quarter, the students had stayed afterward, finding spots in that building to huddle in study groups and prepare for upcoming class discussions and tests.

For the final exam, the professor walked into the room and handed out single sheets of white paper to everyone. "I've taught you what you need to know about business strategy to get your start in the real business world," he said, "but whether you succeed there depends on more than that." He instructed them to write their names on their blank sheets and then provide the answer to just one question: "Who cleans this building? What is her name?" The young Bettinger's eyes widened. He could picture her vaguely, since she had often come into a room to empty its wastebaskets or been in a hallway when he headed for the vending machine. But had they ever spoken?

It turned out her name was Dottie, but he found that out only after failing the exam. And that turned out to be the most enduring lesson from the course. Bettinger says he was particularly abashed because he had come "from a family of Dotties," and should have had the values that teacher was testing for. Looking back on a long career since, he figures he owes much of his success to revising his understanding of what ambitious managers should ask themselves. It isn't: How can I be the smartest strategist? It's more like: Who are all the people my organization depends on to succeed, and what do they need to excel at their work?

My own wake-up call surfaced in the aftermath of that 2014 heart attack I mentioned in the Prologue. In retrospect it's obvious that I was taking on too much in the months leading up to that crisis—mentally, in terms of sheer workload, but also emotionally and physically (traveling across continents two to three times per month on average). Why did I allow things to reach that point? I realized later it was because I had let the wrong question take hold of my life early and across five decades had never brought it clearly out into the cold light of day to examine it. I don't think I am alone in operating in such an autopilot mode, because keystone questions often emerge from habits established as early as childhood.

Many people have grown up with a parent or close relative who, even if he or she resorted only rarely to physical abuse, was a harsh and unpredictable source of psychological torment. It is not uncommon for a kid in such a situation to become skilled at reading mood changes, intervening with distractions, and assuaging others' pain. No wonder, then, that my keystone question—an implicit and powerful one I measured my self-worth against—started out as *How can I keep my father happy?* Without my ever explicitly recognizing the question was there, it evolved to something more generic but ever-present in adult life: *How can I keep everyone around me happy?*

Keeping everyone happy is an absurd thing to demand of oneself, I agree, and a recipe for stress that can only rise as commitments and relationships multiply over years. But to do something about that, one would have to grasp that keystone questions exist and then figure out how to replace a flawed one with a better one. As therapist-consultant Marilee Adams puts it, "Learning to ask the right question is like cracking the code on change." Now that I have done that—with the help of many others, I say with gratitude—I am shedding that heart-stopping load. The keystone question I live by today—*How can I make a positive difference in this person's life right now?*—may sound like a subtle shift but it also allows for the kind of "tough love" that can make someone angry in the moment while hopefully making a positive difference in the end. It pushes me toward a version of kindness that doesn't assign me responsibility for others' happiness.

Our keystone questions, yours and mine, are not set in stone. They can also change over time because our changing circumstances create different possibilities. I asked Nandan Nilekani if there was a question he liked to keep in mind to guide his decisions. He prefaced his answer by admitting: "I'm sort of lucky in my life, in terms of business success and all that." He alluded, of course, to his role in founding Infosys, the global IT company whose market capitalization now exceeds $34 billion. The right question for him has evolved accordingly: "Given my unique position and capabilities, what is it that I can do to have the best possible impact on the most possible people?" Having that as a keystone question has made him a major force in tackling illiteracy. It made it easy for him to say yes when India's prime minister asked him to lead the initiative to give every citizen an officially recognized identity.[2]

Do you know what your own keystone question is? Would you know if it was time to revisit it? And would you recognize a better one if it occurred to you? At the heart of this book is the argument that under certain conditions—at work or in life—better questions are more likely to present themselves. And therefore it makes sense to keep reminding yourself to admit and embrace being a little more wrong, goading yourself to stray into somewhat more uncomfortable environs, and compelling yourself to be more reflectively quiet. Immerse yourself in situations where you feel less right, less comfortable, or less compelled to speak, and your questions will multiply.

Interestingly, these three conditions practically define my avocation of photography, which I took up as a young person to capture events and occasionally make money but now realize benefits me in this unexpected way. Purposeful, focused photographic work not only creates the conditions for catalytic questions to surface; it is inherently a form of questioning itself. One of the most thoughtful conversations I had in researching this book was with Marcus Lyon. He gained early renown as a portrait photographer, capturing revelatory images of people from street children in South America to British royalty and prime ministers. In recent years he has also used his craft to create collages exploring issues of urbanization and mass migration. In his words, he tries "to provoke questions concerning the biggest changes in contemporary society" with his large-scale representations of how globalization works in the modern world.

Lyon's latest book project, *Somos Brasil*, explores the diversity of Brazilian identity at the outset of the twenty-first century. He combines compelling portraits with an image-activated, app-based soundscape, and includes actual, individual DNA maps to tell the stories of over a hundred remarkable Brazilians. A compelling example, is Maria da Penha Maia Fernandes, about whom Lyon writes:

> *Before Maria's name became a law, women were being beaten and suffering death threats inside their own homes without knowing they were victims of crime. Silence within the family and neighbourhood meant that this was a cruel reality of life. Ten years after Law number 11,340 was passed—known as the Maria da Penha law—the climate of fear, pain, and injustice may have only changed a little, but now millions of women have the law on their side and a chance of a new life. Legally empowered, many have gained the courage and incentive to report their violent husbands, partners, and boyfriends to the police. Today violence against women is discussed in schools, symposiums, in the public health systems and in government.*

Now in her seventies, the biopharmacist Maria da Penha Maia Fernandes carries the scars of domestic violence on her body and in her soul. Her ex-husband, a Colombian schoolteacher named Marco Antonio Heredia Viveros, tried to kill her twice—first by shooting her in the back, leaving her paraplegic, and then by electrocuting her. She survived, and has devoted the two decades since to putting him behind bars and fighting for the rights of the abused and ignored. She wants more women to believe that a society with less violence is possible, and more people committed to achieving that. Whenever Lyon photographed one of his remarkable subjects, he tells me, he felt an obligation to make a strong connection to be able to tell their story better. "If you ask the right unlocking question," he has found, "the person you photograph becomes more present and thus can be recorded more powerfully."

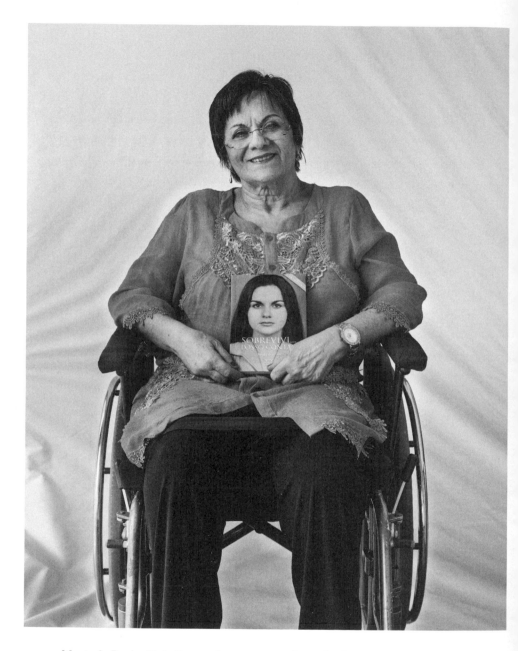

Maria da Penha Maia Fernandes, a portrait from the *Somos Brasil* project.
Marcus Lyon

I began Chapter 6 with my friend Sam Abell—and mentioned that his influence ended up going much further than improving my photographic technique. In some ways I had already sensed that my vocation and avocation were interwoven. As Sam's student, I reflected intensely on how photography connects to arriving at better questions. We subsequently collaborated on a course offering through MIT Executive Education called "Leadership and the Lens: Reframing the Question to Unlock Insight and Impact" in collaboration with Santa Fe Photographic Workshops. Photography is full of metaphorical possibilities: it is easy to transfer a concept like focus, for example, or framing, or depth of field. But beyond the metaphorical, learning to "compose and wait" means consciously deciding to spend some period of time being rather quiet, feeling rather uncomfortable, and accepting that you might just be wrong. It directly serves the purpose of forging better questions.

Learning from Abell, I now look at photographs in a different way, inviting them to challenge my fundamental assumptions with their content. I recently assembled for his review a project I call "Wonder Windows Walls," which attempts to trace a journey from healthy to unhealthy and back to healthy relationships through photographic images. In it there is a particular image I cherish. Having read Fulghum's story about the meaning of life, I always wanted to visit in person the peace institute Papaderos founded at the Orthodox Academy of Crete. While living in Abu Dhabi, my wife and I had the chance to do that in September 2010. We stayed in a home where Cretan descendants of the German resistance lived. They shared old photos and talked about their ancestors' courageous actions and what they suffered. They took us to historical sites where tragic things had happened, including the massacres of entire villages.

On the horizon, you can glimpse the Orthodox Academy of Crete on the edge of the Mediterranean, where Alexandros Papaderos gave his thought-provoking answer to Robert Fulghum's simple question, "What is the meaning of life?"

The heaviness of history was all around us on an island full of rich, natural beauty and welcoming people. One day while wandering in Chania, actively on the hunt for new images to include in my project, I passed by an old metal door that had been painted many times and was immediately intrigued by the pencil-sized hole I saw next to its two rusty locks. It reminded me of some of the haunting portrayals of emotional abuse that photographer Anneè Olofsson included in the exhibit *This Is Who I Am Me and You*. Judging by the pitch-blackness of the hole, that interior space had no light. Meanwhile the vibrant indigo blues and deep goldish-red rust on the outside hit my eyes like the blinding Mediterranean sun, even though I stood in the shade of the alley. I was pulled as if

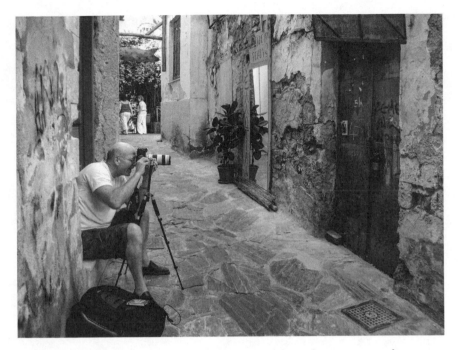

Zora Neale Hurston observed, "There are years that ask questions and years that answer." Little did I know that this cretan door, with its Janusian powers, would offer up a choice—several years later – that would change the course of my life. Suzi Lee

by an electromagnet to this door with its hole, and I snapped images from every angle. The final shot turned out to be stunning; it hangs in our entryway at home.

Just last year a good friend and professional colleague, Bronwyn Fryer, visited us at our home on Boston's north shore. Bronwyn, Suzi, and I talked honestly about our lives, our histories, and our keystone questions. I shared a document that I had written to myself, outlining why I was ready to give up on writing this book. Too much was happening on too many fronts, wearing me down to the point of exhaustion. I admitted that, while on an intellectual level I had shifted my keystone question from being nice to being kind, emotionally I drifted from my new keystone question more often than I'd been willing to admit to myself. All this made for a difficult but inspiring fireside conversation with Bronwyn and Suzi.

Heading downstairs at the end of our visit, we passed by my Chania picture, and at that moment it took on an entirely new meaning for me. The emotional scales finally fell from my eyes. I realized that I had always experienced the image as someone on its inside, immersed in that darkness and looking toward a spot of light. Somehow life, fate, and endless conversations with friends and counselors had opened up my heart to live on its outside. In that very moment I saw I could appreciate, relish, enjoy, and just take in the deep, complex beauty of the door's surface and not be pulled into the darkness of that hole. The self-made shackles came off—not once and for all, but certainly far more than ever before.

I knew then, and know now, that I can choose the questions I live by. Will they create light in my life (and those around me) or (like Eeyore's clouds in *Winnie-the-Pooh*) cast gloom across my landscape? It is up to me to decide.

At the beginning of this book, I suggested that one should publish only if one had discovered important truths that could benefit many readers. But there are other good reasons to write a book's worth of thoughts. I hope that in *Questions Are the Answer* you have found the inspiration to become a better questioner and take away some practical advice from the many creative problem-solvers I have met. In that case I will feel that I have reflected some new light into your life. As for me, I have discovered more than I expected in the process. For as many answers as I gained, I have gained still more questions—and that has made all the difference.

A profound pinhole of light and dark, depending on the angle of one's heart.

ACKNOWLEDGMENTS

At times our own light goes out
and is rekindled by a spark from another person.
Each of us has cause to think with deep gratitude
of those who have lighted the flame within us.
—ALBERT SCHWEITZER

It takes a community to build a questioning capacity. Throughout my life I've had that gift of community. Who has most shaped my own capacity to ask? And who has shaped the opportunity to share that message in this book? So many have stepped forward over the years to answer these questions—for which I am grateful—and the list that follows is far from exhaustive.

Thanks to over two hundred people who took the time to talk with me about the power of inquiry in their lives. Nestled within the millions of transcribed words were profound life stories, each an inspiration to me as I sat down to make sense of what causes people to ask catalytic questions. I wish I could highlight every story, but a constrained book size of 80,000 words makes that impossible. Much wisdom and insight about the stunning power of questions was left on the editing floor—hopefully to be shared later in other forms.

Thanks to thousands of students at ten universities over the past thirty years (California State University, Fullerton; San Diego State University; Penn State Behrend; Turku School of Economics; Dartmouth College; Brigham Young University; Helsinki

School of Economics, now the Aalto University School of Business; London Business School; INSEAD; and MIT) and to tens of thousands of leaders in workshops across the world who have given me inspiration and strength by exploring the terrain of inquiry with honest, open eyes.

Thanks to Stewart Black, Jeff Dyer, Mark Mendenhall, Allen Morrison, and Gary Oddou, collectively, for thirty years of meaningful collaborative research work on how leaders exercise questioning muscles to crack the codes of globalization, transformation, and innovation.

Thanks to colleagues at the MIT Leadership Center—Deborah Ancona, Abby Berenson, Emma Caldwell, Tracy Purinton, and Nelson Repenning—who help me frame new questions about challenge-driven leadership for the twenty-first century and beyond. Thanks to Emilio Castilla, Jake Cohen, S. P. Kothari, Ray Regans, David Schmittlein, and Ezra Zuckerman at the MIT Sloan School of Management for creating a resource path that let this research see the light of day. Thanks to Joi Ito, for insight about the inner workings of the MIT Media Lab and for a fierce commitment to keeping creative, constructive inquiry alive and well at MIT and beyond. Thanks to Jocclyn Bull, Virginia Geiger, Jacky McGoldrick, and Erika Paoletti for working tirelessly to keep the trains on the tracks for a faculty member with ADHD who prefers zigging and zagging.

Thanks to a truly amazing cadre of research assistants, all of whom have sharp minds, great questions, and far more discipline than I could ever hope to muster when it comes to getting things done: Eliza LaRovere, Chris Bingham, Melissa Humes Campbell, Bruce Cardon, Jared Christensen, Janika Dillon, Ben Foulk, Nolan Godfrey, Mark Hamberlin, Spencer Harrison, Julie Hite, Marcie Holloman, Robert Jensen, Kirin Wells Krebs, Kristen

Knight, Todd McIntyre, Jayne Pauga, Spencer Wheelright, Alex Romney, Jake Schroeder, Michael Sharp, Marion Shumway, and Laura Holmstead Stanworth.

Thanks to Gillian St. Leger and Raddiya Lüssi-Begg, former IN-SEAD colleagues, for creatively opening the doors to Room 13 and Handspring Puppetry in Africa. Gillian and Raddiya's unyielding commitment to building a better world caused me to wrestle with questions that count in that part of our world.

Thanks to *Harvard Business Review* editors—Amy Bernstein, Lisa Burrell (now at *Sloan Management Review*), Sarah Green Carmichael, Sarah Cliffe, Susan Donovan, Adi Ignatius, and Melinda Merino—for seeing the light in ideas and focusing them into far brighter ones.

Thanks to thousands of World Economic Forum participants and organizers, especially Jeremy Jurgens, Sylvia Von Gunten, and Andrea Wong, for creating a conversational space where catalytic questions about crucial global challenges get asked and answered.

Thanks to Walt Bettinger, Jonathan Craig, and others at Charles Schwab for highlighting how critical the power of questions can be for any decision we make; to Gil Forer, Mike Inserra, John Rudalzsky, Uschi Schreiber, Mark Weinberger, and others at EY for making every effort to build a better working world by asking better questions; and to Marc Benioff, Simon Mulcahy, and the entire Salesforce Ignite team for taking questions seriously in their quest to create a future with greater opportunity and equality for all.

Thanks to Schon Beechler for asking probing questions that redirected my life's intention thirteen years ago. Her courage, compassion, and contentment remain a wellspring of positive energy.

Thanks to David Breashears for an enduring friendship that

pushes my questions and questioning capacity to the edge of the possible and for his leadership on the 2015 Everest Base Camp and Khumbu Icefall expedition. Thanks also to Ang Phula Sherpa and Chhongnuri (Chhongba) Sherpa for their wise and expert guidance on the expedition, and to Bishnu Sherpa and Jangbu Sherpa for their grit and strength.

Thanks to Mark Widmer for constantly reminding me that life is not meant to be lived within four walls and that the best questions often come in the most unusual circumstances, like rappelling off the center of a 110-foot natural rock arch.

Thanks to Rob Hall, Mike Hawley, and Ricky Valadez for helping me grasp how music, and other art forms, can ask the greatest questions without whispering a spoken word.

Thanks to Roger Lehman for mastering the craft of inquiry as an executive coach, therapist, colleague, and friend. His questions often probe the most tender parts of life, but the initial ouch usually ends up healing a needy and unnoticed emotional wound.

Thanks to Ahmet Bozer for being a "what you see is what you get" leader who cares about everyone's well-being—especially those least noticed but key to any endeavor's success. His gratitude for all fosters a sense of honest inquiry in every aspect of his life.

Thanks to Soraya Salti for making a profound, positive difference in the lives of millions of Arab youth and for living the questions "What's the next frontier?" and "What can we do now?" Her short life was a living testament to the power of questions (and I invite you to help her legacy live on with a contribution to the Soraya Salti Social Impact Scholarship Fund at INSEAD).

Thanks to Hollis Heimbouch at HarperCollins for her love of questions, for believing deeply in the power of an idea long before seeing much of it on paper, and for taking a serious creative leap with photographs in this book—an editorial move that meant the world to me. Thanks to Rebecca Raskin at HarperCollins for her discipline in pulling together countless details every step of the way and for keeping all eyes focused on the finish line. Thanks to Rachel Elinsky and Penny Makras for shaping and sharing the ideas in compelling ways with the world.

Thanks to Ed Catmull for being a beacon of inquiry long before we met and for becoming an even stronger one during the past few years as we've come to know each other better. His calm integrity in the midst of pretty much any storm creates a place where tough questions get raised and tough problems get solved and re-solved—an approach to work and life that comes through loud and clear in his foreword to this book, for which I'm very grateful. Thanks also to Wendy Tanzillo for her gracious, professional, beacon-of-light work as Ed's able executive assistant and to Jared Bush, Andrew Gordon, Marc Greenberg, Don Hall, Jack Hattori, Byron Howard, Wave Johnson, Ann Le Cam, Andrew Millstein, Jim Morris, Guido Quaroni, Denise Ream, Jonas Rivera, Katherine Sarafian, Dan Scanlon, Clark Spencer, and Chris Williams for sharing insights about the inner workings of Pixar and Disney Animation Studios.

Thanks to friends Danny and Susan Stern for being anchors in several life storms and for nurturing this book's core concepts along in their respective agent and public relations roles. Thanks also to Stephanie Heckman and Ned Ward for unwavering, insightful support of catalytic questions as an idea worth reckoning with. Thanks to everyone else at Stern Strategy Group, but especially to Katie Balogh, Mel Blake, Justin Gianninoto, Whitney Jennings, Kristen Soehngen Karp, Dan Masi, and Ania Trzepizur for making mountains move, when necessary, to make things happen.

Thanks to Sam Abell, who single-handedly transformed the

way I took photographs, starting with his first question—"How can I find more of *you* in these images?"—in a mentorship several years ago. He caused me to rethink why I do what I do as a photographer, writer, and sojourner. And in turn, thanks to Reid Callanan, founder and director of Santa Fe Photographic Workshops, who asked the question, "Who would be the perfect complement to Hal's ideas about the intersection of inquiry and photography?" and answered it with an introduction to Sam. Harking back further, thanks to Elden Howlett for going the second and third mile in the 1970s to foster the art of inquiry in my teenage work as a wedding and portrait photographer—and for expecting nothing in return. His encouragement was a gift that keeps on giving to me and so many other young people now grown up (or at least grown old).

Thanks to Kristen Kolakowski (founder of WonderWorks) and Matt Beane for taking the risk one day at the Cambridge Antique Market to co-create (with Suzi) our "Fellowship of the Unbroken Ashtray"—where we work to lighten the load of some of life's most difficult questions.

Thanks to Bonner and Lois Ritchie for caring deeply about my worth and well-being as a spiritual traveler here on earth and for being courageous question marks at crucial points along the way.

Thanks to Sally Barlow for asking over and over, in one form or another, "Where are your feet?" Her professional expertise in seeing around corners by seeing through the past keeps me grounded in a more life-giving present.

Thanks to colleague and friend Clay Christensen for a quiet conversation twenty-five years ago about the compelling power of questions that I hope will continue for a lifetime, and beyond. I always leave his office or home with a new question taking hold, a better quest taking shape, and a recurring gratitude for one of his keystone questions—"How can I help?"—that serves as a wise marker for how to measure a life. Thanks also to Emily Snyder, Brittany McCready, and Cliff Maxwell for their undaunted optimism and behind-the-scenes efforts in the cause of Clay's key concepts.

Thanks to Julia Kirby, one of the best writers on earth. From start to finish, I appreciated her experience (nearly two decades at *Harvard Business Review* and Harvard University Press), insight, optimism, groundedness, wit, and, at the core, love of shaping ideas and sharing them with elegant wisdom. We studied interview transcripts, reanalyzed results from different angles, and explored the journey of my own life's questions to shape a book that would have never seen the light of day without her hard work, intellect, and gift with words. I asked Julia to join me as coauthor early on, and again later in the writing process, but each time she graciously stepped back, simply committed to shaping ideas for ideas' sake, without ego involved. In the end, a miracle worker she was in pulling concepts together and communicating them with conviction.

Thanks to my mother for living a life of adventure on the outer Aleutian Islands and in remote corners of Sweden early on in life—and for then infusing a deep curiosity about the world into every corner of our mobile home, and in time, our house home without wheels. Thanks to my father for his perpetual inventiveness when it came to anything mechanical and for his love of, and mastery of, so many things musical. And the beat goes on. Thanks to my brother, Max, for paving the way that I might dare to ask uncomfortable questions and to my sister, Susan, for creating a safe space to talk about the sometimes unanswerable questions.

Thanks to our children, a blended bunch—Kancie, Matt (Emily), Emilee (Wes), Ryan, Kourtnie (Guy), Amber (Brent), and Jordon

(Brandy)—and grandkids—Coco, Maddie, Kash, Brooklyn, Stella, Rose, Henry, and Eva—each following their own quests with conviction, while scattered across the globe from Seattle to Nairobi.

Last but not least, special thanks to Suzi, for showing me what it means to "live the question" with her deep zest for life, forever and always.

NOTES

CHAPTER 1: WHAT'S HARDER THAN FINDING NEW ANSWERS?

1. Arthur Koestler once noted "the paradox that the more original a discovery the more obvious it seems afterwards." Arthur Koestler, *The Act of Creation* (London: Hutchinson & Co., 1964), 120.
2. Elon Musk, in an interview with Alison van Diggelen, "Transcript of Elon Musk Interview: Iron Man, Growing Up in South Africa," *Fresh Dialogues*, February 7, 2013. Available at http://www.freshdialogues .com/2013/02/07/transcript-of-elon-musk-interview-with-alison -van-diggelen iron man-growing-up-in-south-africa/.
3. Ellen Langer, "Ask a Better Question to Get a Better Answer." Available at http://www.ellenlanger.com/blog/120/ask-a-better-question-to-get-a -better-answer.
4. Kaihan Krippendorff, "4 Steps to Breakthrough Ideas," *Fast Company*, September 6, 2012. Available at https://www.fastcompany.com /3001044/4-steps-breakthrough-ideas.
5. Edgar Schein, *Humble Inquiry: The Gentle Art of Asking Instead of Telling* (San Francisco: Berrett-Koehler, 2013).
6. Robert Pate and Neville Bremer, "Guiding Learning Through Skillful Questioning," *Elementary School Journal* 67 (May 1967): 417–22.
7. Jony Ive, speaking at the *Vanity Fair* New Establishment Summit, as reported by Jillian D'Onfro, "Steve Jobs Used to Ask Jony Ive the Same Question Almost Every Day," *Business Insider*, October 8, 2015. Available at http://www.businessinsider.com/this-is-the-question-steve-jobs- would-ask-jony-ive-every-day-2015-10.
8. Tina Seelig, "How Reframing a Problem Unlocks Innovation," Co.Design, May 19, 2013. Available at https://www.fastcodesign.com/1672354/how -reframing-a-problem-unlocks-innovation.
9. Amitai Etzioni, "Toward a Macrosociology," *Academy of Management Proceedings*, 27th Annual Meeting, Washington, DC (December 27–29, 1967), 12–33.
10. Clayton Christensen, Karen Dillon, Taddy Hall, and David Duncan, *Competing Against Luck: The Story of Innovation and Customer Choice* (New York: HarperBusiness, 2016).

11. Malcolm Gladwell, *Outliers: The Story of Success* (Boston: Little, Brown and Company, 2008), 18.

12. The quotes here come from parent Jack Freeman and appeared in a blog post he wrote about why he participates in a certain fund-raiser. To learn more about Quest Autism Foundation's history and current activities, see its website: http://questnj.org/.

13. Ibrahim Senay, Dolores Albarracin, and Kenji Noguchi, "Motivating Goal-Directed Behavior Through Introspective Self-Talk: The Role of the Interrogative Form of Simple Future Tense," *Psychological Science* 21, no. 4 (April 2010): 499–504.

14. This is a problem I would later explore in a separate project. If interested in the dilemma faced particularly by CEOs, see "Bursting the CEO Bubble," *Harvard Business Review*, March/April 2017.

15. The allusion is to the piece of poetry that gave us the term "movers and shakers." In "Ode" (1873), Arthur O'Shaughnessy wrote: "We are the music-makers, / And we are the dreamers of dreams . . . Yet we are the movers and shakers / Of the world for ever, it seems."

16. Nelson Repenning, Don Kieffer, and James Repenning, "A New Approach to Designing Work," *Sloan Management Review*, Winter 2017.

17. One in this vein I have found especially valuable is Michael Bungay Stanier, *The Coaching Habit: Say Less, Ask More & Change the Way You Lead Forever* (Toronto: Box of Crayons Press, 2016). It outlines seven specific questions to transform the coaching experience.

CHAPTER 2: WHY DON'T WE ASK MORE?

1. Mark Lasswell, "True Colors: Tim Rollins's Odd Life with the Kids of Survival," *New York* magazine, July 29, 1991.

2. Edwin Susskind, "The Role of Question-Asking in the Elementary School Classroom." In *The Psycho-Educational Clinic*, eds. F. Kaplan and S. B. Sarason (New Haven, CT: Yale University Press, 1969).

3. G. L. Fahey, "The Extent of Classroom Questioning Activity of High-School Pupils and the Relation of Such Activity to Other Factors of Pedagogical Significance," *Journal of Educational Psychology* 33, no. 2 (1942): 128–37. Available at http://psycnet.apa.org /doiLanding?doi=10.1037%2Fh0057107. Also see George L. Fahey, "The Questioning Activity of Children," *Journal of Genetic Psychology*, 60 (1942), 337–57, for a review of the early literature on the questions of children, especially in classrooms.

4. William Floyd, "An Analysis of the Oral Questioning Activity in Selected Colorado Primary Classrooms," (unpublished doctoral thesis, Colorado State College, 1960), 6–8.

5. James T. Dillon, "Questioning in Education," a chapter essay in *Questions and Questioning*, ed. Michael Meyer (New York: Walter de Gruyter, 1988).

6. Max Wertheimer, *Productive Thinking*, Enlarged edition, ed. Michael Wertheimer (London: Tavistock, 1961), 214. Emphasis mine.

7. Philip H. Scott, "Teacher Talk and Meaning Making in Science Classrooms: A Vygotskian Analysis and Review," *Studies in Science Education* 32 (1998): 45–80.

8. A. Scott Berg, *Goldwyn: A Biography* (New York: Knopf, 1989), 376.

9. Douglas N. Walton, "Question-Asking Fallacies," a chapter essay (10) in *Questions and Questioning*, ed. Michel Meyer (New York: Walter de Gruyter, 1988), 209.

10. Liz Ryan, "What to Do When Your Manager is a Spineless Wimp," *Forbes*, June 22, 2017. Available at https://www.forbes.com/sites/lizryan /2017/06/22/what-to-do-when-your-manager-is-a-spineless-wimp/#5b a86d673be9.

11. Stacey Lastoe, "The Worst Boss I Ever Had," *Muse*. Available at https:// www.themuse.com/advice/the-worst-boss-i-ever-had-11-true-stories -thatll-make-you-cringe.

12. Barbara Kellerman, *Bad Leadership: What It Is, How It Happens, Why It Matters* (Boston: Harvard Business School Press, 2004), 22.

13. Damon Darlin and Matt Richtel, "Chairwoman Leaves Hewlett in Spying Furor," *New York Times*, September 23, 2006.

14. Maureen Porter and Sally MacIntyre, "What Is, Must Be Best: A Research Note on Conservative or Deferential Responses to Antenatal Care Provision," *Social Science & Medicine* 19 (1984), 1197–1200; William Samuelson and Richard Zeckhauser, "Status Quo Bias in Decision Making," *Journal of Risk and Uncertainty* 1 (1988), 7–59; M. Roca, R. Hogarth, and A. John Maule, "Ambiguity Seeking as a Result of the Status Quo Bias," Department of Economics and Business, Universitat Pompeu Fabra, Economics Working Paper 882 (2005); K. Burmeister and C. Schade, "Are Entrepreneurs' Decisions More Biased? An Experimental Investigation of the Susceptibility to Status Quo Bias," Institute of Entrepreneurial Studies and Innovation Management, Humboldt University-Berlin Working Paper (2006).

15. The quote is from "Carol Dweck Revisits the 'Growth Mindset,'" *Education*

Week, September 23, 2015. More broadly, see Carol Dweck, *Mindset: The New Psychology of Success* (New York: Random House, 2006).

16. Vijay Anand, "Cheat Sheet to Create a Culture of Innovation," Intuit Labs (blog), posted May 2, 2014. Available at https://medium.com/intuit-labs /cheat-sheet-to-create-a-culture-of-innovation-539d53455b53.

17. Christina Pazzanese, "'I Had this Extraordinary Sense of Liberation': Nitin Nohria's Exhilarating Journey," *Harvard Gazette*, April 29, 2015. Available at https://news.harvard.edu/gazette/story/2015/04/i-had-this -extraordinary-sense-of-liberation/.

18. "TK" [anonymous contributor], "Culturalism, Gladwell, and Airplane Crashes," Ask a Korean! (blog), posted July 11, 2013. Available at http:// askakorean.blogspot.com/2013/07/culturalism-gladwell-and-airplane.html.

19. Geert Hofstede, "Dimensionalizing Cultures: The Hofstede Model in Context," *Online Readings in Psychology and Culture* 2, no. 1 (January 2011): 10. Available at https://doi.org/10.9707/2307-0919.1014. The six dimensions along which Hofstede and his colleagues track difference are Power Distance, Uncertainty Avoidance, Individualism/Collectivism, Masculinity/ Femininity, Long/Short Term Orientation, and Indulgence/Restraint.

20. Parker J. Palmer, *Let Your Life Speak: Listening for the Voice of Vocation* (New York: Jossey-Bass, 2000).

21. Neil Postman and Charles Weingartner, *Teaching as a Subversive Activity* (New York: Delacorte Press, 1969), 12.

CHAPTER 3: WHAT IF WE BRAINSTORMED FOR QUESTIONS?

1. More support for this conclusion comes from research on genetically identical twins who were separated at birth. Based on assessment of their innovation skills and impact as adults, it would appear that only one-third of a person's questioning capacity is "born," while two-thirds is "made." Environmental factors at home, school, and work have great influence. See especially Marvin Reznikoff, George Domino, Carolyn Bridges, and Merton Honeyman, "Creative Abilities in Identical and Fraternal Twins," *Behavior Genetics* 3, no. 4 (1973): 365–77. This study looked at creative abilities in 117 pairs of identical and fraternal twins and concluded that about 30 percent of their performance on creativity tests was genetic, in contrast to over 80 percent of their performance on general intelligence (IQ) tests. Other creativity studies of identical twins reinforce the finding that nurture trumps nature as far as creativity goes. See K. McCartney and M. Harris, "Growing Up and Growing Apart: A

Developmental Meta-Analysis of Twin Studies," *Psychological Bulletin* 107, no. 2 (1990): 226–37; F. Barron, *Artists in the Making* (New York: Seminar Press, 1972); S. G. Vandenberg, ed., *Progress in Human Behavior Genetics* (Baltimore: Johns Hopkins University Press, 1968); R. C. Nichols, "Twin Studies of Ability, Personality and Interest," *Homo* 29 (1978): 158–73; N. G. Waller, T. J. Bouchard, D. T. Lykken, A. Tellegen, and D. Blacker, "Creativity, Heritability, and Familiality: Which Word Does Not Belong?" *Psychological Inquiry* 4 (1993): 235–37; N. G. Waller, T. J. Bouchard Jr., D. T. Lykken, A. Tellegen, and D. Blacker, "Why Creativity Does Not Run in Families: A Study of Twins Reared Apart," unpublished manuscript, 1992. For a summary of research in this area, see R. K. Sawyer, *Explaining Creativity: The Science of Human Innovation*, 2nd ed. (New York: Oxford University Press, 2012).

2. James T. Dillon, *Questioning and Teaching: A Manual of Practice* (London: Croom, 1987).

3. The story is recounted in more detail in Ed Catmull, *Creativity, Inc.: Overcoming the Unseen Forces That Stand in the Way of True Inspiration* (New York: Random House, 2014.)

4. Frank Furedi, "Campuses Are Breaking Apart into 'Safe Spaces,'" *Los Angeles Times*, January 5, 2017. Available at http://www.latimes.com /opinion/op-ed/la-oe-furedi-safe-space-20170105-story.html.

5. Amy Edmondson, "Psychological Safety and Learning Behavior in Work Teams," *Administrative Science Quarterly* 44, no. 2 (June 1999): 350 83. Available at https://doi.org/10.2307/2666999.

6. Andy Goldstein, "Oral History: C. Chapin Cutler, Conducted for the Center for the History of Electrical Engineering, May 21, 1993," Interview #160, Institute of Electrical and Electronics Engineers, Inc. Available at http://ethw.org/Oral-History:C._Chapin_Cutler.

7. Charles Duhigg, "What Google Learned from Its Quest to Build the Perfect Team," *New York Times Magazine*, February 25, 2016. Available at https://www.nytimes.com/2016/02/28/magazine/what-google-learned -from-its-quest-to-build-the-perfect-team.html.

CHAPTER 4: WHO REVELS IN BEING WRONG?

1. Steve Morgan, "Cybersecurity Ventures Predicts Cybercrime Damages Will Cost the World $6 Trillion Annually by 2021," Cybersecurity Ventures, October 16, 2017. Available at https://cybersecurityventures .com/hackerpocalypse-cybercrime-report-2016/.

2. Meghan Rosen, "Ancient Armored Fish Revises Early History of Jaws," *ScienceNews*, October 20, 2016. Available at https://www.sciencenews.org /article/ancient-armored-fish-revises-early-history-jaws.

3. Anita L. Tucker and Amy C. Edmondson, "Why Hospitals Don't Learn from Failures: Organizational and Psychological Dynamics That Inhibit System Change," *California Management Review* 45, no. 2 (Winter 2003): 68.

4. What does "Day 1" mean at Amazon? Jeff Bezos answers that question in his 1997 shareholder letter: "Staying in Day 1 requires you to experiment patiently, accept failures, plant seeds, protect saplings, and double down when you see customer delight. A customer-obsessed culture best creates the conditions where all of that can happen."

5. If you're stumped for an answer, check out Randall Munroe's terrific online response (he's the author of *What If?: Serious Scientific Answers to Absurd Hypothetical Questions*).

6. Michelene T. H. Chi, "Three Types of Conceptual Change: Belief Revision, Mental Model Transformation, and Categorical Shift," chapter 3 in Stella Vosniadou, ed., *International Handbook of Research on Conceptual Change* (New York: Routledge, 2008), 67.

7. Ibid., 78.

8. Tim Harford, "How Being Wrong Can Help Us Get It Right," *Financial Times*, February 8, 2017. Available at https://www.ft.com/content /8cac0950-ecfc-11e6-93of-061b01e23655.

9. See, for example, Eli Pariser, *The Filter Bubble: What the Internet Is Hiding from You* (New York: Penguin, 2011).

10. Chuck Klosterman, *Chuck Klosterman X: A Highly Specific, Defiantly Incomplete History of the Early 21st Century* (New York: Penguin, 2017).

11. Chuck Klosterman, *But What If We're Wrong?: Thinking About the Present As If It Were the Past* (New York: Penguin, 2016).

12. Roger L. Martin, "My Eureka Moment with Strategy," *Harvard Business Review*, May 3, 2010.

13. Krista Tippett, "Our Origins and the Weight of Space," transcript of an interview with Lawrence Krauss, April 11, 2013. Available at https://onbeing .org/programs/lawrence-krauss-our-origins-and-the-weight-of-space/.

CHAPTER 5: WHY WOULD ANYONE SEEK DISCOMFORT?

1. Hal Gregersen, "Bursting the CEO Bubble," *Harvard Business Review*, March–April 2017. Available at https://hbr.org/2017/03/bursting-the-ceo -bubble.

2. Nicole M. Hill and Walter Schneider, "Brain Changes in the Development of Expertise: Neuroanatomical and Neurophysiological Evidence About Skill-Based Adaptations," in K. Anders Ericsson, Neil Charness, Paul J. Feltovich, Robert R. Hoffman, eds., *The Cambridge Handbook of Expertise and Expert Performance* (New York: Cambridge, 2006), 653–82.

3. Journal Report, "How Entrepreneurs Come Up with Great Ideas," *Wall Street Journal*, April 29, 2013. Available at https://www.wsj.com/articles /SB10001424127887324445904578283792526004684.

4. Ioan James, "Henri Poincaré (1854–1912)," in *Remarkable Mathematicians: From Euler to von Neumann* (Cambridge, UK: Cambridge University Press, 2002), 239–40. Poincaré's tendency to have flashes of insight while taking breaks from his work was also noted by Arthur Koestler in *The Act of Creation* (London: Hutchinson, 1964).

5. Jackson G. Lu, Modupe Akinola, and Malia F. Mason, "'Switching On' Creativity: Task Switching Can Increase Creativity by Reducing Cognitive Fixation," *Organizational Behavior and Human Decision Processes* 139 (2017): 63–75.

6. Meryl Reis Louis, "Surprise and Sense Making: What Newcomers Experience in Entering Unfamiliar Organizational Settings," *Administrative Science Quarterly* 25, no. 2 (June 1980): 226–51.

7. Mason Carpenter, Gerard Sanders, and Hal Gregersen, "Bundling Human Capital with Organizational Context: The Impact of International Assignment Experience on Multinational Firm Performance and CEO Pay," *Academy of Management Journal* 44, no. 3 (2001): 493–512; Mason Carpenter, Gerard Sanders, and Hal Gregersen, "International Assignment Experience at the Top Can Make a Bottom-line Difference," *Human Resource Management Journal* 39 (2000): 277–85.

8. L. Stroh, M. Mendenhall, J. S. Black, and Hal Gregersen, *International Assignments: An Integration of Strategy, Research & Practice* (Mahwah, NJ: Lawrence Erlbaum, 2005); J. S. Black, H. B. Gregersen, and M. Mendenhall, *Global Assignments: Successfully Expatriating and Repatriating International Managers* (San Francisco: Jossey-Bass, 1992).

9. Diane Haithman, "Cirque Noir," *Los Angeles Times*, December 26, 2004. Available at http://articles.latimes.com/2004/dec/26/entertainment /ca-lepage26.

10. Richard Heller, "Folk Fortune," *Forbes*, September 4, 2000. Available at https://www.forbes.com/forbes/2000/0904/6606066a.html#647f939 6a9fb.

11. Gary Erickson, *Raising the Bar: Integrity and Passion in Life and Business; The Story of Clif Bar & Co.* (New York: Jossey-Bass, 2004).

CHAPTER 6: WILL YOU BE QUIET?

1. Linda Cureton, "If I Want Your Opinion, I Will Give It to You," *Jobber Tech Talk*, October 20, 2015. Available at http://www.jobbertechtalk.com/if-i -want-your-opinion-i-will-give-it-to-you-by-linda-cureton/.
2. Maggie De Pree, "Pitch Lessons from a Cubicle Warrior," Business Fights Poverty (blog), October 28, 2013. Available at http://businessfightspoverty .org/articles/pitch-lessons-from-a-cubicle-warrior/.
3. Clayton Christensen, Taddy Hall, Karen Dillon, and David Duncan, *Competing Against Luck: The Story of Innovation and Customer Choice* (New York: HarperBusiness, 2016), 182.
4. Ellen J. Langer, *Mindfulness* (New York: Addison-Wesley, 1989).
5. Henry Mintzberg, *The Nature of Managerial Work* (New York: Harper & Row, 1973).
6. Oriana Bandiera, Stephen Hansen, Andrea Prat, and Raffaella Sadun, "CEO Behavior and Firm Performance," Harvard Business School Working Paper 17-083 (2017). Available at http://www.hbs.edu/faculty/Publication%20 Files/17-083_b62a7d71-a579-49b7-81bd-d9a1f6b46524.pdf.
7. See Susan Cain, *Quiet: The Power of Introverts in a World That Can't Stop Talking* (New York: Crown, 2012).
8. I have seen this in the two-day, photography-based workshops that Sam Abell and I conduct as MIT Sloan executive education offerings. In "Leadership and the Lens: Reframing the Question to Unlock Insight and Impact," waiting quietly is the hardest skill for participants to learn. Period. See the description at https://executive.mit.edu/openenrollment /program/innovation-and-images-exploring-the-intersections-of -leadership-and-photography/#.WyoFgVVKjIU.
9. Each image emerged from "compose and wait" moments in Jerusalem, Paris, and Boston. Each scene struck me as intriguing so I created a strong composition and waited about twenty minutes for something surprising to come along. Either people and/or boats entered the scene to create a seemingly "inevitable" image. In our workshop at MIT (in collaboration with Santa Fe Photographic Workshops), "Leadership and the Lens: Reframing the Question to Unlock Insight and Impact," Sam Abell and I regularly notice that "waiting" is one of the hardest lessons for leaders to live. Life doesn't dish out "wait time." Rather,

it's a conscious choice, crucial for crafting photographs and catalytic questions.

CHAPTER 7: HOW DO YOU CHANNEL THE ENERGY?

1. Danielle Sacks, "Patagonia CEO Rose Marcario Fights the Fights Worth Fighting," *Fast Company*, January 6, 2015. Available at https://www.fastcompany.com/3039739/patagonia-ceo-rose-marcario-fights-the-fights-worth-fighting.
2. Lisa Jardine, *Ingenious Pursuits: Building the Scientific Revolution* (New York: Nan A. Talese, 1999), 7.
3. Yvon Chouinard, *Let My People Go Surfing: The Education of a Reluctant Businessman* (New York: Penguin, 2005).
4. For a quick grounding in the methods of design thinking, which has become a mainstay approach used by innovators in entrepreneurial, corporate, and nonprofit settings, see Tim Brown, "Design Thinking," *Harvard Business Review*, June 2008. Brown is chief executive officer and president of the design company IDEO, where he pioneered the method.
5. Net promoter score is a simple measure produced by surveying actual customers on their likelihood to recommend, or promote, a product or service they purchased to others. For an explanation by the consultant who introduced it, see Fred Reichheld, "The One Number You Need to Grow," *Harvard Business Review*, December 2003.
6. C. E. Shalley, J. Zhou, and G. R. Oldham, "The Effects of Personal and Contextual Characteristics on Creativity: Where Should We Go from Here?" *Journal of Management* 30 (2004): 933–58.
7. A. M. Isen, "On the Relationship Between Affect and Creative Problem Solving," in S. Russ, ed., *Affect, Creative Experience and Psychological Adjustment* (Philadelphia: Brunner/Mazel, 1999), 3–17.
8. Valeria Biasi, Paolo Bonaiuto, and James M. Levin, "Relation Between Stress Conditions, Uncertainty and Incongruity Intolerance, Rigidity and Mental Health: Experimental Demonstrations," *Health* 7, no. 1 (January 14, 2015): 71–84.
9. Jose-Maria Fernandez, Roger M. Stein, and Andrew W. Lo, "Commercializing Biomedical Research Through Securitization Techniques," *Nature Biotechnology* 30 (2012): 964–75. Available at doi:10.1038/nbt.2374.
10. Teresa Amabile and Steven Kramer, *The Progress Principle: Using Small Wins to Ignite Joy, Engagement, and Creativity at Work* (Boston: Harvard Business Review Press, 2011).

11. Robert I. Sutton and Huggy Rao, *Scaling Up Excellence: Getting to More Without Settling for Less* (New York: Crown Business, 2014).

12. Judith Samuelson, "Larry Fink's Letter to CEOs Is About More Than 'Social Initiatives,'" *Quartz@Work*, January 18, 2018. Available at https://work.qz .com/1182544/larry-finks-letter-to-ceos-is-about-more-than-social -initiatives/.

13. Ray Dalio, *Principles: Life and Work* (New York: Simon & Schuster, 2017), 415.

14. Paul J. Zak, "Why Your Brain Loves Good Storytelling," *Harvard Business Review*, October 28, 2014.

15. For any readers interested to learn more about Mo Willems and the appeal of his work, I recommend Rivka Galchen, "Mo Willems's Funny Failures," *New Yorker*, February 6, 2017. Available at https://www.newyorker.com /magazine/2017/02/06/mo-willems-funny-failures.

16. Chris Anderson, *TED Talks: The Official TED Guide to Public Speaking* (New York: Houghton Mifflin Harcourt, 2016), 64.

CHAPTER 8: CAN WE RAISE A NEXT GENERATION OF QUESTIONERS?

1. The quote was reported by his friend Donald Sheff in a letter to the editor of the *New York Times*: "Izzy, Did You Ask a Good Question Today?," January 19, 1988. Available at http://www.nytimes.com/1988/01/19/opinion/l -izzy-did-you-ask-a-good-question-today-712388.html.

2. Dan Rothstein and Luz Santana, *Make Just One Change: Teach Students to Ask Their Own Questions* (Cambridge, MA: Harvard Education Press, 2011).

3. For example, Marilee Adams takes a similar approach for teachers in her book, *Teaching That Changes Lives: 12 Mindset Tools for Igniting the Love of Learning* (San Francisco: Berrett-Koehler, 2013).

4. James T. Dillon, of the University of California, Riverside, studied this phenomenon. See, for example, his essay "Questioning in Education," in Michel Meyer, ed., *Questions and Questioning* (Berlin: Walter de Gruyter, 1988), 98–118.

5. For an account of that experiment, see Dale Russakoff, *The Prize: Who's in Charge of America's Schools?* (New York: Houghton Mifflin Harcourt, 2015).

6. Mary Budd Rowe, "Wait-Time and Rewards as Instructional Variables, Their Influence on Language, Logic, and Fate Control: Part One—Wait-Time," *Journal of Research in Science Teaching* 11, no. 2 (June 1974): 81–94. Available at https://doi.org/10.1002/tea.3660110202.

7. Karron G. Lewis, "Developing Questioning Skills," in *Teachers and Students—Sourcebook* (Austin: Center for Teaching Effectiveness, the University of Texas at Austin, 2002). Available at http://www.ecapteach.com/survival%20traiining/lesson_07/questioning.pdf.

8. Sophie von Stumm, Benedikt Hell, and Tomas Chamorro-Premuzic, "The Hungry Mind: Intellectual Curiosity Is the Third Pillar of Academic Performance," *Perspectives on Psychological Science* 6, no. 6 (2011): 574–88. Available at https://www.researchgate.net/publication/234218535_The_Hungry_Mind_—_Intellectual_Curiosity_Is_the_Third_Pillar_of_Academic_Performance. See also B. G. Charlton, "Why Are Modern Scientists So Dull?: How Science Selects for Perseverance and Sociability at the Expense of Intelligence and Creativity," *Medical Hypotheses* 72 (2009), 237–43.

9. Christopher Uhl and Dana L. Stuchul, *Teaching as if Life Matters: The Promise of a New Education Culture* (Baltimore: Johns Hopkins University Press, 2011), 75.

10. Angeline Stoll Lillard, *Montessori: The Science Behind the Genius* (Oxford, UK: Oxford University Press, 2007), 129.

11. Greg Windle, "Workshop School Wins National Innovation Grant," *Philadelphia Public School Notebook*, March 7, 2016. Available at http://thenotebook.org/latest0/2016/03/07/art-of-teaching-learning-workshop-school.

12. For more of Salti's thinking on the subject of youth unemployment and the value of teaching entrepreneurship, see Amanda Pike's extended interview with her for *Frontline/World*. Available at http://www.pbs.org/frontlineworld/stories/egypt804/interview/extended.html.

13. Echoing my conclusions about Salti's continuing impact on others, Sean Rush, former president and CEO of Junior Achievement Worldwide, recently shared: "Aside from being a dear friend and colleague, Soraya inspired not only young people but *me* to question the *status quo* in our own organization and in the world around us. As a woman in the Middle East, she questioned, challenged and inspired countless young people to move beyond traditional definitions of success. Soraya lives on through the robust INJAZ organization that continues to transform Middle Eastern youth attitudes about their future. She was and is a beacon of hope in a troubled part of our world."

14. Dhirendra Kumar, "The Art of Questioning," *Value Research*, April 5, 2017. Available at https://www.valueresearchonline.com/story/h2_storyview.asp?str=30352&&utm_medium=vro.in.

15. Tony Wagner, *Creating Innovators: The Making of Young People Who Will Change the World* (New York: Scribner, 2012).

16. Note, by the way, that Bezos grabbed the URL relentless.com when he was setting up Amazon. It's an indication perhaps of how much that word resonates with him that he believes it might be a useful URL to him in the future.

17. David McCullough, *The Wright Brothers* (New York: Simon & Schuster, 2015), 18.

18. Ken Bain, *What the Best College Students Do* (Cambridge, MA: Harvard University Press, 2012), 159.

19. Owen Fiss, *Pillars of Justice* (Cambridge, MA: Harvard University Press, 2017).

20. See J. Bonner Ritchie and S. C. Hammond, "We (Still) Need a World of Scholar-Leaders: 25 Years of Reframing Education," *Journal of Management Inquiry* 14 (2005), 6–12.

21. Interview with John Hunt, *Lürzer's Archive*, issue 3 (2010). Available at https://www.luerzersarchive.com/en/magazine/interview/john-hunt-126.html.

22. Antoine de Saint-Exupéry, *The Little Prince* (New York: Harcourt, Brace & World, 1943).

23. If devoting four minutes a day to focused questioning sounds reasonable to you, and you could use some of the encouragement that comes with a like-minded community, please join us at https://4-24project.org/.

CHAPTER 9: WHY NOT AIM FOR THE BIGGEST QUESTIONS?

1. People generally extend the quotation to its sneering next sentence: "No great and enduring volume can ever be written on the flea, though many there be who have tried it." But I prefer the soaring sentences that preceded it: "Such, and so magnifying, is the virtue of a large and liberal theme! We expand to its bulk." Herman Melville, *Moby-Dick, or the White Whale* (Boston: St. Botolph Society, 1892), 428.

2. Andrew Solomon "The Middle of Things: Advice for Young Writers," *New Yorker*, March 11, 2015. Available at https://www.newyorker.com/books/page-turner/the-middle-of-things-advice-for-young-writers.

3. For more of the XPRIZE backstory, see Michael Belfiore, *Rocketeers: How a Visionary Band of Business Leaders, Engineers, and Pilots Is Boldly Privatizing Space* (Washington, DC: Smithsonian, 2007); Julian Guthrie, *How to Make a Spaceship: A Band of Renegades, an Epic Race, and the Birth of Private Spaceflight* (New York: Penguin, 2016).

4. Oprah Winfrey, "What Oprah Knows for Sure About Life's Big Questions," Oprah.com, December 12, 2017. Available at http://www.oprah.com /inspiration/what-oprah-knows-for-sure-about-lifes-big-questions #ixzz5ILDBCed5.
5. Gary Zukav, *The Seat of the Soul: 25th Anniversary Edition* (New York: Simon & Schuster, 2014), xiv.

EPILOGUE: WHAT WILL YOU ASK OF YOURSELF?

1. Robert Fulghum, *What on Earth Have I Done?: Stories, Observations, and Affirmations* (New York: St. Martin's Press, 2007), 290–91.
2. While an identity card may not seem aspirational to a Westerner who was automatically issued at birth a Social Security number or the equivalent— and may even be regarded with suspicion by someone who worries about the potential abuse of such a database—it can literally be life-changing for those whose lack of official standing has cut them off from opportunities or assistance.

INDEX

NOTE: Page numbers in italics indicate a photograph. Page numbers followed by "n" indicate a note on that page.

Abell, Sam, 151–52, *153*, 174, 277
Acton, Lord, 45
Adams, Douglas, 248
Adams, Marilee, 126, 273
Akinola, Modupe, 138
Alphabet's X unit, 22–23
Amabile, Teresa, 188–89
Amazon, *105, 106*, 296n4
Anand, Vijay, 51
Anderson, Chris, 198
Ang Phula Sherpa, *6, 7*
Ansari XPRIZE, 255–56, *257*, 259
answers
    day care onsite for employees, 180
    finding better answers, 12–13
    growth mindset vs. fixed
        mindset, 47–49
    question as key to, 176–77
    value in questions they inspire, xiii
approachability, 163–65
Argomento polling software, 74
armored fish fossil, 101
Art of the Idea, The (Hunt), 233
ASK conference, 165
assumptions, 22–25, 107–8, 160,
    162, 187, 206
attitude adjustments, 95
authentic voice, 8–9
authoritative questions, 38–39

back-layer approach, 151–52
Bad Leadership (Kellerman), 46
Bain, Ken, 229–30

Baldwin, James, 268
Bali beach with lightbulb, *133*
Barlow, Sally, 90–91
Barron, Hal, 161–62
Beginner's mind, 29–30
Beighton, Nick, 140–41, 155, 164
Bell Labs, 92
Benioff, Marc
    Airing of Grievances group, 82–83
    on beginner's mind, 29–30
    on culture of innovation, 193
    on giving back to others, 80
    and Gregersen, at Davos, 145, 156
    and Ignite sessions, 79–80, 81
    on listening, 156
    meditation practice, 171
    questions for Salesforce team,
        80–81, 83
    and Robbins, 193
    sabbatical in Hawaii, 80
Bennis, Warren, 104
Berkshire Hathaway HomeServices
    Ignite session, 79
Bettinger, Walt, 120–22, 234, 271–72
Bezos, Jeff, 122, 226–27, 301n16
biblical story of Saul, 194
biomimicry, 14
Blakely, Sara, 119, 270–71
Blefari, Gino, 79
blindness experience, 11–12
Bloom's taxonomy, 19, 20
Bowers, Betsy, 219
Bozer, Ahmet, 149

brainstorming for questions
    overview, 60
    conditions for, 61–63, *64, 65, 66,*
      67, 294*n1*
    creating conditions for, 93–95
    diversity of perspectives, 184
    on equality, 59–60
    family sessions in different
      places, 77–78
    "five whys" sequence, 71
    generating the questions, 69–70
    Pixar's Brain Trust and Notes Day,
      ix–x, 86–88, 111–12
    Question Burst session/reset,
      67–74, 79, 96–97, 186
    setting the stage, 67–69
    team off-sites, 78–81
    unpacking the questions, 70–71
    See also safe space for questions
brainstorming questions, 183–84
Brain Trust sessions at Pixar, ix–x,
    86–87, 111–12
Brand, Stewart, 110
breakthrough solutions, 33
Breashears, David, 5, 8
Bremer, Neville, 20
brunch club, 31–32, 57
brutally honest reports (BHRs), 121
bubble, living in the, 127–30
Bush, Jared, 112, *113*, 114
But What If We're Wrong?
    (Klosterman), 116–17

Campbell, Joseph, 126
candor, 111–12, 120–22
Caol Primary School, Scotland, *214, 215*
Carpenter, Mason, 143
Carson, Rachel, 244
Carter, Dean, 179–80
catalytic questions
    overview, 4, 21–22
    brainstorming for, 73

    in *Creativity, Inc.,* ix–x
    in Einstein's process, 38
    power-seeking people vs., 48, 49–50
    self-questioning, 176
    starting a green business with,
      177–79
    from staying in wrongness,
      100–103
    what do great parents leave their
      children, 78
Catmull, Ed
    overview, ix–xiii, 83
    culture of candor, 86
    on distractions, 138–39
    meditation practice, 170–71
    and perpetual-inquiry machine, 89
    promoting candor, 110–11
    reading books, 168–69
    See also Pixar
certitude, 115, 116–20
challenge-centered learning model,
    206, 209–12, 220–22
Change Your Questions, Change Your
    Life (Adams), 126
channeling the energy
    asking the right question, 176–77
    cascading the questions, 182–86
    emotional arc management, 186–90
    emulating great coaches, 191–92
    escalating the questions, 177–81
    innovation capital and
      questioning capital, 193–96
    with storytelling, 196–200, *200, 201*
charter schools, 210
Chase, Robin, 139
cheap seats, 146–47
Chi, Michelene, 104, 107–8
children
    cultural inhibition of questions,
      36–39, 58, 109
    fear of MRI resolved with decor,
      198–200, *200, 201*

keystone question, 272–73
question journal, 224
reading books with, 228–29
"reading" with memorization
    skills, 108–9
research on twins, 294n1
teaching values to, 78
See also schools and education
children as good questioners
overview, 242
expecting different questions,
    240–42
extracurricular questioning,
    209–11, 219–22
managers teaching questioning
    skills, 232–35, 236, 237, 238,
    239–40
Room 13 International model,
    212–13, 213, 214, 215, 216,
    217–19, 218
See also schools and education
Children's Hospital of Pittsburgh,
    199–200, 200, 201
Chiquet, Maureen, 93
Chouinard, Yvon, 177–78
Christensen, Ann, 209
Christensen, Clay
    on asking the right question, 61–62
    on behaviors, 61
    and Gregersen, 3
    on passive data, 165, 166
    on questions and answers, 17
    reframing questions, 25
    research of innovator behaviors,
        3–4, 28–29, 61, 210
Cirque du Monde, 219–20
Cirque du Soleil, 132–34, 146
clearness committee, 55–57
climate change and activism,
    124–26, 140
closed vs. open questions, 20–22,
    29, 38–39, 138

clown/court jester at Cirque du
    Soleil headquarters, 134
coal mine tour, 125–26
Coco (film), 134–35
cognitive biases, 114–15
cognitive psychologists, 23–24
cohesiveness, 91
collectivist vs. individualist
    cultures, 54–55
colleges, 211, 229–32
Collier, Haroon, 216
conceptual change, 104, 107–9
confirmation bias, 114–15
conflict, benefit of, 139–42
controlling questions, 36–37, 38, 43–45
convergent vs. divergent questions,
    20–22, 29, 38–39, 138
Cook, Scott, 170
core cultural values, 179–81
Craig, Jonathan, 72–73
Creating Innovators (Wagner), 224
creative breakthroughs, 13–17, 33
creative thinking
    and childhood experiences, 226
    from great questions, 20, 26, 48
    making space for, 89, 118, 136–37,
        152, 172, 298n8
    and meditation practice, 171
    modeling, 239–40
    in start-ups, 115
creativity
    creating context, 152
    epiphany moments, 118–19,
        125–26, 135, 137, 186–87, 266
    from experience of conflict, 139
    from exposure to new things, 131–36
    and meditation, 171
    and positive mood, 187
Creativity, Inc. (Catmull), ix
creativity and insights
    candor as requirement for,
        110–12, 114

creating an environment for, 63, 67
from nature, 14
and power of questions, 4
See also safe space for questions
criticism, receptivity to, 111–12, 114, 146
cross-cultural differences, 53–55
crucible experiences, 104
Csikszentmihalyi, Mihaly, 139
culturalism, 53–55, 62, 103. *See also*
social conditioning
Cureton, Linda, 154
Cutler, C. Chapin, 92
cybercrime, 98–100
Cybereason, 98–100

Dalio, Ray, 195–96
Day 1 work at Amazon, *105, 106,* 296n4
day care onsite for employees, 180
Dell, Michael, 3–4
democratizing other nations, 61
De Pree, Maggie, 156–57
designing team off-sites, 79–81, 93
design thinking
as approach to innovation, 51–52
at Hyatt Hotels, 182–86
at Pixar, 87
device-free time, 57
dialogic questions, 38–39
"Dialogue in the Dark" opening,
Shanghai, 11–12
Diamandis, Peter, 211–12, 255
Dietz, Doug, 198–200, *200, 201*
digital. *See* technology
Dillon, James T., 37, 73–74, 204
Dintersmith, Ted, 36–37
discomfort, 181. *See also* seeking
discomfort
Disney Animation Building, *113*
Disney Animation story trust, x, 112,
114
Disneyland Park "Nikon Picture
Spot," *49*

distraction, powers of, 136–39
Div, Lior
on approachability, 164
assuming he's missing
something, 98
and cybercrime, 98–100
on discovering his boundaries, 130
dyslexia challenges, 108–9
on happiness vs. satisfaction, 270
on raising children, 229
raising the comfort level with
failure, 119
Di Valerio, Scott, 162
divergent vs. convergent questions,
20–22, 29, 38–39, 138
"dreamers of dreams"
(O'Shaughnessy), 30, 292n15
Drucker, Peter, 3, 11, 166
drug discovery process financing
quest, 187–88
Drury, Rod, 94, 115, 135
Dweck, Carol, 47–48
Dwyer, Matt, 181
Dyer, Jeff, 3–4, 28–29, 61, 143, 210

Eastman, George, 13–14
Edmondson, Amy, 91, 102–3
Ed Tech, 209
education. *See* schools and education
EG conference, 146–47
Einstein, Albert, 22, 37–38
e-learning tools, 209
embrace failure school of thought,
118–19
emotions
collecting data about, 186
emotional arc management, 186–90
identifying the impact of, 69, 70,
74, 75, 76
shifting someone's internal
environment, 191–92
utilization of, at Pixar, 86–87

employees and employment
answer suppression, 44–45
boss criticizes thinking time, 167
candor requirement, 111–12,
120–22
Cirque du Soleil's court jester
clown, 134
Facebook's employees question
time, 57
making work more meaningful,
180–81
managers teaching questioning
skills, 232–35, *236*, *237*, *238*,
239–40
of noisy complainers, 102–3
question suppression, 39
empowering students, 207–8
empowering women, 223
endangered species protection, 50
energy. *See* channeling the energy
epiphany moments, 118–19, 125–26,
135, 137, 186–87, 266
equality, brainstorming about, 59–60
Erickson, Gary, 148–49, 150
Escape Bar prototype, Hyatt Hotels,
184–85
Etzioni, Amitai, 24
Everest (IMAX film), 5, 8
extra cognition, 136–37
extracurricular questioning, 209–11,
219–22
EY, 234–35, *236*, *237*, *238*

Facebook's employees question
time, 57
Fahey, George, 37
Fairley, Rob, 212
families
brainstorming sessions in
different places, 77–78
family meeting to work through
problems, 228

parenting, 27–28, 96–97
questioning skills in the home,
225–29
saying no to a "great idea," 154
table-talk routine, 57
Fast Company magazine, 18
Fernandes, Maria da Penha Maia,
275, 276
Fernandez-Ruiz, Reese, 261–64, 267
Fidelity Investments, 252–54
Fink, Larry, 194
first-principles thinking, 24–25,
245–46
Fiss, Owen, 230–32
"five whys" sequence (Toyoda;
variation by Ray), 71
fixed mindset vs. growth mindset,
47–49
Floyd, William D., 37
focusing on a problem and the need
to solve it, x
focusing on solutions, 143–45, 189
Forbes magazine, 44
foreign countries, value of living in,
143, 149
4–24 Project, 241
Freeman, Jack, 27, 292n12
Freyer, Hunter, *107*
Fryer, Bronwyn, 279–80
Fulghum, Robert, 268–70
fundamental questions, 264–67

Gadiesh, Orit, 208–9
Gallup poll of worker engagement, 180
Gardner, John, 58
generating questions, 69–70
genesis questions, 263
Gentile, Chris, 18
Getzels, Jacob W., 139
Ghandour, Fadi, 143–45, 196–97
Gladwell, Malcolm, 26
Gohar, Kian, 256, 258

Goldbert, Ken, 57
GoldieBlox, 32
Goldwyn, Samuel, 40–41
Goodall, Jane, 124
Google's Project Aristotle, 92
Gordon, Andrew, 155–56, 197–98
Gram Vikas, 130
Greene, Diane, 226
Gregersen, Hal
    4–24 Project, 241
    and Abell, photography mentor,
        151–52, *153*, 277, 298*n*8
    and Benioff, at Davos, 145, 156
    heart attack, 5, 272
    images taken in "compose and
        wait" moments, *173*, *174*, *174*
    keystone question, 272–73
    Mount Everest experience, 5, 6, 7,
        8, 147–48
    picture of, at Zappos, *66*, 67
    qualifications of, 1–4
    researching and coauthoring *The
        Innovator's DNA*, 3–4, 28–29,
        61, 210
    research on effect of living in a
        foreign country, 143
    as stay-at-home dad, 145
    teaching social entrepreneurs in
        France and UAE, 220–22
    "Wonder Windows Walls"
        photograph exhibition,
        277–80, *278*, *279*, *281*
growth mindset vs. fixed mindset,
    47–49

Hamburg street scene, *42*
Handspring Puppet Company, 250–52
Handspring Trust for Puppetry Arts,
    251–52
Hapinoy, 263
Harford, Tim, 110
Hauger, Simon, 210–11

Hawley, Michael, 146–47, 155, 175
Heinecke, Andreas, 12
Hellman, Lillian, 40–41
Hernandez, Miguel, *64*
heuristics, 103–4, *105*, *106*, 107–9
Hewlett-Packard, 46
hierarchies and the questioning
    process, 40–41, *42*, 43–45
Highest Goal, The (Ray), 71
high-impact entrepreneurs, 252
High Tech High School, 210
Hitchhiker's Guide to the Galaxy, The
    (Adams), 248
Hofstede, Geert, 53–54, 294*n*19
Holacracy, 63
Howard, Byron, 112, *113*
Hsieh, Tony, 62–63, 67
human nature
    assuming something is missing
        or you are wrong, 98, 100
    and awareness of what you know
        you don't know, 15–16, 47, 109,
        122
    certitude in spite of a history of
        being wrong, 116–17
    choosing exhilarating
        experiences, 128–29
    cognitive biases, 114–15
    comfort seeking, 127–28, 130
    and crucible experiences, 104
    fixed vs. growth mindset, 47–50
    and mysteries, 123
    power-seeking people, 40–41, *42*,
        43–45
    resistance to correction, 110–12, 114
    See also social conditioning
humble inquiry technique, 19
Hunsaker, Kevin T., 46
Hunt, John, 218–19, 233
Hurston, Zora Neale, 279
Hwang, Victor, 132, 135–36
Hyatt Hotels, 182–86

Hyatt Thinking, 182–85
Hyperloop, 131, 246–47

Idea Brunch club, 31–32, 57
ideas
    from advisory council of science
        fiction writers, 258–59
    brainstorming and prototyping,
        183–85
    cross-fertilization of, 246
    discovering new ideas, 129–30
    nature as source of, 14
    from openness to criticism, 146
    See also creativity
Ignite sessions designed by
    Salesforce, 79–80, 81
Ikea, 147
Imran, Mir, 226
India, 52–53, 273–74, 303n2
individualist vs. collectivist
    cultures, 54–55
inequality and power distance, 54
innovation
    overview, 8, 58
    building a culture of, 193–96
    creating differentiation with, 30–31
    design-thinking approach, 51–52,
        87
    from lunch with Harry Nyquist, 92
    need for, 31–32
    in photography, 13–14
    and questioning behavior, 28–31
    See also seeking discomfort
Innovation Realized (EY client
    retreat), 236, 238
Innovator's Dilemma, The
    (Christensen), 61
Innovator's DNA, The (Gregersen,
    Christensen, and Dyer), 3–4,
    28–29, 61, 210
Inserra, Mike, 94–95
insights

from asking a different question, 15
    epiphany moments, 118–19,
        125–26, 135, 137, 186–87, 266
    from new questions, 245
    teaching facts with insight
        background, 206
    turning into a practical reality,
        26–27
    See also creativity and insights
inspiration, creating, 131–32
instincts, 114–15
integrative thinking, 117–18
Intuit, 51–52
isolation, 89–90, 121, 122, 127–30, 142
Ito, Joi, 260–61, 267
Ive, Jony, 21

Jamieson, Marie, 217
Jardine, Lisa, 176
Jerusalem, 173
Jobs, Steve, 21, 155–56, 270
Johnson, Abigail, 252–54
Jones, Basil, 250–52
Junior Achievement Worldwide,
    220–22, 301n13

Kalven, Harry, 230–31
Kamprad, Ingvar, 147
Kapsin, Kathleen, 199
Karp, Jeff, 14, 120, 136
Kate Spade, 131–32
Kefover, Bill, 92
Kellerman, Barbara, 46
Kessy, Doreen, 223
Kewtown Primary School, Athlone,
    Cape Town, South Africa, 213, 216
keystone questions
    examples of, 268–74
    identifying your keystone
        question, 274–75, 276, 277–80,
        278, 279, 281
Kids of Survival (K.O.S.), 34–35

Klosterman, Chuck, 116–17
Kodak, 13–14, 16, 48–49
Kohler, Adrian, 250–52
Kramer, Steven, 188–89
Krauss, Lawrence, 123
Kumar, Dhirendra, 222–23

Lafley, A. G., 153
Lakewood Heritage Center, Lakewood, Colorado, 219
Laliberté, Guy, 131–34, 162
Lamarre, Daniel, 133–34, 146, 162, 220
Langer, Ellen, 17
Langer, Robert, 232
LaRovere, Joan, 264–65
leadership
    overview, 8
    allocating their finite time and attention, 254
    asking to be educated, 121
    average time spent on each task, 167–68
    building a culture of questioning, 88–89, 141
    creating differentiation through innovation, 30–31
    effect of insulation, 128
    encouraging openness and honesty, 111–12, 121–22, 140–41
    going undercover, 141–42
    high-impact entrepreneurs, 252
    humble inquiry technique, 19
    innovation capital and questioning capital, 193–96
    and isolation, 89–90, 121, 122, 127–30, 142
    leaders' quest experience, 124–26, 140
    making others the smartest, 162
    modeling for your team, 239–40
    spending time with employees, 143–45

talking to spectacularly different people, 145–46
teaching questioning skills, 232–35, 239–40
See also listening and observing
"Leadership and the Lens" (MIT Executive Education course), 277, 298n8
Le Cam, Ann, 171
Lee, Suzi, 279, 279–80
Legend, John, 243
legitimate questions, 34–35
Let My People Go Surfing (Chouinard), 178
Levin, Lindsay, 124–26, 140
Lewis, Karron, 207
Lillard, Angeline Stoll, 209–10
Lion's Den Cirque du Soleil shows, 146
listening and observing
    actively seeking passive data, 165–67, 182–83
    back-layer approach, 151–52, 173, 174
    becoming approachable, 163–65
    clearing your head and heart, 170–71
    at Hyatt Hotels, 182–83
    listening for the unexpected, 155–58
    and mediation practice, 158–61
    pausing to leave room for others, 158
    preparing for surprises, 161–63
    reading daily and deeply, 168–70
    shutting down others with vocalization, 153–55, 172
    silent mode thinking time, 167–68
    the sound of silence, 172, 298n8
Little Prince, The (Saint-Exupéry), 240–41
Lo, Andrew, 2, 187–88
Los Angeles Times newspaper, 90
Lu, Jackson G., 138
Lyon, Marcus, 274–75, 276

Madame Zazou, 134
Madiath, Joe, 130
Mahfouz, Naguib, 59
Make Just One Change (Rothstein and Santana), 203–4
Marcario, Rose, 175–76, 179, 181
Maria da Penha law in Brazil, 275
Marjory Stoneman Douglas High School shooting, Parkland, Florida, 207–8
Maryniak, Gregg, 255
Mason, Malia, 138
matrix of knowledge of a situation, 15–16. *See also* what you know you don't know
McChrystal, Stanley, 164–65
McCullough, David, 227
McDermott, Bill, 46, 139–40, 195
mediation, 158–61, 170–71
meditation practice, 170–71
Melville, Herman, 247, 302*n1*
mental models, updating, 103–4, *105, 106, 107*–9
military, 29, 39
Miller, Donald, 9
Million Miles in a Thousand Years, A (Miller), 9
mindfulness, 95, 166–67
Mindset (Dweck), 47–48
Mintzberg, Henry, 167
MIT, 2, 277, 298*n8*
MIT Media Lab, 260–61
Moby-Dick (Melville), 247, 302*n1*
Mohri, Lionel, 51–52
Montessori method, 209–10
Morgan, Steve, 99
Morris, Jim, 112
Most Likely to Succeed (Wagner and Dintersmith), 36–37
motivating others, 26–28
Mount Everest, *5, 6, 7,* 8
Mulcahy, Simon, 29–30, 128, 158

Murthy, Narayana, 30–31
Musk, Elon, 17, 24–25, 131, 245–48, 246–47
mysteries, 123

nature as source of ideas, 14
negative threats, 15–17, 192
Negroponte, Nicholas, 260–61
net promoter score, 185, 299*n5*
New York magazine, 34–35
New York Times magazine, 92
Nilekani, Nandan, 128, 163, 273–74, 303*n2*
Nohria, Nitin, 52–53
noisy complainers, 102–3
Notes Day at Pixar, 87–88
nursery rhyme, 151
nurses following doctor's orders, 43
Nyquist, Harry, 92

observing. *See* listening and observing
Olofsson, Anneè, 278
Omidyar, Pierre, 4
open vs. closed questions, 20–22, 29, 38–39, 138
Opposable Mind, The (Martin), 117–18
Origins Project, 123
Orthodox Academy of Crete, 277, 278
O'Shaughnessy, Arthur, 30, 292*n15*
Outliers (Gladwell), 26

Palmer, Parker, 55–57, 60
Papaderos, Alexandros, 268–70, 277
parenting, 27–28, 96–97
passive data, 165–67, 182–83
Patagonia, 177–81
Pate, Robert, 20
Patrick Deval, 158
Perez, Bea, 57, 228
performance measurement, 185
photography innovations, 13–14

Piazza, Tony, 158–61, 250
Picasso, 9, 17–18
Pillars of Justice (Fiss), 230–31
Pixar
  overview, 83, *84, 85, 86,* 88–89
  Brain Trust, ix–x, 86–87, 111–12
  candor as key to sustaining
    performance, 111–12
  Notes Day, 87–88
  staff immersion in pertinent new
    things, 134–35
  See also Catmull, Ed
Plattner, Hasso, 110
Poincaré, Henri, 136–38
polarization of views, 117–18,
  124–26, 140
positive opportunities
  creating better questions, 16–20
  energy fueled by, 186–90
  Question Burst sessions as, 70
  See also brainstorming for
    questions; reframing
    questions
Postman, Neil, 58, 202
power distance, 54
power of questions
  overview, 19–20, 185, 247–48
  asking the right question, 61–62,
    161–62, 169, 176–77, 188–89,
    294n1
  for creative breakthroughs, 13–17, 33
  for dislodging negative feelings, 70
  Hyatt Hotels asking, "What do
    women want.," 182–83
  mission statements as limiting
    answers, xii
  and negative threats, 15–17
  producing protégés who think, 232
  as theme at EY, 234–35
  unlocking new insights and
    positive behavior change, 4
power-seeking people and the

questioning process, 40–41, *42,*
  43–45
Principles (Dalio), 195–96
problem-solving self-reliance,
  226–27, 301n13
Productive Thinking (Wertheimer),
  37–38
progress as energizing, 188–89
Project Aristotle, Google, 92
project-centered learning model,
  206, 209–12, 220–22
prototyping, 183–85
psychological safety, 91, 92. *See also*
  human nature
psychological torment, 272–73, 275

Q/A ratio, 28
Quakers' clearness committee,
  55–57
Qualcomm Tricorder XPRIZE, 256,
  258, 259
Quest Autism Foundation, 27–28
question box exercise, 205–6, 235, 239
Question Burst session/reset, 67–74,
  79, 96–97, 186
questioners, 17–20, 40–45, 51,
  207–9, 233–34. *See also* children
  as good questioners
Questioning and Teaching (Dillon), 73–74
questioning capital, 194–96,
  247–48
questioning mode, 30
questioning skills
  overview, 1, 33
  focusing on, 17–20
  managers teaching, 232–35, *236,*
    237, 238, 239–40
question journal, 224
questions
  overview, xi–xii
  about what you know you don't
    know, 15–16, 47, 109, 122

for breaking down assumptions,
22–25, 107–8
building and maintaining
fluidity, 149
creating a shift in focus with,
191–92
exciting and engaging others
with, 26–28
fixed vs. growth mindset, 47–48
follow-on questions, 190
genesis questions, 263
highlighting questions that
resulted in change, 206
as indicator of future success, 196
open vs. closed, 20–22, 29,
38–39, 138
for resentment aversion, 34–35
responses based on who's asking,
193–96
for retaining self-worth, x–xi
social conditioning vs., 36–39,
41, 43, 58, 93

Rabi, Isidor, 202–3
Rags2Riches, 262
Rao, Hayagreeva "Huggy," 189–90
rape picture by thirteen-year-old
South African boy, 217
Ray, Michael, 71
reading books, 168–70, 198, 228–29
recruiting and motivating others,
26–28
reframing questions
overview, 4, 126–27
breaking down assumptions, 22–25
for breakthrough solutions, 33,
166, 239
creating better questions, 16–20, 118
helping a disabled man share his
disability, 12
in mediation, 158–59
monitoring intent of adversaries, 99

overcoming children's fear of
MRIs, 198–200, 200, 201
psychologists shifting from the
wrong to the strong, 244
Salesforce Ignite sessions, 79–80
and subsequent emotional arc,
186–90
unleashing energy, 26
Renner, Mary Beech, 131–32
reverse mentoring, 94–95
Rhinos Without Borders, 50
Rilke, Rainer Maria, 249
Ritchie, Bonner, 2–3, 168
Robbins, Tony, 191–92, 196
Robinson, Sir Ken, 98
Rollins, Tim, 34–35
Room 13 International model, 212–
13, 213, 214, 215, 216, 217–19, 218
Rothstein, Dan, 203–4
Rowe, Mary Budd, 206–7
Rudaizky, John, 234–35
Ruiz, Mark, 261–64
Rumsfeld, Donald, 16
Rush, Sean, 301n13
Rutan, Burt, 256

safe space for questions
overview, 50–53, 55–57
asking uncomfortable questions,
253
defining "safe," 91
designing, 93–95
at Fidelity Investments, 253
"five whys" sequence, 71
focusing on solutions, 143–45
in group psychotherapy, 90–91
isolation from others vs., 89–90
for opening mental processes, 77
at Pixar, ix–x, 86–88, 111–12
tactful response to wrongness,
122
virtual space, 94

safe space for questions (*cont.*)
See also brainstorming for
questions
Saint-Exupéry, Antoine de, 240–41
Salesforce, 79–83. *See also* Benioff,
Marc
Salti, Soraya, 221–22, 301n13
Samuelson, Judith, 194
Sanders, Gerard, 143
Santana, Luz, 203–4
SAP, 139–40
Sapebuso Primary School, Soweto,
South Africa, *216*, 217
Sarafian, Katherine, 87–88
scaling opportunities, 189–90
Scanlon, Dan, *84*
Schaal, Carrie, 227
Schein, Edgar, 19, 166–67
schools and education
and building questioning
capacity, 19–20
campus challenge, 229–32
celebrating questioners, 207–9
college campuses and political
views, 89–90
educational reform, 203–6
e-learning tools, 209
highlighting questions that
resulted in change, 206
increasing wait time, 206–7
the Internet and questioning
skills, 222–25
Montessori method, 209–10
question box exercise, 205–6,
235, 239
questioning skills in the home,
225–29
question suppression from first
grade on, 36–39, 58, 204
and uncertainty avoidance, 54
utilizing project-centered
learning, 206, 209–12, 220–22

Scott, Philip, 38
Seat of the Soul, The (Zukav), 266
seeking discomfort
overview, 131, 148, 149–50
for benefit of conflict, 139–42
bubble/insulation vs., 127–30
disciplined approach, 143–48
leaders' quest experience,
124–26, 140
living in a foreign country, 143, 149
for powers of distraction, 136–39
for stimulating surprises, 131–36
Seelig, Tina, 22–25
self-aware error makers, 102–3
Seligman, Martin, 244
Semenchuk, Jeff, 182–85, 189
setting the stage at a Question Burst
session, 67–69
Shlain, Tiffany, 57, 224–25
Silent Springs (Carson), 244
Sippey, Michael, 129–30, 228–29
Slutkin, Gary, 243–44
Smith, Brad, 51, 67
social conditioning
asking questions as part of, 205
culturalism, 53–55, 62, 103
culturalism as, 53–54
do not ask questions, 36–39, 41,
43, 58, 93, 109
play by the rules, 46–47
social entrepreneurs, 261–64
social media, 57, 225
Solomon, Andrew, 249
solutions
breakthrough solutions, 13–17, 33
created by parents of autistic
children, 27–28
false leads, 187–88
prototypes with available
materials, 184–85
and Question Burst exercise, 68
Somos Brasil (Lyon), 274–75, 276

sound of silence, 172, 298*n*8. *See also*
listening and observing
South Africa, *213, 216,* 217–19, *218,*
250–52
space. *See* safe space for questions
SpaceShipOne, 256, *257*
space travel, Ansari XPRIZE for,
255–56
*Specialty Competencies in Group
Psychology* (Barlow), 90–91
Spence, Pamela, 235
Spheres (creative rainforest space), *106*
Spock, S'chn, T'gai, *64*
Sterling, Debbie, 31–32, *57,* 226
Stern, Claude, 159–60
storytelling skills, 196–200, *200, 201*
story trust, Disney Animation, x,
112, 114
stressors, 127–28, 130, 136, 187
Stuart, Chris, 79
Stuchul, Dana L., 208
Stumm, Sophie von, 208
surprises, 131–36, 161–63
Susskind, Edwin, 37
sustainable differentiation, 31
Sutton, Bob, 45, 136, 189–90

Tanzania, 223
TBWA, 213, 217–19, 233
team off-sites, 78–81
technology
the cloud appears, 139–40
discovering new ideas, 129–30
e-learning tools, 209
the Internet and questioning
skills, 222–25
and polarization of views, 117
social media, *57,* 225
TED talks, 198–99
Teller, Astro, 23
Tennyson, Alfred, Lord, 29
Tesla, 248

thinking
building habits of mind, 171
design-thinking approach to
innovation, 51–52, 87
extra cognition, 136–37
first-principles thinking, 24–25
integrative thinking, 117–18
outside the box, *66,* 101, 122
silent mode thinking time,
167–68
See also creative thinking; design
thinking
Thomas, Bob, 104
Thoreau, Henry David, 8–9
Tigner, Rick, 141–42
toxic questions, 20–22, 45
Toyoda, Sakichi, 71
transformative questions
the big picture, 252–54
the business of questioning,
255–56, 256–61, *257, 258*
Chicago's murders as a public
health problem, 243–44
fundamental questions, 264–67
living the questions now, 249–52
pesticides make earth unfit for all
life, 244
psychologists shifting from the
wrong to the strong, 244
of social entrepreneurs, 261–64
Trend Group at Cirque du Soleil,
132–33
Tucker, Anita, 102–3

Uhl, Christopher, 208
Unbongo Kids (TV series in Tanzania),
223
uncertainty, creating, 109–12, *113,*
114–15, 123
uncertainty avoidance, 54
Undercover Boss (TV show), 141–42
universities, 211, 229–32

unpacking questions at a Question
Burst session, 70–71

values
core cultural values and actions,
179–81
leading your children with, 78
vantage point differences, 121
Virtue Foundation, 264–65
Visioneers Summits, 259
vocalization, shutting down others
with, 153–55

Wagner, Tony, 36–37, 223–24
Walden (Thoreau), 8–9
Wall Street Journal conference,
Singapore, 28–29
Walton, Douglas, 41
War Horse (Handspring Puppet
Company), 250–52
Watson, Phil, 22, 23
weaponized questions, 40–41, 43
Weick, Karl, 70
Weinberger, Mark, 30, 235
Weingartner, Charles, 202
Weird Ideas That Work (Sutton), 136
Wertheimer, Max, 37–38
What Age Can You Start Being An Artist?
(documentary), 213
what you know you don't know, 15–16,
47, 109, 122
opening the door to, 153
Wiesel, Elie, 1
Wiesner, Jerome, 260–61
Wilke, Jeff, 103–4, 140
Willems, Mo, 198
Winfrey, Oprah, 265–67
Wizard of Oz, The (film), 34, 43–44
women
empowering with digital tech, 223
Hyatt Hotels' accommodations
for, 182–86

marginalization in law school
class, 231–32
"Wonder Windows Walls"
photograph exhibition
(Gregersen), 277–80, *278, 279, 281*
Woodward, Bob, 119–20
Woolridge, Adrian, 119–20
Workshop School, West
Philadelphia, 205–6, 209, 210–11
World is Flat, The (Friedman), 224
Wright, Orville, 227
Wright, Rod, 213
wrongness, 98–123
among scientists, 123
checking your certitude, 115,
116–20
as a condition, 100–102
continued acceptance of flaws and
failures, 102–3, 108
creating uncertainty, 109–12, *113,
114–15*
increasing comfort level with, 119
misconceptions and category
mistakes, 104, 107–8
reveling in, 98–100, 118–19
stale mental models, 103–4, *105,
106,* 107–9
system integration of, 120–22
utilizing, 119–20

XPRIZE, 255–56, *257, 258,* 258–59
XPRIZE Foundation, 259, 261
X unit, Alphabet's, 22–23

Yellow Cab, 16

Zak, Paul, *197*
Zappos, 62–63, *64, 65, 66,* 67
Zootopia (film), 112
Zuckerberg, Mark, 57, 204–5
Zukav, Gary, 266

ABOUT THE AUTHOR

HAL GREGERSEN is the executive director of the MIT Leadership Center and a senior lecturer in leadership and innovation at the MIT Sloan School of Management. As an inspirational speaker, he has worked with such renowned organizations as Chanel, Disney, Patagonia, UNICEF, and the World Economic Forum, and has been recognized by Thinkers50 as one of the world's most innovative minds. He has authored or coauthored ten books, translated into fifteen languages, including the bestseller *The Innovator's DNA*. Hal and his wife, Suzi Lee, lived in England, France, and the UAE before landing on Boston's North Shore, where he pursues his lifelong avocation of photography and she works as a sculptor.